Breached!

Breached!

Why Data Security Law Fails and How to Improve It

DANIEL J. SOLOVE

& WOODROW HARTZOG

OXFORD
UNIVERSITY PRESS

OXFORD
UNIVERSITY PRESS

Oxford University Press is a department of the University of Oxford. It furthers
the University's objective of excellence in research, scholarship, and education
by publishing worldwide. Oxford is a registered trade mark of Oxford University
Press in the UK and certain other countries.

Published in the United States of America by Oxford University Press
198 Madison Avenue, New York, NY 10016, United States of America.

© Daniel J. Solove and Woodrow Hartzog 2022

CIP data is on file at the Library of Congress
ISBN 978-0-19-094055-3

9 8 7 6 5 4 3 2 1

Printed by LSC communications, United States of America

To Pamela and Griffin—DJS

To Mom and Dad—WH

TABLE OF CONTENTS

Introduction

Chronicle of a Breach Foretold

Sometimes the thing we are looking for is right in front of us and yet we still don't see it. A great novella by Gabriel Garcia Marquez called *Chronicle of a Death Foretold* begins with the vicious fatal stabbing of the main character. The rest of the story reveals that all the warning signs about the murder were in plain sight yet ignored by everyone. The murder was readily preventable—but, because of human nature, it was almost inevitable.

The story of most data breaches follows the same pattern. We have read about thousands of data breaches, and the moral of most of these stories boils down to the same thing: The breaches were preventable, but people made blunders. What is quite remarkable about these stories is that they haven't evolved that much in decades. The same mistakes keep happening again and again. After so many years, and so many laws to regulate data security, why haven't the stories changed?

Let us begin with a classic data breach tale involving one of the largest and most notable breaches of its time—the Target breach of 2013. The story has many of the common themes of data breach stories, and what makes it particularly fascinating is that it is a sinister version of a David-and-Goliath story. Target was Goliath, and it was well-fortified. With its extensive resources and defenses, Target was far more protected than most organizations. Yet, it still failed. This fact should send shivers down our spines.

In mid-December 2013, right in the middle of the holiday shopping season, executives at Target found out some dreaded news: Target had been hacked. It was cruel irony that the second-largest discount store chain in the United States quite literally had a target sign on it—Target's logo is a red and white bullseye. The hackers hit it with an arrow straight into the center.

Executives at Target learned about the breach from Department of Justice officials, who informed them that stolen data from Target was appearing online and that reports of fraudulent credit card charges were starting to pop up.[1] Quite concerned, the Target executives immediately hired a forensics firm to investigate.

What they discovered was devastating. Target's computer system had been infected with malware, and there had been a data breach. It wasn't just a small breach, or a sizeable one, or even a big one—it was a breach of epic proportions.[2] Target had the dubious distinction of having suffered the largest retail data breach in U.S. history.[3]

Over the course of two weeks starting in November 2013, hackers had stolen detailed information for about 40 million credit and debit card accounts, as well as personal information on about 70 million Target customers.[4] The hackers had begun to sell their tremendous data haul on black-market fraud websites.

The timing couldn't have been worse for Target. It suffered the single largest decline of holiday transactions since it first began reporting the statistic.[5] Target sales plummeted during a season which traditionally accounts for 20 to 40 percent of a retailer's annual sales.[6] To stop the bleeding, Target offered a 10 percent discount across the board. Nevertheless, the damage was catastrophic. The company's profits for the holiday shopping period fell a whopping 46 percent.[7]

The pain was just beginning. On top of the lost profits, costs associated with the breach topped $200 million by mid-February 2014. These costs would rise significantly due to bank reimbursement demands, regulatory fines, and direct customer service costs.[8] About 90 lawsuits were filed, leading to massive lawyer bills.[9]

What made this all the more unnerving for Target is that it had devoted quite a lot of time and resources to its information security. Target had more than 300 information security staff members. The company had maintained a large security operations center in Minneapolis, Minnesota, and had a team of security specialists in Bangalore that monitored its computer network 24/7. In May 2013—just six months before the hack—Target had implemented expensive and sophisticated malware detection software from FireEye.[10]

With all this security—an investment of millions of dollars, state-of-the-art security software, hundreds of security personnel, and round-the-clock monitoring—how did Target fail?

A common narrative told to the public is that this entire debacle could be traced to just one person who let the hackers slip in. In caper movies, the criminals often have an inside guy who leaves the doors open. But the person who let the hackers into Target wasn't even a Target employee and wasn't bent on mischief. The person worked for Fazio Mechanical, a Pennsylvania-based HVAC company, a third-party vendor hired by Target. The Fazio employee fell for a phishing trick and opened an attachment in a fraudulent email the hackers had sent to him. Hidden in the email attachment lurked the Citadel Trojan horse—a malicious software program that took root in Fazio's computers.[11]

The Citadel Trojan horse was nothing novel—it was a variant of a well-known malware package called ZeuS and is readily detectable by any major enterprise anti-virus software. But Fazio lacked the massive security infrastructure that Target had, allowing the malware to remain undetected on the Fazio computers. Through the Trojan horse, the hackers obtained Fazio's log-in credentials for Target's system.

With access to Target, the hackers unleashed a different malware program, one they bought on the black market for just a few thousand dollars.[12] Experts such as McAfee director Jim Walker characterized the malware as "absolutely unsophisticated and uninteresting."[13]

At first, the malware went undetected, and it began compiling millions of records during peak business hours. This data was being readied to be transferred to the hackers' location in Eastern Europe. But very soon, FireEye flagged the malware and issued an alert. Target's security team in Bangalore noted the alert and notified the security center in Minneapolis. But the red light was ignored.

FireEye flagged as many as five different versions of the malware. The alerts even provided the addresses for the "staging ground" servers, and a gaffe by the hackers meant that the malware code contained usernames and passwords for these servers, meaning Target security could have logged on and seen the stolen data for themselves.[14] Unfortunately, the alerts all went unheeded. Furthermore, given that several alerts were issued before any data were actually removed from the Target systems, FireEye's automated malware deletion feature could have ended the assault without the need for any human action. However, the Target security team had turned that feature off, preferring a final manual overview of security decisions.[15]

With FireEye's red lights blinking furiously, the hackers began moving the stolen data on December 2, 2013. The malware continued to exfiltrate data freely for almost two weeks. Law enforcement officials from the Department of Justice contacted Target about the breach on December 12, armed not only with reports of fraudulent credit card charges, but also actual stolen data recovered from the dump servers, which the hackers had neglected to wipe.[16]

The aftermath of the breach caused tremendous financial damage to Target. It remains unknown what the precise cost of the breach was, but an estimate in Target's annual report of March 2016 put the figure at $291 million.[17] The company's reputation was harmed. The CIO resigned. For customers, there was increased risk of future fraud. Daily spending and withdrawal limits had to be placed on many affected accounts, and new credit cards had to be issued, causing consumers significant time loss while updating their card information everywhere.[18]

The breach went down in the annals of data breach history—one for the record books. But it would soon be overshadowed by even bigger breaches.

THE SYSTEM IS DOWN

On paper, the hackers never should have been able to breach Target. The hackers used cheap methods, such as readily detectable malware that wasn't state-of-the-art. They were quite sloppy and made careless mistakes. Target had much better technological tools and a large and sophisticated team. It conducted phishing tests and employed forensic investigators. The hackers were grossly outspent and outnumbered. Yet Target was still felled.

At first glance, it seems that Target's Achilles' heel was one employee at one of its third-party vendors. Most large companies have hundreds of third-party vendors. This person made just one wrong click of the mouse, and that was all the hackers needed. Had that one person not clicked, then a data breach leading to more than half-a-billion dollars might not have occurred. That's one very expensive mouse click!

However, a prolonged look reveals a host of systemic vulnerabilities. Although on a checklist Target looked healthy, it lost because one key factor wasn't accounted for—human behavior. Spending millions of dollars and installing high-tech software still couldn't prevent the humans from their fateful blunders.

It doesn't necessarily take technical wizardry or great skill to be a highly successful criminal on the Internet. Technologies and data ecosystems are so fragile and flawed that it is far too easy for hackers to break in. The black market is overflowing with cybercrime start-up kits.[19] Just download the tools and it's off to the races. Because crime committed using the Internet is rarely tracked down and enforced, in most cases, the fraudsters get away with it.

WE HAVE MUCH TO LOSE

The stakes for data security are enormous. Data breaches, by which we mean the unauthorized exposure, disclosure, or loss of personal information, are not only more numerous; they are more damaging. Every year, millions of people are victimized by identity theft. Their personal data is used by fraudsters to impersonate them. Victims suffer because their credit files become polluted with delinquent bills. Creditors go after victims for the unpaid bills, and victims struggle to prove that the bills weren't theirs. Identity thieves also steal people's identities to obtain medical care, and this has resulted in people losing their health insurance. There are cases where the police have arrested victims because their police records were tainted by the identity thieves.

Ransomware attacks are rising dramatically. Ransomware works by encrypting files on people's computers so that the files are unreadable and inaccessible. The data is held hostage. To get the data back, victims must pay the hackers a ransom. Ransomware is incredibly profitable for hackers. It is a frightening world where at any moment, all our computer files—our documents, our precious photos and videos, our music, our most important information—can be held hostage for a ransom. In 2018, the city of Atlanta, Georgia, spent $2.6 million to recover from a ransomware attack on the city's systems that asked for the rough equivalent of about $50,000 worth of the electronic currency Bitcoin.[20]

Malicious hackers can readily frame people when data is compromised. They can put incriminating files onto people's computers and then tip off law enforcement authorities.[21] Hackers can also access your most private photos and writings and publish them to the world.[22] They can take over your computer and use it to spam other people or to serve as a conduit through which to commit crimes.

As more devices, appliances, and vehicles are hooked up to the Internet, physical safety is at grave risk.[23] Hackers can break into our home devices. They can peer at our children through our baby cameras. They can snoop around through our home security cameras. They can listen in on us through our home assistant devices. They can gain control of our cars. They can also hack into implantable devices in our bodies, such as pacemakers or insulin pumps.

As more and more of our sensitive data is maintained in vast dossiers about us, as our biometric information is gathered and stored—such as our fingerprints, eye scans, facial data, and DNA—what will the future look like if organizations can't keep it secure?

In *Minority Report*, a 2002 movie based upon a short story by Philip K. Dick, the protagonist John Anderton is on the run, being pursued exhaustively by the authorities. The movie is set in the future—2054—where the government and businesses use extensive surveillance technologies. To evade capture via ever-present retinal scanners, John must undergo an operation to replace both of his eyes. The procedure is rather gruesome, but it is necessary given the pervasive use of biometric identification in the story.

Imagine the data breach notification letters of the future:

> *We regret to inform you that we have suffered a breach, and hackers have obtained your retinal data, which they could use to impersonate you and gain access to accounts. To guard against future harm, we recommend that you immediately schedule an operation to replace your eyes.*

We are hurtling forward into a perilous future, with organizations collecting more data and with the consequences of its misuse becoming more dire—and even deadly.

DATA SECURITY LAW'S GRAND ENTRANCE

During the past two decades, policymakers have rushed out a body of law to address the worsening data security nightmare. The most significant development is the rise of data breach notification laws, which require organizations that are breached to notify regulators, affected individuals, and sometimes the media. Breach notification is immensely popular; every state in America, as well as many countries, now have these laws. Unfortunately, breach notification merely alerts victims that their data was compromised in a breach. It doesn't cure the harm; it just informs people of the danger.

Then come the class action lawsuits. Sometimes mere hours after a breach is made public, attorneys file lawsuits against companies on behalf of those whose data was compromised. Many of the suits fail. Others end up settling, with companies paying to save on the cost of litigating the case. Consumers often don't receive any significant benefits or compensation.

In the Target case, the consumer lawsuits for the breach settled for a pittance—just $10 million. The settlement was a fee paid not on the merits of the case but to make it go away. The Target breach affected between 70 and 110 million individuals, which means that the recovery amounted to just a few pennies per person.[24] Victims did not see significant restitution as the settlement only applied to the reimbursement of notoriously elusive "documented damages" and reimbursements for "lost time," which is often not given much value.

After breaches, regulators also step in to enforce, but many times regulators take a pass. There are too many breaches each year, and regulators only have the resources to go after a small fraction of them. When regulators step in, their penalties often just increase the cost of the breach to a small or modest degree. For example, a group of state regulators settled with Target for $18.5 million.[25] With the Target breach costs at an estimated $291 million, this regulatory penalty represents less than 10 percent of the total. Even if regulators or individual litigants were to recover more in penalties and damages, it's not clear that things would be any different. Of course, greater monetary pain after a data breach might provide a stronger incentive to keep data secure, but organizations already face significant costs for breaches, and the additional incentive is not likely going to be a game changer. Target was already taking security quite seriously and devoting significant resources to it. Target failed not because of a lack of commitment to data security but because it made mistakes.

Breaches set in motion a series of legal responses that often drag on for years and mire organizations in millions of dollars in expenses. By this time, however, it is far too late. The damage has been done, and the law mostly serves to heighten the expense to companies. While it is important to make sure that organizations internalize the risks they create, the law isn't addressing all other actors that create risk. To make matters worse, the law often fails to help individual victims whose data was compromised in the breach.

Despite data security law's obsession with data breaches, the law doesn't seem to be reducing the size, severity, or number of breaches. Data breaches are steadily increasing.[26] The news is inundated with stories about data breaches that were readily preventable through rather inexpensive, non-cumbersome means. Why aren't data breaches slowing down? Why doesn't the law seem to be making any difference?

THE ARGUMENT OF THIS BOOK AND A ROADMAP

This is a book about how to improve the law's approach to data security. Our goal is to reorient the way the law addresses actors who create and participate in systems that leave personal information vulnerable to exposure and misuse.

Our book is not about cybersecurity in the broadest sense of the term, which applies to all forms of security with systems that use the Internet.[27] Instead, our focus is on *data security*, a significant piece of the cybersecurity pie that involves personal data. Data security law is largely part of privacy, data protection, and consumer protection frameworks like the Federal Trade Commission's (FTC) enforcement of rules against deceptive and unfair trade practices, the European Union's General Data Protection Regulation (GDPR), statutes that govern entities using personal data like the Health Insurance Portability and Accountability Act (HIPAA), and the law of torts that provides a remedy for negligent data practices.[28]

Although there is a lot of overlap between optimal regulation for data security and cybersecurity, there are important differences. The risk thresholds, threat modeling, actors affected, and type and magnitude of harm can differ when personal data is involved rather than when supply chains, machinery, or infrastructure are involved. It thus makes sense in some contexts to treat data security as unique from other areas of cybersecurity, and the law does so. Data security law emerges more from privacy law than cybersecurity law.

Unfortunately, data security law currently exists in an awkward space between cybersecurity and privacy. Being in this space has been a detriment to data security law, which has often failed to incorporate the strengths of both cybersecurity and privacy. Laws addressing privacy issues often include data security as part of their framework. Because the legislative lens is on privacy, legislators typically focus on the individual. Breach notification dominates data security law. The security rules are often vague and sparse. In contrast, cybersecurity law frequently includes more robust security rules based on systems-focused security frameworks.

In a cruelly ironic way, data security law also fails to draw strengths from privacy law. Data security remains quite siloed from privacy. When it is part of privacy laws, data security is often cabined to narrow sections. Data security law has not fully incorporated privacy law's evolving recognition about designing to accommodate human behavior and protecting human values beyond confidentiality. To make matters worse, the protections in privacy law often fall short in ways that are bad for data security.

The fact that data security is often part of the fabric of privacy law is a missed opportunity. Lawmakers could draw from privacy law's toolbox to bring a richer and more nuanced approach to securing personal data. Yet so far, they have not.

In this book, we hope to bring data security law out of this "no man's land" to better reflect the overlapping wisdom of privacy and cybersecurity. Because we focus mainly on personal data, we largely leave to others more general critical cybersecurity issues such as infrastructure security, industrial espionage, cyberwarfare, computer crime, trade secrets and proprietary data, and the nuanced debates surrounding the market for and disclosure of security vulnerabilities.[29] Of course, these issues overlap with data security problems.[30] But in this book we are examining the data security piece of the pie.

We also are not seeking to critique the established strategies technologists have developed to protect information. Nor are we proposing new technological approaches to the field of cybersecurity. Rather, as legal scholars, we are drawing from existing security knowledge that the law often fails to embrace. Because we are not technology experts, we will not delve too deeply into technical specifics of data security. Instead, our goal is to develop principles and theories that can guide the law for the foreseeable future. In this book, we propose a general approach lawmakers and judges can take to improve the security of personal data, and we outline a broad set of principles to bring coherence and consistency to a body of law that for too long has been focusing in the wrong direction.

Our argument is built around one overarching point: To improve the rules for securing personal information, policymakers must counter-intuitively shift the law's focus beyond data breaches. Too much of the current law of data security places the breach at the center of everything. Turning data security law into the "law of breaches" has the effect of over-emphasizing the conduct of the breached entities while ignoring the other actors and factors that contributed to the breach. We present an alternative, broader vision of data security policy in three areas: accountability, redress, and technological design.

It is tempting to say to organizations: "Come on, just be more secure!" But data security is notoriously complicated and needs a great deal of calibration. Ironically, some attempts by lawmakers and industry to add more security can actually make systems more vulnerable.[31] Security measures come with difficult costs and tradeoffs, so the choice of which ones to use and how many is quite challenging.

Data security is a delicate dance between technology and people. The ideal amount of data security is not necessarily to be as secure as possible and avoid a breach at all costs. In most cases, it is a poor policy choice for an organization to have the strongest possible security because the tradeoffs are too significant. It is easy to underappreciate the costs of many security measures because costs are often thought of in monetary terms. But the biggest costs of many security measures are that they can reduce functionality, make things inefficient and inconvenient, and be difficult and time-consuming.

One of the challenges with data security is that there are no absolute answers, as we are dealing with a continuum of risk and an ongoing cat-and-mouse game between attackers and defenders. Policy choices depend upon not only an assessment of risk but also an assessment of the costs of addressing those risks. A complicated balancing must take place.

Current data security rules fail to address risk effectively. In many circumstances, the law penalizes breaches with little regard to considerations of risk and balance. Other times, the law levies no penalty against organizations even though their actions created enormous unwarranted risks.

We contend that there is a better role for law to play. The main lesson of this book is that time and again, data security law and policy are missing the bigger picture. Lawmakers should move beyond the reactionary "blaming the breached" and hold accountable all the actors in the data ecosystem that contribute to the problem. They should break down the silos between privacy and security. They should promote human-centric security that accounts for the way people actually think and act.

Part I of this book focuses on the challenges to data security and why the law is not adequately addressing these challenges.

In Chapter 2, we provide a brief history of data security in this century. We discuss how and why data breaches started to capture news media headlines. In our brief sweep through the past two decades, we cover the most historic breaches and the new security threats that emerged. When looking at the big picture, the war against data breaches is being lost, one battle at a time. There is a lot to learn from data breach stories; there are common plot lines that clearly show us why data security is so often failing.

In Chapter 3, we survey the law and policy of data security and analyze its strengths and weaknesses. We conclude that despite some small successes, law and policy are generally failing to combat the data security threats we face. Data security law is too reactionary. The law often merely increases the cost of data breaches but fails to do enough to prevent them. Moreover, the law has failed to protect individuals who are being put at greater risk by inadequate data security.

In Part II of this book, we propose a different approach to data security that we call "holistic data security." Under this approach, the law would apply earlier, more frequently, to more actors, and to more activity.

In Chapter 4, we introduce our approach, holistic data security, which focuses on the mitigation of risk in an entire data ecosystem. Instead of concentrating solely on individualized harm and specific breaches, data security law should aim to ensure the wellbeing and resilience of the data ecosystem. Our approach draws insights from fields that focus on entire systems, such as public health.[32] Both data security and public health rules seek to keep a complex and dynamic system safe and thriving. Both frameworks address complex, opaque, and ever-shifting risks that make attributing causation and effective enforcement at the individual level difficult. Both fields are tasked with mitigating the spread of "viruses." Yet public health law seeks to sustain the health of an entire population by mandating practices that reduce risk across the board.[33] Meanwhile, data security law struggles to look beyond the place where a virus took hold, addressing only the last links in the chain.

In Chapter 5, we contend that lawmakers and courts can better distribute responsibility among all the different actors who play a role in the problem of data security even if they are not proximate to an actual breach. Data breaches are not just caused by the particular organizations that have the breach. Breaches are the product of many actors—it takes a village to create a breach. We provide a survey of these various actors and their contributions to the problem.

Unfortunately, the law doesn't hold most of the actors accountable. Policymakers often focus rather myopically on the particular organizations being breached, and they often overlook the fact that data security is a systemic problem.

In Chapter 6, we argue that policymakers also often fail to address practices by other organizations that increase the harm of data breaches to people as well as increase the costs. We can't eliminate all breaches, but we can significantly reduce the harm that they cause.

In Chapter 7, we address the relationship between privacy and security. Privacy is a key and underappreciated aspect of data security. Right now, there is a schism between privacy and security in companies. Privacy functions are commonly addressed by the compliance and legal departments, while security is handled by the information technology department. The two areas are commonly split apart and rarely speak to each other.

We should bridge data security and privacy and make them go hand-in-hand in both law and policy. Strong privacy rules help create accountability for the collection, use, and dissemination of personal information and can reduce vulnerabilities and risk by minimizing the use and retention of personal information. Good privacy strengthens security.

In Chapter 8, we argue that although most failures in data security involve human error, policymakers are not designing security measures with humans in mind. Instead, humans are expected to do things that are beyond the bounds of normal cognition. Far too little emphasis and resources are given to educating people about their role in data security. The result is that policymakers have failed to address the greatest security vulnerability—the human factor.

Consider again the Target breach. On a checklist, Target looked healthy—it had good policies, a large security team, significant resources, and strong security software. Spending millions of dollars and installing high-tech software still couldn't prevent human blunders. Humans turned off the software. Humans ignored the blinking red lights. A human clicked on the wrong link.

Rethinking law with humans at the center is not just a simple rethink—it goes to the very core of our law and policy regarding data security. It means that many of our existing policies are flawed and that a number of commonly accepted good security practices are, in fact, bad.

■

In this book, we are calling for policymakers to take a new direction, a fundamental shift in focus. Along the way, we suggest some specific things that the law should require, but we are not aiming to provide a laundry list of particular measures. Our focus is on the big picture. We propose a different way of thinking about data security, and we set forth our vision for how the law can take a different approach.

A Broader Understanding of Data Security

The Data Breach Epidemic

D ata breaches have been an epidemic. Every year brings count-less headlines about companies whose safeguards have been de-feated, resulting in the exposure of personal data. Every year the breaches grow bigger and more numerous. What's worse is that we haven't reached the peak yet—the curve just keeps going up, with no end in sight.

Organizations and policymakers can't be faulted for ignoring the problem. Over the years, many organizations have dramatically increased their spending on security. Policymakers have sprung into action, enacting a myriad of new data security and breach notification laws during the past 15 years. But the problem keeps growing.

It is difficult to fully understand the scope of the problem. Stats on data breaches differ quite substantially, so it is hard to obtain precise num-bers. Additionally, the metric for measuring the extent of the data breach problem is unclear. Some commentators point to the number of breaches in a given year and others point to the number of records breached. Both figures are subject to some flux and contingency, especially the number of records breached, because one enormous breach can significantly impact that number.

Additionally, breaches are often attributed to the year in which they are announced, but this date often is long after the breach occurred. For example, the Yahoo breaches occurred in 2013 and 2014 but weren't fully reported until 2016 and 2017.

Is there any wisdom to be gleaned from these statistics? Comparisons from one year to the next have often been made, with each year often being designated as the worst. Despite the lack of precision in the data, the trend over time has been clear—a notable increase in the number of breaches and the number of records breached.[1] For example, in 2005, there were 136 reported breaches involving about 55 million records.[2] In 2018, there were 668 reported beaches involving about 1.37 billion records. We have yet to see any signs that this terrible trajectory will improve.

A BRIEF HISTORY OF DATA BREACHES

Ever since data breaches started to be reported, the stories have proceeded in an endless parade of horrors. The unofficial beginning of the data breach nightmare occurred in 2005 with the announcement of the ChoicePoint breach. ChoicePoint, a Big Data company that amassed extensive profiles of personal data on people, was breached when fraudsters masqueraded as legitimate customers and obtained records on about 162,000 individuals.[3]

ChoicePoint's announcement of its breach was one of the first public disclosures by an organization that it had been infiltrated. Before 2005, there were certainly many data breaches, but companies weren't required to report them, so there isn't much recorded history. These were akin to prehistoric times. In 2005, light began to shine on the dark underworld of data security.

After the announcement of the ChoicePoint breach, several other companies came forward with their data breaches. Bank of America announced a breach involving 1.2 million records. DSW, a retailer, disclosed a hack that compromised 1.4 million records. Citigroup announced a breach involving 3.9 million records. These breaches seemed to be large until Card Systems Solutions announced that it had 40 million records hacked.

Although there were accounts of a few breaches prior to 2005, it wasn't until this year that the mainstream news started to focus on data breaches. California's breach notification law—and the rapid passage of similar laws in other states—prompted many organizations to finally air their dirty laundry. Data breaches finally received public attention. InfoWorld and other publications proclaimed 2005 to be "The Year of the Data Breach."[4] It wouldn't be the last.

In 2006, the average cost of a breach was estimated at exceeding $3 million. As concerns about data breaches mounted, many state lawmakers were jolted into action and passed breach notification laws.[5]

The saga continued in 2007. The data economy blossomed. Netflix had just begun its streaming service, and Apple introduced the iPhone. But the fraudsters were also having a banner year. According to an article by the Associated Press: "The loss or theft of personal data such as credit card and Social Security Numbers soared to unprecedented levels in 2007."[6]

A gang of hackers infiltrated the computer system of supermarket chain Hannaford Brothers and accessed 4.2 million records.[7] Retailer TJ Maxx suffered an enormous breach of credit card information, which was noted at the time to be the "largest hack ever." Initial reports pegged the number of records at 45 million.[8] This huge figure was shocking at the time, but ironically, it was far lower than the actual tally, which was later revised to 94 million. TD Ameritrade's database of 6.3 million clients was compromised through malware.[9]

In 2008, data breaches increased by 47 percent from 2007.[10] Bank of New York Mellon lost a box of back-up tapes with personal data, including Social Security Numbers. The tapes weren't encrypted, and 12.5 million records were compromised. The breach prompted the governor of Connecticut to declare: "It is simply outrageous that this mountain of information was not better protected."[11]

Forbes awarded 2009 the title of "Year of the Mega Data Breach."[12] The European Union implemented a data breach notification regime by amending its e-Privacy directive.[13] The largest breach announcement of the year was a hack of Heartland Payment Systems involving 130 million records. The breach cost the company more than $200 million dollars, and its stock dropped by more than 77 percent within a few months of announcing the breach.[14]

A breach at software company RockYou exposed user account data of 32 million people. Hackers were thrilled to discover that RockYou stored the data in plain text without encryption.[15]

A hacker broke into a database maintained by the state of Virginia to track prescription drug abuse. The hacker deleted 8 million patient records and demanded $10 million in ransom to recover them:

> I have your [expletive] in *my* possession, right now, are 8,257,378 patient records and a total of 35,548,087 prescriptions. Also, I made an encrypted backup and deleted the original. Unfortunately for Virginia, their backups seem to have gone missing, too. Uhoh :(For $10 million, I will gladly send along the password.[16]

This incident appears to be an early harbinger of the ransomware epidemic that would spread exponentially a few years later.

2010 was another gigantic year in data breach history. According to a report by Experian, data breaches were "happening on a bigger scale and affecting more consumers than ever." The report noted that 26 percent of consumers received a breach notification letter. More than 25 percent of affected individuals had to replace a debit or credit card.[17]

The computer virus Stuxnet showed just how vulnerable technical systems were to attack. The virus caused real world physical effects when it disrupted the centrifuges in an Iranian uranium enrichment plant.[18]

Many pundits proclaimed 2011 as the "Year of the Data Breach."[19] The loose collectives Anonymous and LulzSec introduced the world to "hacktivism," while more profit-minded hackers set their sights on healthcare. Health data breaches increased by 97 percent in 2011.[20]

Even data security firms weren't immune from breaches. RSA Security, which provided security to 40 million businesses, was hacked. A hacker sent phishing emails with the subject "2011 Recruitment Plan" to a few employees. The spam filter caught the email, but one employee retrieved it from the spam folder and clicked on the attached Excel document, infecting the system with malware.[21] The malware enabled the hacker to access the system and obtain credentials to break into other systems.

One fateful click also resulted in one of the largest breaches of the year. At Epsilon, an email marketing company, an employee clicked on a phishing email, enabling hackers to access 60 million records.[22] The cost of the breach was estimated to be in the billions.[23]

Fueling the rise of data breaches, illicit markets for stolen data began to emerge. Criminals could sell their spoils of personal data, and other criminals could buy key pieces of data to help them plunder. The personal data peddled in this crooked bazaar could be used for answering password recovery questions to steal passwords or for filling out fraudulent credit card applications. Fraudsters could also purchase user passwords from previously hacked sites; these passwords are valuable because people often use the same password on multiple accounts. Markets in stolen data thus became a source of revenue for criminals, as well as a place for criminals to acquire data to help them hack other companies.

The most prominent of these underground markets was the Silk Road. Created in 2011 by Ross Ulbricht, a recent college graduate who longed to be an entrepreneur, Silk Road was an online marketplace that existed in the nether regions of cyberspace colloquially known as the "Dark Web." The Dark Web originated in the early 2000s. Because users could remain anonymous and be difficult to trace, the Dark Web became a virtual bazaar for hacked personal data.[24] Silk Road quickly grew to become a major marketplace in the Dark Web.

Donning the pseudonym Dread Pirate Roberts (from the book and movie, *The Princess Bride*), Ulbricht hoped to develop Silk Road into a libertarian utopia beyond the restrictive authority of governments.[25] Silk Road was made possible by the rise of cryptocurrency, such as Bitcoin, which enabled financial transactions that could be nearly impossible to trace.

Silk Road quickly became a cesspool for drug trafficking, murder-for-hire, and other illegal activities. People could even hire hackers to hack for them.[26] The "Hacking Pack" was also for sale, which contained more than 100 hacking tools and software programs.[27]

At one point, a Silk Road user was able to figure out the identities of other Silk Road users and started to blackmail Ulbricht by threatening to release the names publicly. Ulbricht reached out to another Silk Road user to kill the blackmailer.[28]

Ultimately, Ulbricht was caught, convicted, and sentenced to a double life sentence without the possibility of parole. Silk Road was shut down. But the Dark Web is a much vaster place, and new illicit marketplaces have emerged where hackers can readily sell the personal data they plunder.

In 2012, breaches continued at a torrid pace. *VentureBeat* proclaimed 2012 to be a "big, bad year for online security breaches."[29] Hackers broke into LinkedIn, accessed its user passwords, and posted 6.5 million of them on a hacker forum. The passwords were not sufficiently encrypted,

Figure 2.1

and many were cracked quickly.[30] Not much happened afterwards, so the damage appeared to be small, but four years later, 117 million LinkedIn passwords suddenly appeared online.[31]

Later in 2012, Dropbox was hacked, resulting in a breach of more than 68 million user login credentials. The breach was actually a downstream effect of the LinkedIn breach. A Dropbox employee was using the same password from LinkedIn for his workplace Dropbox account. Armed with the password from the LinkedIn breach, hackers broke into Dropbox's network through this employee account.[32]

Ransomware began to flourish in 2012. Ransomware is malware that encrypts data on a computer system or device. The victim must pay a ransom to get the key to decrypt (unencrypt) the data. Originating in 1989, ransomware suddenly escalated from an obscure occurrence to one of the leading threats online.[33]

PC World awarded 2013 with the title of the "Year of the Personal Data Breach."[34] Symantec upped the ante and gave this year the title of "Year of the Mega Data Breach."[35] According to Symantec, "Attacks against businesses of all sizes grew, with an overall increase of 91 percent from 2012."[36] Malware and malicious apps for mobile devices grew substantially

Figure 2.2

in 2013. Ransomware grew like a weed, with a 500 percent increase from 2012.[37]

Target was one of the biggest and most notable breaches of the year, involving 110 million records. Hackers stole login information of 38 million people from Adobe, including passwords and credit card data. Later, an enormous file was posted anonymously online that included login credentials of more than 150 million accounts.[38] Hackers broke into a backup server with inadequate protection because the same encryption key was used for all passwords. Adobe was planning to fix the issue, but it never got around to it.[39]

In 2014, many media entities proclaimed the year to be the "Year of the Data Breach."[40] Hackers released hundreds of private, often nude, photos of women celebrities online, demonstrating that breaches can be acutely harmful and reflective of the gendered Internet attacks on women.[41] Two more states passed breach notification laws, but the breaches kept coming.[42]

One of the most notable breaches announced in 2014 was the Home Depot breach. Criminals remotely stole payment card data from self-checkout kiosks for about half a year until Home Depot discovered the activity. As with many other breaches, the initial hole in Home Depot's armor was an external vendor, where the thieves were able to obtain network credentials. From there, because of a poorly segmented network, the cybercrooks were able to work their way around as if in a giant playground.[43]

JP Morgan Chase was also breached, exposing 76 million records in "the largest intrusion of an American bank to date." Hackers broke in with stolen login credentials from one employee, then exploited a neglected database that hadn't been upgraded to require two-factor authentication. This simple upgrade could have stopped this debacle from happening, but it was overlooked. JP Morgan Chase spent $250 million per year on security, but it was felled by a small oversight.[44]

Sony Pictures was attacked in retaliation for its upcoming release of a comedy about North Korean leader Kim Jong Un. Attackers backed by the North Korean government broke in by stealing an administrator's credentials through a phishing scheme.[45] On the morning of November 24, 2014, Sony employees turned on their computers to see a red skeleton and a message threatening to release the data publicly.[46] The hackers made good on their threat, publicly posting private emails of Sony employees, including emails by executives, some of whom made insulting comments about celebrities and others.

According to a Symantec report on ransomware, "Between 2013 and 2014, there was a 250 percent increase in new crypto ransomware families on the threat landscape." As the Symantec report observes: "Never before in the history of humankind have people across the world been subjected to extortion on a massive scale as they are today."[47] The fact that so many companies were being infiltrated led FBI director James Comey to state: "There are two kinds of big companies in the United States. There are those who've been hacked . . . and those who don't know they've been hacked."[48]

The year 2015 earned the title of "the year of the data breach"—a title that nearly every year has earned.[49] One study noted: "In 2010, you had a one in nine chance of becoming a victim of identity theft after your financial or personal information was swiped. Today, your odds have increased to one in three."[50]

The health plan Anthem had a breach of 80 million patient records involving very sensitive data. Hackers broke in when one employee clicked on a phishing email.[51] The breach was noted as the "largest healthcare breach in history."[52] On the very same day that Anthem announced its breach, Premera Blue Cross discovered it had been hacked, compromising 11 million records.[53]

Hackers also attacked Ashley Madison, a website for facilitating extramarital affairs. They obtained 32 million records and posted them online. Although some people had paid a fee to Ashley Madison to delete all their data, the company hadn't done so.[54] Ashley Madison also used weak encryption to store sensitive data. After the hackers posted the data online, several of the people exposed committed suicide.[55]

Experian also announced a major breach involving 15 million people's Social Security Numbers and other personal data. Ironically, the breach was announced at the beginning of National Cybersecurity Awareness Month.[56]

In 2016, the total number of records compromised in recorded breaches in all years surpassed 6 billion. *Bloomberg News* proclaimed that 2016 was a "record year."[57] Mossack Fonesca, a Panamanian law firm, had a breach that involved 11.5 million records of wealthy clients from many countries who were seeking to evade taxes. The incident was dubbed the "Panama Papers" breach.[58]

In one of the tardiest breach announcements in history, Yahoo announced a series of breaches that occurred in 2013 and 2014 involving 3 billion records, making this the largest series of breaches in the history of humankind. In 2018, the SEC fined Yahoo for covering up the breach for several years, failing to inform investors, and not fully investigating the breach. The fine is notable for being the SEC's first fine for failing to disclose a data breach, but the fine was just for $35 million, which is low considering the egregiousness of Yahoo's actions.[59]

The ransomware epidemic continued, prompting the FBI to issue a warning and request to be informed about new ransomware infections.[60] Ransomware attacks averaged 4,000 per day. The year began with a 300 percent increase in daily ransomware attacks compared to 2015.[61] Where ransomware attacks previously targeted mainly smaller businesses and demanded small ransoms of a few hundred to a few thousand dollars, the criminals began to shift to targeting larger organizations and demanding higher ransoms. They also attacked hospitals. Hollywood Presbyterian Medical Center paid attackers $17,000 in bitcoin in February 2016. By 2020, ransom demands on hospitals or healthcare entities would top $1 million.[62]

While politically motivated hacks—"hacktivism"—gained prominence in 2011 with the growth of Anonymous, politically motivated hacks in 2016 targeted major parties. Prominent members of the Democratic Party were hacked in 2016, including John Podesta, chairman of Hilary Clinton's presidential campaign. Sponsored by the Russian government, hackers sent phishing emails to more than 100 members of Clinton's campaign. When the hackers had trouble infiltrating official campaign email accounts, the hackers turned to targeting people through their personal email accounts, which they used to break in.[63] The hacked emails were subsequently provided to WikiLeaks, which published 20,000 of the hacked emails.

In 2017, the story was more of the same. As the Online Trust Alliance noted: "Surprising no one, 2017 marked another 'worst year ever' in personal data breaches and cyber incidents around the world."[64] The total all-time number of breaches reported surpassed 5,000 and involved more than 7.8 billion records compromised.[65] There are 7.6 billion people on Earth, so 2017 saw the total number of compromised records surpass the total world population.

Equifax had an enormous breach involving personal data of about 147 million people. The breach was caused by hackers who broke in through an unpatched software vulnerability.[66] Hackers stole data of 50 million riders and 7 million drivers from Uber. Uber's CEO paid the hackers $100,000 to keep the incident secret, a cover-up that resulted in his ouster and in criminal charges against the chief security officer.[67]

Bloomberg News proclaimed 2018 to be the "year of the data breach."[68] Alabama became the final U.S. state to pass a breach notification law.[69] The General Data Protection Regulation (GDPR) went into effect, resulting in data protection authorities all over Europe being overwhelmed with notifications due to the law's strict breach reporting requirements.[70] More than a dozen organizations had breaches involving more than 100 million records each.[71] One breach involved 1.1 billion records of India's national identification database.[72] Criminals were offering access to people's personal data for a fee, as well as software that could print out identification cards necessary for certain government services.

Marriott announced a breach of 500 million records. The breach began in the Starwood hotel chain's system back in 2014. Marriott acquired Starwood in 2016, but the breach wasn't discovered until 2018.[73] The hackers used a Trojan horse, which allowed them to remotely access the system. The hackers were able to gain access to credit card data and passport numbers, which unfortunately were unencrypted.[74]

In 2019, the number of breaches increased by more than 50 percent from the past four years.[75] As early as August 2019, the year was proclaimed to be a "landmark" year.[76] According to *Risk Based Security*: "On May 2, 2019, we hit a data breach milestone. The Cyber Risk Analytics research team added the 40,000th breach entry to our ever-expanding data breach database."[77] Continuing the trend, 2019 was labeled "the worst year on record" for data breach activity—"more breaches reported, more data exposed, and more credentials dumped online."[78]

Early in the year, a large treasure trove of 773 million email and 21 million passwords were posted in a hacker forum online. The data was called "Collection #1."[79] Hackers obtained 20 million records from the American Medical Collection Agency (AMCA). Due to the anticipated costs of the data breach, AMCA filed for bankruptcy protection, an ironic move because its business was debt collection.[80]

In the fall of 2019, the FBI warned: "Ransomware attacks are becoming more targeted, sophisticated, and costly, even as the overall frequency of attacks remains consistent."[81] Even worse, a new form of ransomware emerged. Unlike ransomware that just locks up your files, this new type of ransomware attack (dubbed "double extortion") also threatens to release personal data to the public.[82] When organizations refused to pay ransoms late in 2019, hackers behind Maze ransomware started posting the personal data online.[83]

A NEVER-ENDING SAGA

The saga over the past 15 years reads like a Shakespearean tragedy. Or, perhaps more aptly, it has the plot of a typical work of Franz Kafka—things start out badly, then get worse.

The Privacy Rights Clearinghouse, a public interest organization, keeps a database of publicly reported data breaches. When this manuscript was finalized, more than 9,000 data breaches have been reported involving more than 11.6 billion records.[84] There are many other organizations keeping track, and their numbers are just as ugly—if not uglier.

TABLE 2.1 A CHRONOLOGY OF DATA BREACHES BY THE
PRIVACY RIGHTS CLEARINGHOUSE

Year	Number of Reported Breaches	Number of Records Compromised
2005	136	55,101,241
2006	482	68,580,749
2007	455	149,957,907
2008	355	130,896,900
2009	270	251,575,814
2010	801	140,937,393
2011	793	447,901,379
2012	885	298,766,788
2013	889	158,787,838
2014	868	1,313,623,460
2015	540	318,795,437
2016	822	4,815,010,518
2017	766	2,048,397,757
2018	668	1,369,452,404
2019	stats not yet available	stats not yet available
2020	stats not yet available	stats not yet available

The numbers fluctuate each year, but the general trend is more breaches and compromised records with no improvement in sight.[85]

We should note that the numbers reflect reported breaches. Many breaches aren't reported, either because they don't fit the requirement to report or because they are unknown. According to an estimate by the Online Trust Alliance, the actual number of security incidents is more than 20 times the number of reported breaches.[86] Reported breaches are thus the tip of a much larger iceberg.

Each year brings more bad news. Each year steals the crown for the most awful year for data breaches. Are there any records left that haven't been compromised? Will we ever have a good year?

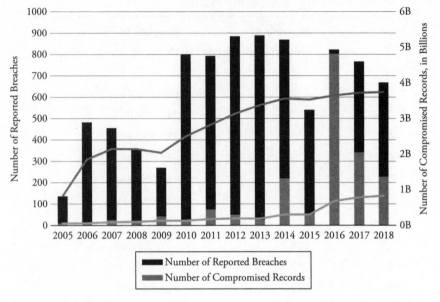

Figure 2.3

Figure 2.4

THE COMMON PLOTS OF DATA BREACH STORIES

If you are getting tired of hearing similar data breach stories over and over again, welcome to the world of data security. By now, you might have been hoping for something new. But, alas, to quote the eminent data breach expert, Yogi Berra, it has been "déjà vu all over again."

In a famous book, *The Seven Basic Plots*, Christopher Booker concludes that all stories use one of only seven plot structures.[87] A similar book could be written about data breaches, which seem to follow a few basic patterns again and again.

The Big Spend Wasn't Enough

Many organizations spent a lot of money on security yet still had big lapses in oversight. Throwing cash at the problem didn't stop the breaches.

Some organizations didn't seem to care at all, but even those that did devote a lot of resources to security were lacking. They would buy expensive shiny armor, but then forget to put on key pieces like the breastplate.

Human Error Opened the Door

Many breaches were facilitated by human error. Humans fell for a phishing scam. Humans failed to patch vulnerable software promptly. Humans lost devices with data on them. Humans misconfigured servers. One of the major imbalances in the world of data security is that defenders need to constantly protect the entire perimeter—every entry point and vulnerability. Meanwhile attackers need just one entry point and only must be successful once.

Vendors Were a Weak Link

Many large organizations had sophisticated defenses, but hackers figured out that they had a big vulnerability—their vendors that had access to their computer system. The vendors, typically small- to medium-sized companies that provided ancillary services to larger companies, had much weaker security. This allowed hackers to break into the vendors, steal their credentials, and then use these credentials to break into a company's computer system.

Too Much Data Was Being Kept (and Stored Together)

Many organizations were collecting data that they shouldn't have been collecting or retaining it when they should have been deleting it. Breaches grew bigger and bigger, mainly because organizations increased the quantities of records they maintained.

Organizations have been collecting and using data faster than they have been able to keep it secure—just like during the Industrial Revolution when factories sprouted up long before safety and pollution controls were introduced. Law professor Danielle Citron has called these bloated databases "reservoirs of danger"—an allusion to the precarious but profitable underregulated water dams during the Industrial Age.[88]

To make matters worse, many organizations stored the vast troves of data they were amassing all in one place. Because data wasn't adequately segmented, once the hackers broke in, they could quickly hit the mother lode and access everything.

Devices Always Seemed to Disappear

Lost or stolen devices played a big role in breaches. Storywriter and playwright Anton Chekhov famously noted that if there is a gun in Act One of a play, it surely will be fired by Act Three. When personal data is loaded onto a portable device such as a laptop or a thumb drive, it is often lost or stolen. These thefts are a disaster if the data on them isn't encrypted.

Data Was Not Encrypted

Many breaches involved failing to encrypt data. In a study from 2004, only 15 percent of organizations had an enterprise-wide encryption strategy. By 2014, 36 percent had such a strategy. Given the breach experience in the decade between 2004 and 2014, it is shocking that 64 percent still lacked a strategy.[89]

One Click Was All It Took

Phishing played a big role in data breaches. For many breaches, all it took was one gullible employee to click, and the hackers were able to get inside. For large organizations with thousands of employees, the risk can be enormous. And yet, despite the huge risk, many organizations have not been focusing enough on phishing prevention.

Lessons Weren't Learned

Despite the parade of horror stories, organizations have continued to make the same mistakes and have kept getting burned. Short-term thinking, as well as an *it-won't-happen-to-me* attitude, have been pervasive. For example, despite the fact that human error is an aspect of most data breaches, many organizations have failed to train employees about data security. In the healthcare sector, despite HIPAA's requirement to have security training, a quarter of U.S. healthcare employees have never received such training. It's even worse in Canada, where 40 percent of employers in the health care sector do not receive training. Of those that do, it's often not frequent enough—only 38 percent were trained annually.[90] These stats are not from 2000 or 2005—they are from 2019, after years and years where the healthcare industry experienced relentless hacking attacks and security blunders.

Breaches Often Involved Careless Simple Mistakes

There is an even broader, more overarching lesson to be learned from the miserable past 15 years in data security. Most of the breaches involved rather small, overlooked mistakes. It can be easy to get caught up focusing on the Leviathan and miss the low-hanging fruit. This low-hanging fruit consists of rather simple and easy-to-fix vulnerabilities and bad practices.

After reviewing more than 1,000 data breaches from 2018, the Online Trust Alliance (OTA) found that more than 95 percent could have been avoided.[91]

Although many organizations fear a diabolical hacker who can break into anything, what they should fear most are the small, careless errors that are continually being made. But the diffuse nature of the risks make them difficult for individual organizations to address.

■

Over the past 15 years of reported data breaches, there have been many new threats and technological developments, but what is quite remarkable is how the same common mistakes keep getting made again and again.

The Failure of Data Security Law

I t began with a seemingly small theft. A laptop computer went missing from the Veterans Affairs Medical Center. This theft, however, turned out to be anything but small. An employee had put the personal information of about 7,400 patients on the computer—their names, birthdates, physical description, age, weight, race, and the last four digits of their Social Security Numbers, among other things. To make matters worse, the information was unencrypted, which meant that the thief could readily access it.[1] Putting unencrypted personal information on a laptop— especially sensitive patient data at a hospital—is a big security no-no. But it happens all the time because people often act carelessly.

As is typical procedure following many data breaches, the medical center notified all the patients whose information was on the missing laptop. In every state in the U.S., the law requires that individuals be notified if their personal data is lost, leaked, or improperly accessed. The medical center offered free credit monitoring to all the patients for one year.

The problem, though, is that credit monitoring for just one year doesn't really address all the harm to the patients. Credit monitoring is a service that consumer reporting agencies provide that alerts people if there is unusual activity in their credit report. Credit monitoring doesn't immunize against fraud; it only provides an alert if there is suspicious activity. The period of one year is very limited. Criminals can use personal information to conduct fraud at any time, possibly many years in the future. Because credit monitoring sounds protective, it actually risks lulling people into a false sense of security. You can have your identity stolen, your tax refund intercepted, your sensitive information leaked, and your personal hard drive with all your documents and data locked up behind ransomware without credit monitoring triggering an alert.

Later, Dorn VAMC officials lost four boxes of pathology reports with information on about 2,000 patients. These boxes contained names, Social Security Numbers, and medical diagnoses. As with the laptop breach, Dorn VAMC notified the individuals and provided one year of free credit monitoring. The credit monitoring here did nothing to rectify the fact that patients' intimate health information was compromised.

A group of affected people sued Dorn VAMC. They argued that the breach caused them "embarrassment, inconvenience, unfairness, mental distress and threat of current and future substantial harm from identity theft and other misuse of their personal information." The plaintiffs argued that they had to spend time monitoring their accounts and purchasing various services to protect themselves from potential fraud.

Addressing both incidents together, the court noted that the data breaches were "disconcerting," but the plaintiffs had not suffered harm. The plaintiffs claimed that the lost data put them at greater risk for future fraud and identity theft. The court concluded, however, that this claim was "too speculative" because the plaintiffs had not yet been victimized by fraud. The fact that plaintiffs spent money for services to protect themselves was "self-imposed"—an attempt to "manufacture" a harm. The plaintiffs were thus out of luck.

This case demonstrates how badly the law of data security fails. The law failed to prevent the data breaches, which were readily preventable. The law failed to hold the medical center accountable for its inability to keep the data secure. The law required patients to be notified of the breach, but it failed to protect them from the harm the breach caused. The law also failed to compensate the patients for their lost time, anxiety, the increased risk of fraud they faced, their lost privacy over their personal and health information, and their expenditure of money to protect themselves. In almost every way, the law failed.

In this chapter, we examine personal data security law. This relatively new body of law has developed quickly, mostly in the last few decades. It is a sprawling framework, involving numerous types of laws at the federal and state levels, as well as internationally. Broadly speaking, there are three types of data security laws:

Breach Notification Laws

Laws that require organizations to notify various government authorities and affected individuals in the event of a data breach.

Security Safeguards Laws

Laws that require substantive administrative, physical, and technical measures to secure personal data.

Private Litigation

Lawsuits brought by affected individuals who are harmed by a data breach.

Our goal isn't to explore the law in intricate detail; treatises are written for this purpose. Instead, we aim to show some of the key themes of this law and draw some big picture conclusions. With data security law, the forest is often ignored for the trees, and laws keep sprouting up based on trendiness rather than good policy.

Each type of security law accomplishes some good things, but each type has many weaknesses. We are not arguing that existing security law should be abandoned. Nor are we arguing for completely different types of security law. Instead, the shortcomings of these types of law are actually due to a more overarching problem: *Data security law has an unhealthy obsession with data breaches.* This obsession has, ironically, been the primary reason why the law has failed to stop the deluge of data breaches. The more obsessed with breaches the law has become, the more the law has failed to deal with them.

BREACH NOTIFICATION LAWS

In February 2005, people in California started to receive letters from ChoicePoint, a company most had never heard of. ChoicePoint's business involved collecting personal data from numerous sources to compile extensive dossiers on millions of people. Companies and government agencies could sign up to access this data.

Among other things, ChoicePoint provided organizations with background check services for use in hiring. It stored the name, address, Social Security Number, driver's license number, credit report, and other information on virtually every adult in the United States.

Individuals, however, had no idea that ChoicePoint was gathering and selling all this data about them. ChoicePoint wasn't the only company doing this. In fact, many companies were engaged in this activity, and companies are still doing it today. This type of data aggregation and analytics is now referred to as "Big Data." Back in 2005, the activities of companies such as ChoicePoint weren't well known to most people.

The fraudsters in the ChoicePoint breach walked right in the front door. They pretended to be a legitimate business, which signed on as a client. The fraudsters were able to obtain personal data on approximately 162,000 people. The criminals then used the data for identity theft. At least 750 individuals suffered identity theft that was traced back to this breach.[2]

By today's standards, this breach was tiny; it pales in comparison to Yahoo's breach of more than one billion people or to other breaches with hundreds of millions of people. Yet, in 2005, when the breach was announced, it was a gargantuan story. At the time, the ACLU stated that the breach "may have been the biggest release of personal information to data thieves ever."[3]

The story captivated the media. Far from a fleeting headline, the ChoicePoint breach was the story that wouldn't go away. Unlike most news stories in this century, it lingered in the media for months. Why was this breach different? There had been countless other breaches before ChoicePoint, so why all the fuss?

The reason was because of a unique and innovative law that California passed in 2003.[4] The law required public and private organizations to notify Californians when the "unauthorized acquisition of computerized data" compromises "personal information maintained by the person or business."[5] The law didn't specify a deadline to notify people; organizations had to act without "undue delay."[6]

Prior to the California law, most breaches were dirt swept under the rug. They were certainly occurring, but they were ugly secrets whispered in the corridors. Why would a company publicly announce it had lost control over peoples' data if it didn't have to?

With California's law, for the first time the dirty laundry was starting to be hung out in public. The ChoicePoint breach angered people because it was not just about security; it was also about privacy. A company they hadn't heard of was collecting their data. People were upset they didn't know about it. They were upset because there was no benefit to them by ChoicePoint's collection of their data. All this was on top of the fact that the breach led to their data being in the hands of fraudsters. People were outraged.

ChoicePoint sent the initial breach notification letter just to the 35,000 California residents who were affected. Only California residents had been notified because California was the only state that required it.[7] Soon after, the Attorneys General from 19 other states began to clamor for their citizens to also be notified. They sent a letter to ChoicePoint demanding that every victim be notified.[8] Facing increasing criticism, ChoicePoint notified all affected individuals. In the month following the disclosure of the ChoicePoint breach, four major companies disclosed data breaches, including Bank of America.[9]

The Dramatic Rise of Breach Notification Laws

Breach notification has been the fastest growing and trendiest type of data security law. These laws continue to spread around the world. The laws have been evolving to include more types of personal data and to shorten the time organizations have to report data breaches and notify affected individuals.

Soon after the ChoicePoint breach, breach notification laws started sprouting up in other states. Every state wanted in on the action. By the end of 2005, 20 states and Puerto Rico had passed their own data breach laws, modeled largely on California's law.[10] By the end of 2006, more states passed data breach notification legislation, bringing the total to 33 states.[11] By the end of 2008, all but six states had passed data breach notification laws, with the rest gradually adopting laws at the rate of approximately one per year. In 2018, Alabama and South Dakota became the last two states to pass breach notification laws. Thus, within the span of 15 years, all 50 states, the District of Columbia, Guam, Puerto Rico, and the Virgin Islands passed breach notification laws.

This is truly a remarkable development. It is rare that all states reach a consensus about the need for a particular type of law, and it is quite amazing that they all managed to pass legislation in such a short span of time.

At the federal level, there was considerable talk about passing a breach notification law, but Congress has been gridlocked in partisan bickering for much of the time since 2000. During a brief window of legislative activity when the Democrats controlled both houses of Congress in 2009, a breach notification requirement was passed as part of the HITECH Act (which was part of the law known as Obamacare). The U.S. Department of Health and Human Services, pursuant to the HITECH Act, promulgated the HIPAA Breach Notification Rule on January 25, 2013.[12] This was the first federal breach notification requirement, though it only applied to health data regulated by HIPAA. Had Congress not been so broken in the early 21st century, it likely would have passed a broader federal breach notification law.

Breach notification also has proven to be quite popular abroad. Unlike many types of U.S. privacy and security laws, which are viewed by much of the world as weak and incoherent, countries have eagerly sought to emulate the United States in breach notification. The EU incorporated breach notification as part of its major privacy legislation—the General Data Protection Regulation (GDPR).

Breach notification has been a huge hit. Mandated disclosure laws like this one are popular at least in part because they don't eat up a lot of resources for enforcement, and they relieve lawmakers from making some difficult case-by-case decisions.[13] You have probably received quite a few data breach notification letters. If you haven't, then you might want to call the *Guinness Book of World Records* for being the only human alive not to have received a breach letter. In case you haven't received such a letter—or more likely haven't read any of these letters—here's a brief overview of what the typical letter says: It begins by saying that the organization regrets to inform you that your data was lost or stolen or improperly accessed, describes the type of data involved, briefly relays what is known about the incident, provides a phone number hotline to call for more information, and often offers one year of free credit monitoring. And that's it, even if you get that much.

The organization sending these letters hope that after a quick groan, you will throw the letter in the trash and move on with your day. Indeed, the costs for organizations are lower if fewer people call the hotline or request credit monitoring, so the letters are written to avoid making people feel uneasy or alarmed.

Breach notification is now a basic part of the canon for data security law. That lone California law sparked a trend that has launched billions of letters. If there's an undisputed winner in all this, it's the post office.

Variations in Breach Notification Laws

Although breach notification laws all have some form of notification in common, the laws are far from uniform, and their approaches have evolved over the years.

Breach notification laws differ significantly on how they define a "data breach"—the type of incident that triggers notification. Generally speaking, most states define a breach either as any unauthorized access to personal information or as acquisition of personal information.[14] Many states adopt some form of a harm requirement along the lines of the "CIA" security triad (intrusions that compromise the confidentiality, integrity, or availability of personal data).[15] However, enough ambiguity remains in many definitions of a security breach that it is not fully clear if a breach occurs merely when unauthorized people gain access to a data storage system or whether the data must be exposed to significant risk (even if harm has not yet occurrred).[16]

California's breach law requires that personal data be "reasonably believed" to have been "acquired" by an unauthorized party.[17] According to guidance by the California Office of Privacy Protection, factors to demonstrate acquisition of personal data include indications that the data is "in the physical possession and control of an unauthorized person" or "has been downloaded or copied" or "was used by an unauthorized person."[18] Many U.S. states have followed this approach and define a breach as involving the acquisition of personal data.

The problem with requiring the acquisition of data is that sometimes unauthorized people look at data yet do not copy it. The goal might have been just to learn information. But many laws do not consider such actions to be a breach. Frequently, all that can be known is that a hacker broke in and improperly accessed the data; whether the hacker copied it or used it is unknown. Nor is it known what the hacker might do in the future. In other words, the hacker could have acquired the data, but it is quite difficult to know for sure.

Other notification laws require notification only if here is a "misuse" of personal data or a reasonable likelihood of misuse.[19] HIPAA's breach notification standard requires notification when there is a risk greater than a "low risk" that information is "compromised."[20] The EU's General Data Protection Regulation (GDPR) requires notification whenever data has been improperly accessed, destroyed, lost, or altered that will "result in a risk to the rights and freedoms of natural persons."[21]

Another way that notification laws vary is in how they define "personal information." Notification is required only for breaches involving personal information. In the U.S., most states define personal information as an individual's first name or first initial and last name in combination with an additional data element, such as a Social Security Number, driver's license number, or financial account information with the applicable PIN or access code for same. Recently, however, many states have amended their statute's definition of personal information to include additional data elements, such as biometric health information, username, email address, and password.

In the EU, the GDPR has a broader concept of personal information. Using the term "personal data," the GDPR's definition encompasses "any information relating to an identified or identifiable natural person." Personal data is "identifiable" when it is possible to identify people directly or indirectly" from the information.[22] The GDPR's definition is much more sensible compared to the way many U.S. notification laws have defined personal information. There are many instances under U.S. laws where information can be linked to people and can be used to cause them harm yet don't fall under the statutory definitions of personal information.

Once a notification law is triggered—by a type of incident affecting personal information—the laws further vary in how quickly they require notification. Many laws mandate notification "without delay" or "as soon as practicable." In the United States, a sizeable minority of states (about 40 percent) have timelines. Florida and Ohio were the first states to mandate a maximum time (45 days) between the identification of a breach and notification of the affected parties. Both laws were passed in 2005. In 2006, Wisconsin and Colorado set time limits of 45 days and 30 days, respectively.

Before 2014, only these four states had set time limits. But then, in 2014 and over the next few years, 14 more states added timelines ranging from 15 to 90 days, with most still mandating 45 days. Recently, timelines have been shrinking. The GDPR, for example, requires notification of the authorities within 72 hours after discovering the breach.[23]

Notification laws also diverge in who can sue following a violation of the law. In the U.S., 10 states and the District of Columbia explicitly allow for a private right of action in their laws.[24] Most states lack a private right of action.

Problems with Breach Notification Laws

Breach notification laws are quite popular, but do they work well? In at least one way, they do. Breach notification laws have added much greater transparency to data breaches. The increased transparency has been tremendously important, shedding much-needed light on the extensiveness of the data breach epidemic and the inadequacy of the data security of many organizations. They also at least provide a reputational incentive to encourage executives to invest some resources into avoiding data breaches.

Unfortunately, in many other respects, breach notification falls short. Breach notification laws ultimately do not require good security; they merely require organizations to provide information about data breaches.

INADEQUATE PROTECTION OF CONSUMERS

A main purported goal of breach notification is to help protect consumers, but it is not clear that the laws achieve this purpose. Recall the Target breach that we discussed earlier. Under the law of most states, Target was required to individually notify affected customers. Target sent out a letter from its CEO that stated, in part:

> Target learned in mid-December that criminals forced their way into our systems and took guest information, including debit and credit card data. Late last week, as part of our ongoing investigation, we learned that additional information, including name, mailing address, phone number or email address, was also taken. I am writing to make you aware that your name, mailing address, phone number or email address may have been taken during the intrusion.

People are affected by so many breaches, and they receive letters like this all the time. The letters say little to help people assess their risk, and there is often not much people can do except to keep a more watchful eye on their credit, change their passwords, and hope that nothing bad happens to them in the future.

People also experience "breach notification fatigue." Receiving countless notices becomes tiresome, making some people throw up their hands and think that all is hopeless.[25] People might not respond with as much concern or take protective steps after receiving so many breach notifications.

Notification timelines are getting shorter as a way to make laws tougher. The GDPR requires companies to send notifications without "undue delay" but not later than 72 hours after becoming aware of the breach. The Federal Deposit Insurance Corporation (FDIC) has proposed a 36-hour time frame.[26] But shorter timelines aren't always beneficial. In the initial days following a breach, not enough is known about the nature, size, and scope of the data breach to report details accurately. Too much attention is placed on how to make the notification and not enough on figuring out what went wrong and how to stop the bleeding.

States and countries are racing to create the shortest possible reporting and notification deadlines. Reporting often occurs too soon to provide accurate, meaningful information.

Even when people do receive a notice, there often isn't much they can do about the breach. People can change their passwords and keep an eye on their credit card transactions, but they can't change their fingerprints, and Social Security Numbers are very difficult to change.

Unproductive Increase in the Costs of a Breach

A byproduct of breach notification is that it increases the costs and pain of a breach. Reporting a breach to all the different regulators involved is a cumbersome and complicated task—and it's very expensive. A myriad of different deadlines and requirements must be met—and often in a very short period of time.

Notification letters are quite costly to send, especially for large breaches involving tens of millions of people. Breach notification in essence works like a strict liability fine, as it involves costs regardless of whether an organization was at fault for a breach. Organizations must pay costs to notify based on the size of the breach not based on how careless they were.

Lawmakers often aim to deter careless conduct by making fault the trigger for liability. The idea is to increase costs for those acting carelessly.

Because the costs of notification are not based upon a company's fault, however, notification rules impose the same costs on everyone. Those who have strong security must face the same costs as those who have poor security.[27] This is a lost opportunity to incentivize better data security. Of course, other laws can penalize fault, such as private litigation, but as we will discuss later, this type of law isn't working very well either.

When California first conceived of breach notification, few knew the full scope of our data vulnerability. The breach notification law was a critical intervention at the right time. But our understanding of the problem has evolved over time and so too must our rules. Breach notification provides valuable transparency and some reputational incentives to invest in meaningful data safeguards, but it achieves these goals at a tremendously high expense, siphoning resources and money from other measures to address security. Breach notification is also problematic when policymakers view it as the primary response to data breaches. Breach notification is being asked to do far more than it is capable of. It provides transparency, but it doesn't provide prevention, protection, or a fix.

Too much money and resources are spent on notification with not enough being achieved. There are ways to provide transparency at a

Figure 3.1

fraction of the time and cost. For example, lawmakers might remove the requirement for notifying individuals about a data breach in lieu of more robust public disclosure requirements that ensure high visibility of a breach in the media and by regulators. Although breach notification produces light, it also generates a lot of unnecessary heat. Resources could be better allocated to other security measures that would help improve data security.

SECURITY SAFEGUARDS LAWS

A second type of data security law is what we refer to as *security safeguards* laws. These types of laws existed long before breach notification laws. They are the workhorse of data security law.

Safeguards laws differ from breach notification laws because safeguards laws involve administrative, physical, and technical data security standards. Breach notification is mainly about providing information about data breaches.

Security safeguards were incorporated into many of the privacy laws of the 1970s, 1980s, and 1990s. It is important to note that security was often dealt with in *privacy* laws rather than separate security laws. These days, things have changed, and legislatures often pass independent security laws.

The reason why security was included in privacy laws traces back to the original set of Fair Information Practice Principles (FIPPs), which have formed the backbone of most data privacy laws. The FIPPs were famously articulated in the 1973 Report by the U.S. Department of Health, Education, and Welfare (HEW). The report, *Records, Computers, and the Rights of Citizens*, was an early attempt to address the rights and responsibilities associated with keeping data about individuals. The report recommended the passage of a code of FIPPs, which have been highly influential in shaping countless privacy laws. Among the FIPPs was the following: "Any organization creating, maintaining, using, or disseminating records of identifiable personal data must assure the reliability of the data for their intended use and must take reasonable precautions to prevent misuse of the data."[28]

Whether included in privacy laws or, later on, in separate security laws, the security safeguards approach to regulating data security aims to require organizations to implement security safeguards to protect personal data. This approach differs significantly from breach notification, which focuses only on providing notice that a data breach has occurred. Security safeguards involve various best practices that organizations should undertake regarding data security. Examples of safeguards include having a chief security officer, having a comprehensive security program, having key policies for security, controlling access to data, encrypting data, backing up data, properly retaining and destroying data, and so on.

Types of Security Safeguards Laws

Broadly, there are two approaches to security safeguards laws: (1) the standards approach, and (2) the reasonableness approach. The standards approach provides a list of particular safeguards that organizations must implement. In contrast, the reasonableness approach broadly mandates "reasonable" data security safeguards but doesn't specify particular ones. This approach tackles the issues case-by-case. Over time, though, as reasonableness laws are enforced, specific security measures emerge from the cases.

THE STANDARDS APPROACH

Security laws that use a standards approach specify a series of security safeguards that must be followed. For example, the Homeland Security Act, which included the Federal Information Security Management Act (FISMA) of 2002, adopts this approach. FISMA requires all federal agencies "to develop, document, and implement an agency-wide program to provide information security for the information and information systems that support the operations and assets of the agency."[29]

The Health Insurance Portability and Accountability Act (HIPAA) regulations in the early 2000s adopts a hybrid standards approach. The HIPAA Privacy Rule uses the reasonableness approach, merely stating that administrative, technical, and physical safeguards should be used. But the HIPAA Security Rule of 2003 uses the standards approach, including a detailed list of 18 administrative, technical, and physical standards as well as 36 implementation specifications, which indicate more specifically how to comply with a standard.[30] For example, companies must "Implement technical policies and procedures for electronic information systems that maintain electronic protected health information to allow access only to those persons or software programs that have been granted access rights."[31]

States have also enacted data security laws, some of which take a standards approach.[32] The most notable state security law was passed by Massachusetts in 2007—the first state-level safeguards law. The law sets forth a series of various administrative, physical, and technical safeguards such as maintaining a written information security program, conducting risk assessments, and auditing third-party service providers, among other things.[33] The security laws of Oregon and Nevada also employ a standards approach.[34]

The standards approach is only used in a handful of security laws. Lawmakers and rulemaking agencies are reluctant to pin down specifics when the state of data security is constantly evolving due to new threats and technologies. By far, the most common approach is the reasonableness approach.

The Reasonableness Approach

Under the reasonableness approach, laws typically require organizations to protect personal data with "reasonable" or "appropriate" or "adequate" safeguards. These words essentially mean the same thing, and they establish a standard that is open-ended and vague. In applying this standard to particular cases, regulators look to common practices.[35]

An early example of the reasonableness approach is the Privacy Act of 1974, which requires that federal governmental agencies "establish appropriate administrative, technical, and physical safeguards to insure the security and confidentiality of records."[36] The Federal Communications Commission (FCC) has adopted a reasonableness approach to enforcing against security violations by companies providing radio, television, phone, and cable services.[37] States have also enacted a number of data security laws, most of which take a reasonableness approach.[38]

The most significant and prevalent user of the reasonableness approach is the U.S. Federal Trade Commission (FTC). Since the late 1990s, the FTC has used its broad authority under the FTC Act to bring enforcement actions against companies that have had unreasonable data security. The FTC Act grants the FTC the authority to enforce against companies that engage in a "deceptive" or "unfair" trade practice. The FTC's early cases involved claiming "deception" when a company promised "reasonable" data security in its privacy policy yet failed to live up to this promise.[39] A deceptive act or practice is a material "representation, omission or practice that is likely to mislead the consumer acting reasonably in the circumstances, to the consumer's detriment."[40]

For example, in 2002, the FTC brought an enforcement action against Eli Lilly, a pharmaceutical company. Eli Lilly manufactured Prozac, a drug used for treating depression. Eli Lilly offered customers a service that would send them email reminders to refill their prescriptions. The company later decided to stop the service, and it sent out an email to notify all subscribers. Unfortunately, Eli Lilly made one of the most basic blunders of email—it put all the individuals in the "To" line of the message rather than in the "BCC" line. The result was that all users of this service now knew each other's identity. The FTC faulted Eli Lilly for not living up to its promises to maintain the confidentiality and security of people's personal data because Eli Lilly failed to adequately train and oversee its employee who sent the email.[41]

Later on, beginning with *In the Matter of TJX Companies, Inc.* in 2008, the FTC began enforcing reasonable security in the absence of any particular promises made by companies.[42] The FTC has claimed that unreasonable security is an "unfair" trade practice that "causes or is likely to cause substantial injury to consumers which is not reasonably avoidable by consumers themselves and is not outweighed by countervailing benefits to consumers or competition."[43]

Interestingly, in determining which security practices are unreasonable, the FTC has relied heavily upon the National Institute of Standards and Technology (NIST) Special Publication 800-53.[44] This framework consists of a series of standards. Over time, as the FTC has determined that various security practices are unreasonable, it is possible to develop a list of the practices that the FTC has deemed to be reasonable and unreasonable. This list begins to resemble a standards approach.[45]

The FTC also enforces the Safeguards Rule of the Gramm-Leach-Bliley Act (GLBA), which requires financial institutions to adopt "administrative, technical, and physical safeguards that are appropriate to [the institution's] size and complexity, the nature and scope of [institutional] activities, and the sensitivity of any customer information at issue."[46] Although the rule has a few specific requirements, it mostly takes a reasonableness approach.

A more recent enforcer of data security to join the party is the Securities and Exchange Commission (SEC), which started to become active in 2014.[47] Instead of issuing a set of security requirements, the SEC has used a reasonableness approach. In 2015, the SEC faulted an investment advisor for failing to adopt written cybersecurity policies and procedures reasonably designed to protect customer records and information.[48]

Problems with Safeguards Laws

Regardless of their approach, safeguards laws have struggled to contain the data security problem.

UNHELPFUL VAGUENESS VS. MECHANICAL RIGIDITY
A big debate for safeguards laws consists of the choice between the reasonableness approach and the standards approach. The problem with the reasonableness approach is that many companies find it too vague and lacking

in sufficient guidance about what they ought to do. They beg for a checklist so that they can check the boxes and feel assured that they are complying.

On the other hand, standards approaches are critiqued for being too rigid. Security threats are evolving, and best practices for security have changed over time, so a rigid list might not keep up with current technology and practice. Lawmakers and policymakers are not always nimble enough and lack the expertise to come up with an up-to-date and comprehensive set of standards. There might be items on a list that don't quite fit specific organizations or contexts.

Not all standards approaches fall into this trap. The HIPAA Security Rule's standards are quite broad, allowing for a lot of flexibility in how they are applied by specific organizations. With this balance, a standards approach can avoid the pitfalls of being too vague or too rigid.

Unfortunately, standards approaches can fail if organizations undertake a check-the-box compliance strategy. Organizations can check off everything in a list of standards yet have poor measures to address each standard. Compliance efforts often falter by focusing on quantity rather than quality. As we will discuss later, security isn't just a game of box checking; it's about establishing a careful balance between tradeoffs. While industry standards for data security often recognize those tradeoffs, there are far too many incentives for companies to implement these standards in a minimal check-the-box manner.

Ignoring Safeguards

Even when the law requires certain security practices and these practices are really effective, there still is an alarming number of organizations that don't do them. For example, in 2014, the U.S. Department of Health and Human Services began conducting random audits under the HIPAA Security Rule. The results were awful: 58 out of 59 audited organizations were found to have one or more failures to comply with the Security Rule.[49]

The requirements of many laws—having a comprehensive security program, doing routine security assessments, training the workforce, and so on—are not controversial. They are near universally recognized as worthwhile measures. Yet, they are often just ignored.

ENFORCEMENT IS TOO LATE

A bigger shortcoming of safeguards laws stems from the way they are enforced. The enforcement of safeguards laws is generally triggered by a data breach. The result is that enforcement of these laws mainly adds to the pain of a breach. Breaches are already very costly and painful, so when regulators come along and add a little more to the pain, it often is not a game changer. This is especially true because the penalties are often far smaller than the overall costs of the breach.

The fines imposed on organizations for poor security leading to a data breach are often a slap on the wrist. One article colorfully described the penalty that Australian regulators imposed on Adobe for its 2013 breach of user passwords: "The commissioner has flogged Adobe with wet lettuce, telling it to straighten up and fly right to make sure this kind of thing doesn't happen again."[50] Adobe's fine in Australia was $1.3 million, pocket change for a huge company like Adobe.[51] In most cases, fines are often a fraction of the total costs for a breach. Regulatory penalties ultimately raise the costs of a breach by a small percentage, but not enough to make a material difference.

Perhaps if costs and pain were ratcheted up even more, then these laws would work better. But costs and pain for breaches have continually risen throughout the years, and the situation isn't improving. As we will discuss later, breaches are the product of many actors and not 100 percent the fault of the breached organization. There are limits on what organizations can do to prevent breaches.

Enforcing after a breach is often the worst time to bring an enforcement action. Certainly, there should be vigorous enforcement for covering up a breach or lying about a breach. But post-breach enforcement is often an exercise in redundancy. Organizations that suffer breaches are often already engaging in soul-searching and exploring how to improve in the future. Instead, enforcement could be much more effective before breaches occur, prompting organizations to do the kind of rigorous thinking about their security practices at a time when it can help prevent breaches.

Additionally, the enforcement of safeguards laws does little to help compensate victims. In 2019, for example, the FTC reached a settlement with Equifax for its breach where victims could be compensated by being paid $125 or receiving 10 years of credit monitoring.

People rushed to claim their $125. There was an unfortunate catch, however. The fund to pay victims was only funded with $31 million, and people's payments would be reduced if too many put in claims. The FTC tried to put lipstick on this pig by trying to convince people of the value of the free credit monitoring.[52]

Equifax also agreed to pay up to $425 million (and possibly more) to people harmed by the data breach. But proving harm has long been a challenge, as we will discuss later on.

Thus, the typical story with data security enforcement involves regulators collecting some money that is dumped into government treasuries, with barely anything going to consumers.

PRIVATE LITIGATION

In the years following the ChoicePoint breach, another body of law bubbled up out of nearly nowhere—waves of private litigation after nearly every major data breach. Over the past 15 years, there has been an extensive amount of data breach litigation.

The Rise of Data Breach Lawsuits

Lawsuits usually follow quickly after breaches. For example, in the aftermath of its breach, Target faced 140 lawsuits. One lawsuit was even filed the day after the breach was announced to the public. Target eventually settled the consolidated consumer lawsuits for $10 million.

One study of about 230 lawsuits for data security breaches from 2004–2014 found more than "86 different causes of actions brought by plaintiffs for essentially the same kind of event."[53] Causes of action involved tort, contract, state statutes, and federal statutes.

Problems with Private Litigation

In theory, the way that data breach litigation is supposed to work is to empower consumers to seek redress for harms from data breaches and to supplement regulatory enforcement with private enforcement in the courts. Thus far, however, private litigation has failed to make a meaningful difference in improving data security. Litigation has increased the costs of data breaches but has accomplished little else.

CASES IMPROPERLY DISMISSED FOR LACK OF HARM

The key issue in data breach cases is harm. Most causes of action that plaintiffs can sue under require what is known as a "legally cognizable harm." Even if a defendant acted wrongly, the law often requires a plaintiff to prove that the defendant's actions caused harm. Courts have often struggled to understand the harm from data breaches, so data breach cases have often been dismissed.[54]

In federal court, plaintiffs must make an additional preliminary showing of harm to proceed with their case. Plaintiffs must establish "standing" to be able to sue in federal court.[55] For standing, plaintiffs must demonstrate an "injury in fact" that is "concrete and particularized" and "actual or imminent, not conjectural or hypothetical."[56]

Data breach plaintiffs argued that the exposure of their data has caused them emotional distress. Many courts, however, are reluctant to recognize harm that consists purely of emotional distress.[57] In the words of one court, "Emotional distress in the wake of a security breach is insufficient to establish standing."[58] Courts seem so quick to dismiss claims of anxiety over a data breach that they ignore many other areas of law where anxiety alone is recognized as a cognizable harm.[59]

Plaintiffs have also alleged that the exposure of their data has subjected them to an increased risk of harm from identity theft, fraud, or other injury. Many courts, however, require harms to be "vested"—already materialized in the here and now.[60]

Additionally, plaintiffs argue that the exposure of their data has resulted in their having to expend time and money to prevent future fraud, such as signing up for credit monitoring, contacting credit reporting agencies and placing fraud alerts on their accounts, and so on. Courts have been skeptical of these claims too.

A classic example is *Reilly v. Ceridian Corp*. Reilly was an employee of a law firm that was a customer of Ceridian, a payroll processing firm. After an attacker compromised its servers, Ceridian notified its customers that their personal information was affected. Reilly and other victims argued that they suffered injuries resulting from an increased risk of identity theft. The court rejected their argument, holding that the harm was too distant because the plaintiffs' "conjectures" about being victimized by identity theft hadn't yet "come true."[61] The plaintiffs' fears were based "on entirely speculative, future actions of an unknown third-party."[62] The court further stated: "Here, no evidence suggests that the data has been—or will ever be—misused. The present test is actuality, not hypothetical speculations concerning the possibility of future injury."[63]

A 2013 Supreme Court case, *Clapper v. Amnesty International USA*, has had an enormous influence on data breach cases even though the case had nothing to do with data breaches. A group of attorneys, journalists, and others contended that government surveillance violated their constitutional rights. They could not establish that they were definitely under surveillance, but they had a legitimate reason to suspect that they were under surveillance because they represented or spoke to individuals who the government viewed as suspicious.

The U.S. Supreme Court held that plaintiffs lacked standing because they could not demonstrate that "future surveillance is certainly impending." The Court found that the plaintiffs could only "speculate" as to future surveillance.

The plaintiffs also contended that they were injured because they had to take measures to avoid the risk that they were under surveillance. For example, instead of talking to clients on the phone, they had traveled to meet them in person. The Court, however, held that plaintiffs "cannot manufacture standing by incurring costs in anticipation of non-imminent harm."[64]

After *Clapper*, several courts have used *Clapper's* reasoning to deny standing to plaintiffs in data breach cases when plaintiffs claim injury due to an increased risk of future harm or expenditures to reduce the risk of future harm.

For example, in one case, thieves stole backup tapes with the medical data of more than 4 million service members. The tapes also included Social Security Numbers, addresses, birth dates, and phone numbers, along with extensive health information. An employee of a company had put the tapes in his car—an all-too-common blunder.[65]

A group of 33 plaintiffs sued. One of the plaintiffs alleged that loans were fraudulently taken out in his name by using his Social Security Number, birth date, address, and other data from the tapes. Two plaintiffs claimed that marketers contacted them by phone and email about their medical conditions. Other plaintiffs alleged other harms. Many plaintiffs argued the exposure of their medical information to an unknown third party was an injury in itself. Several plaintiffs argued that they spent time and money monitoring their credit and bank accounts after the incident.

The court took issue with several plaintiffs who argued a risk of future identity theft because "the likelihood that any individual Plaintiff will suffer harm remains entirely speculative." The court elaborated that whether the plaintiffs will be harmed is "entirely dependent on the actions of an unknown third party—namely, the thief. At this point, we do not know who she was, how much she knows about computers, or what she has done with the tapes." The court later noted that "Unfortunately, there is simply no way to know until either the crook is apprehended or the data is actually used."[66]

The problem is that thieves like this are rarely apprehended. Although the court noted that it is "reasonable to fear the worst in the wake of such a theft," the court still concluded that "Plaintiffs thus do not have standing based on risk alone, even if their fears are rational." The court also stated: "Nor is the cost involved in preventing future harm enough to confer standing, even when such efforts are sensible. There is, after all, nothing unreasonable about monitoring your credit after a data breach." But the court ultimately concluded it was bound by *Clapper* and could not recognize harm for increased risk for identity theft.[67]

Other courts have held that *Clapper* doesn't foreclose finding harm on these theories. For example, in *Remijas v. Neiman Marcus Group*, the Seventh Circuit held that the plaintiffs could pursue their lawsuit when hackers broke into Neiman Marcus's database.[68] As the court stated: "Why else would hackers break into [an organization's] database and steal consumers' private information? Presumably, the purpose of the hack is, sooner or later, to make fraudulent charges or assume those consumers' identities."[69]

The story before *Clapper* was that courts were deeply divided and about whether data breaches caused harm. The story after *Clapper* didn't change very much—courts remained divided.

In 2016, another Supreme Court case attempted to add more clarity to the issue of standing. In *Spokeo, Inc. v. Robins*, the Court declared that there must be "concrete" harm for standing, yet it acknowledged that "intangible harm," and even the "risk" of harm, could be sufficient to establish a concrete harm if intangible injury has a "close relationship to a harm that has traditionally been regarded as providing a basis for a lawsuit in English or American courts.[70] The Supreme Court, however, failed to elaborate much further. No guidance was provided to distinguish intangible harms that are sufficient for standing from ones that are not. *Spokeo* ended up resolving nothing.

After *Spokeo*, the courts have remained divided on the issue of standing. The law is thus deadlocked with two drastically different resolutions on standing and harm.

One of the major challenges in data breach cases is that hackers are rarely caught. Their precise motives might never be known. Personal data can circulate in dark corners for a long time because information, such as dates of birth, mothers' maiden names, and Social Security Numbers, doesn't change. Because there are many breaches, it also becomes difficult to trace a harm to one particular breach. The hackers aren't going to voluntarily step forward and explain where they got their data and what they are going to do with it. Courts that demand that plaintiffs prove harm in this way are demanding the impossible.

FAILURE TO HELP VICTIMS

When lawsuits succeed, they rarely do much to compensate victims even if they occasionally manage to have a small impact deterring future bad behavior.

Litigation is mostly resolved via settlement. A study of 230 lawsuits for data security breaches from 2004–2014 showed a settlement rate of 50 percent. The settlement rate during this time was particularly interesting because most cases during this period were being dismissed for lack of harm. Even cases that weren't strong settled for millions of dollars—mainly because of the high costs of litigating a case, even if victorious.

The settlements do little to help victims, even if they act as a deterrent for companies. They amount to just cents to a few dollars per victim, and most victims don't receive a penny. For example, Ashley Madison, an online "dating" service for adulterers, settled with users for $11.2 million for its 2015 breach involving 37 million people's personal data.[71] Anthem, a large health plan, settled for $115 million for a breach involving nearly 80 million records.[72]

Just like the safeguards laws and breach notification laws, lawsuits can ratchet up the cost and pain, but often just by a marginal percentage and not enough to be a significant additional deterrent. Lawsuits make a breach feel worse, but they don't do much for consumers.

As with the other types of data security law, the problems with private litigation aren't inherent and unfixable. Private litigation has the potential to have a positive impact. But thus far, cases are stuck on the issue of harm, and they are dismissed or settled before they can progress to developing duties and standards. Litigation is focused almost entirely on the organizations that are breached, but these organizations are only partly responsible for the problem.

AN UNHEALTHY OBSESSION WITH THE BREACH

After a data breach, the law will spring into action. Breach notification laws will often be triggered, requiring notification of a breach. Regulatory agencies will launch an investigation and might bring an enforcement action. A blizzard of lawsuits will likely be filed.

This combination—a triple punch in the gut—is expensive and demanding of resources. That would be okay if the rules and enforcement fostered a secure data ecosystem. But it's not working.

Since the ChoicePoint breach was announced in 2005, there have been two broad trends. First, data breach laws have proliferated. Countless new laws have been passed, and enforcement has increased. Second, data breaches are occurring more frequently and at an increasing size and scale. The same breach-causing mistakes are being made. Even with more data breach laws than ever on the books, we are still setting records for data security failures.

One conclusion to draw from the law's failure is that the situation is hopeless: The law can't do much, and we are doomed. But we reach another conclusion, one that is much more hopeful: The law can do a lot to improve data security, but it requires a major shift in focus and approach.

Although the law fails for a number of reasons, there is an overarching theme behind the law's failure—data security law focuses too much on the breach. For example, breach notification laws revolve around the breach. Attorneys file hundreds of lawsuits in the wake of a data breach. The FTC and Department of Health and Human Services (HHS) typically use the data breach as the launching point of their enforcement actions. It was the breach that sparked and fueled so much of the law's development. Unfortunately, the more the law has obsessed over data breaches, the less effective the law becomes in stopping them.

As the number, size, and severity of data breaches continues to rise year after year, policymakers are doubling down on this approach to regulating data security. Breach notification laws are proliferating, expanding, and strengthening in numbers. More regulators are pouncing on breaches. Breach lawsuits continue to multiply. Unfortunately, this approach is leading to a dead end.

The law must take a new direction. It needs a new focus. Ironically, to reduce data breaches, the law must stop obsessing over them.

PART II

Holistic Data Security Law

The Big Picture

System and Structure

Rachel followed all the advice on good data security. She chose strong passwords. She used two-factor authentication, where a code was sent to her phone whenever a login was attempted from a new device. With two-factor authentication, she felt assured that her accounts couldn't be broken into. But she would soon discover that she was very wrong.

On a warm September night in Salt Lake City, Rachel was getting ready for bed when her phone lost service. She received a strange message from her mobile phone service carrier telling her that the SIM card for her phone number had been updated.[1] Rachel took the natural step and turned the phone off and on again. It didn't work. Rachel asked her husband to call her number using his phone. Her phone didn't ring.

Rachel soon discovered that she had multiple emails saying that her passwords on various accounts had been reset—accounts that required two-factor authentication to change the password. What was odd was that her phone hadn't buzzed with texts of codes for resetting the passwords. Her phone had remained silent.

Suddenly, her husband Adam's phone rang. The caller asked for Rachel. Adam asked what was happening. "We're . . . in the process of destroying your life," the caller declared. "If you know what's good for you, put your wife on the phone." The caller threatened to destroy Adam and Rachel's credit. The caller rattled off the names and addresses of their friends and relatives. "What would happen if we hurt them?" the caller asked. "What would happen if we destroyed their credit and then we left them a message saying it was because of you?"[2]

How did the hackers take over her phone while it was in her possession at all times? How did they circumvent two-factor authentication? How did they commandeer Rachel's accounts in just a matter of minutes?

Rachel was the victim of an emerging hacking attack known as "SIM swapping" or "SIM hijacking." People's phone numbers are one of the biggest vulnerabilities they have, given the growing use of two-factor authentication. The hackers broke into her phone account and switched her number to a different phone. Then, they started to reset all the passwords from her accounts. The two-factor authentication codes all came to *their* phone, not Rachel's. In this way, the hackers were able to seize her accounts at Instagram, Amazon, eBay, PayPal, Netflix, and Hulu.

SIM card attacks usually begin with a hacker tricking a customer's cell phone carrier into transferring the customer's phone number. The hacker calls the cell phone carrier's tech support number pretending to be the target. The hacker explains to the company's employee that they lost their SIM card. A SIM card is the commonly used shorthand for a *subscriber identification module*, which is a circuit integrated into a cell phone or other mobile device that links a phone number to a particular device. The SIM card is how calling your phone number will ring your particular mobile device rather than another one.

In a SIM attack, the hacker requests that the customer's phone number be transferred to a new SIM card. The carrier's employee will usually ask a few questions to verify the identity of the customer—maybe asking for the customer's Social Security Number or home address. These pieces of information are easy for hackers to obtain—they are often readily available in public records or for sale on the Dark Web because of a previous data breach. Once the hacker has answered the verification questions, the employee transfers the phone number to the new SIM card.[3] All texts and phone calls to the customer will then no longer go to the customer's phone—they will go to the hacker's phone. From there, the hacker can start breaking into the customer's accounts.

Several points of vulnerability enable hackers to carry out SIM card attacks. Personal data such as addresses, dates of birth, and other information is readily available to hackers due to inadequate privacy protections, poor restrictions on the availability of public records, and weak security at other companies. The cell phone carrier's customer support system and the phones themselves were not optimally designed to protect against this attack. Security expert Bruce Schneier wrote of SIM attacks, "It's a classic security vs. usability trade-off. The phone companies want to provide easy customer service for their legitimate customers, and that system is what's being exploited by the SIM hijackers. Companies could make the fraud harder, but it would necessarily also make it harder for legitimate customers to modify their accounts."[4]

The two-factor authentication schemes that are reliant upon text messaging are also vulnerable to this attack. The fact that companies and systems continue to leverage peoples' Social Security Numbers (which are easily compromised and hard to change) as ways to verify their identity is another big vulnerability that hackers readily exploit. The SIM card attack is thus the product of vulnerabilities marbled throughout the entire data ecosystem.

With a few exceptions, data security law generally doesn't look too far beyond the blast radius of a data breach. The law often fails to hold the right actors responsible, often worsening the damage that data breaches cause. Obsessed with data breaches, the law fails to take the right preventative steps and fails to assign responsibility on the actors who can prevent and mitigate the harm of a data breach.

With its focus on the breach, the law penalizes organizations that suffer breaches, with the aim being to serve as a deterrent for future breaches.

Although this approach certainly accomplishes some degree of deterrence and incentivizes improved security, it is far from enough. Even organizations with good security are breached. It is hard to defend against persistent attacks. Eventually, even very security-savvy organizations will make mistakes. There will always be weak spots in the security armor or careless blunders. Organizations can certainly do better, but being perfect is almost impossible, especially for organizations with a large workforce and many vendors. Pushing organizations to improve can help but there is a point of diminishing returns. Even the organizations with the best security programs will stumble.

In this chapter, we propose that improving data security requires seeing it quite differently. In what we call "holistic data security," we contend that data breaches aren't a series of isolated incidents as they often are assumed to be. Data breaches are the product of the data ecosystem, which is perversely structured in ways that not only to fail to prevent data breaches but make it easier for them to occur and heighten the damage they cause. We contend that the law must dramatically widen its scope. It must move away from its narrow focus on data breaches. It must become more involved earlier on. It must apply to the full range of actors that contribute to the problem. In short, the law must address the structural points where the system is failing.

STOPPING ALL DATA BREACHES ISN'T THE RIGHT GOAL FOR THE LAW

What do we want data security law to accomplish? Many might reply: "Stop all data breaches. The ideal is perfect security. Data should never be compromised." This is essentially what the law is proclaiming: "DON'T GET BREACHED!" By ratcheting up the cost and pain for breaches, the law is declaring: "If you get breached, you will pay more. It'll hurt more. So, do everything possible not to get breached."

The language and imagery of data security reinforces this view. If you do a search for the keyword "security," you will be inundated by thousands of images of locks and safes. Security is often analogized to locking some-thing in a big vault or padlocking it in a fortified place. People think that to have data security, you must put the data in an impenetrable location, in a castle surrounded by a moat high up on a cliff guarded by thousands of knights.

Although at first blush the goal of perfect security seems desirable, it is actually the wrong goal, and it is based on a fundamental misunder-standing of what data security is about.[5] When security is properly under-stood, we will see that it is more of an art than a science, more about how to deftly balance tradeoffs and opposing goals. These tradeoffs can't be denied if we want good data security policy. We can't have perfect security, and we wouldn't want it either.

Why We Don't Want Perfect Security

It seems odd to claim that perfect security isn't good. Nobody wants intruders or unauthorized access or data loss or theft. So why shouldn't we strive for perfect security?

The reason is that security isn't the only goal for data systems. Just as important as keeping the bad actors out is allowing the good actors in. Why bother keeping personal data if nobody could ever see it or use it?

We want to use and transfer data quickly and easily, we want ease and convenience. But quick, easy, and convenient are a recipe for security debacles. If you make it more convenient for good guys to access data, then you often make it more convenient for bad guys to access it too. Every time data is stored, there's a security risk. Every time access to data is granted, there's a security risk. Every time data is transferred, there's a security risk. Anything involving the Internet is risky. Email is risky. Sharing files is risky. Nearly everything that is efficient, productive, con-venient, or useful is risky.

A security professional who locks all the data away or makes it very cumbersome to access would prevent an organization from functioning. Imagine a patient being wheeled into the ER, with the doctors having to go through time-consuming steps to get the information they need about the patient. If data is too locked up or if access to data is too slow and cumbersome, then people can't do their work—and the security professional will soon be out of work.

People may say that they want extreme security, but they also want convenience. People want these conflicting things, and they don't like being told that they can't have their cake and eat it, too.

Law professor Guido Calabresi poses an interesting hypothetical. He asks you to imagine that you are the leader of a country. An evil deity comes to you and asks you whether you will accept a special gift for your country—a magical machine that would make life much easier and more convenient. "Of course," you say. "But there's a catch," the evil deity says. The gift would come at a great cost: 40,000 lives lost every year. Would you accept the gift?

"Absolutely not!" most people would declare. When people say no, Calabresi asks: *What's the difference between the gift and the automobile?* Cars make life much more convenient, but car crashes kill about 40,000 people per year.[6] Society accepts this "gift" despite the costs. Calabresi calls this a "tragic choice."

We accept great costs for convenience, but it is very uncomfortable to admit it. We could make cars a lot safer by designing them so they couldn't go faster than 15 mph and with bumpers 10 times bigger. There are many safeguards that could be implemented, but at the cost of a large sacrifice of utility.

Security is somewhat like the car. We want convenience and speed, but these things come at a tragic cost. We can't ignore these tradeoffs. Pretending that they don't exist will result in poorer data security because the interests on the other side won't just disappear if ignored. People will look for workarounds that will often undermine security.

We should thus be honest about the goals of data security law. We don't want data security at all costs. We don't want to do what it takes to stop all breaches. We must accept a certain amount of risk to access and use data quickly and conveniently. The key, of course, is just how much risk we should accept and how much utility we want.

To complicate matters, there is no ideal balance that works for all people and all organizations. The fact that there is no one-size-fits-all security balance doesn't mean that we can't assess whether a balance is good or bad. There are some balances that are clearly off kilter. We can evaluate and improve balances, but the key to getting it right is to understand that we are balancing competing priorities.

Data Security Is About Humans, Not Technology

When many people think about data security, they often think of hackers in hoodies furiously typing on computers. But technology is just one part of data security. At its core, data security is about humans. People are the largest component of the data security risk equation, and people are one of the most challenging variables to control.

Technology is often thought of first when it comes to data security. From firewalls to encryption to access controls, there is an array of technologies that can help protect against intruders or improper access to data. At universities, the main place to study data security is within the computer science and engineering programs. Certifications for data security are often tech-heavy, including lots of lines of code, cables, and navigating user interfaces.

Data security, however, is not really a war between technologies that attack and technologies that protect. Instead, data security is a struggle with people using technologies. Most data breaches involve human error. It is humans who fail to encrypt or that choose poor encryption. It is humans who fail to patch software. It is humans who put data on portable devices and lose them or fail to keep them in safe places. It is humans who are susceptible to being manipulated, deceived, and defrauded though targeted attacks.[7]

Data Security Is About Risk Management

An employee at the United Kingdom's National Health Service (NHS) lost a USB memory device while delivering it from a clinic to the local administrative offices. The device contained the health records of approximately 6,360 people. Fortunately, the device was encrypted. Unfortunately, the employee had stuck a note on the side of the device with the password to decrypt it.

On paper, NHS was also doing the right things regarding security—it was encrypting USB devices. Encryption is a wonderful tool because if a device is lost or stolen, the data is unreadable. Encryption, however, doesn't work like magic—it can still be thwarted if people select bad passwords or fail to protect their passwords.

The NHS employee likely knew better than to paste his password to the device. Why, then, did such a ridiculous blunder happen? Even when people know better, they still do careless things. They recognize a suspicious link or attachment, yet they still click on it. They know they are not supposed to write down passwords on sticky notes and attach them to computers or devices, yet they do so anyway. Why are people so careless?

People are careless because good security is often cumbersome and inconvenient. One of the basic tendencies of human nature is that the more inconvenient something is, the less people will do it. The law, as well as security officials, often neglect to account for this reality.

This is why security policies and measures can look fine on paper but fail in practice. Suppose a law mandates encryption for personal data on portable devices. An organization follows the law. So far, so good. The organization has checked the box on a checklist of best security practices. The organization might even require a complex password for the device—check! In a training video shown to new employees a sentence is uttered about not writing down passwords—check! On paper, it all looks quite good. All boxes are checked. And yet, it can fail, as we learned from the NHS case.

The organization or the security team typically don't take the blame. The blame goes to the person who unwisely wrote down the password and stuck it to the device. Blaming the employee, however, is one reason why data security so often fails. The employee may have been foolish and careless, but he should have been considered a known variable. His behavior was foreseeable.

The problem is that there are Hobson's choices with so much of data security. For example, with passwords, if you make the password easy, and the employee will remember it. But then the password can be more readily cracked. Make the password longer and more complex, but then the employee can't remember it. The employee will struggle to figure out what to do. If the only advice the employee is given is "don't write the password down," this isn't helpful. The employee needs to find a way to remember the password, but it's too difficult to remember. The employee will inevitably write it down. Who wouldn't? Employers often advise employees to use unique passwords for different accounts and devices, so the employee probably found it necessary to put the password near the device.[8]

How could this problem have been averted? Telling people not to write down passwords is unrealistic. People won't remember them. They must write them down somewhere. There must be a better way to make it easy for the employee to remember the password for the device. If organizations were to help the employee do this rather than demand a more difficult, inconvenient, or impossible task, then there is a much better chance the employee won't use a runaround.

Far too often, security advice is given in training to make the optics look good for the organization. Organizations can always claim that it told employees the right things. Training becomes a waste dump for intricate security advice that only the most assiduous people will follow. On paper, an organization can point to a training program that says all the right things. It looks good to show to regulators. "We told our employees not to write down passwords," the company can explain to regulators after the breach. "Our foolish employee didn't listen, so it's not our fault." Unfortunately, in this context, the focus on making everything look good on paper is terrible in practice.

People often think of data security as a set of clear choices as opposed to privacy, which is seen as a set of muddy policy issues. Data security, however, is actually quite muddy itself—it involves difficult policy decisions about risks and tradeoffs.

Managing human behavior is immensely challenging. People are hard to control. They need to be educated. They need to care. But people forget.

Figure 4.1

They have lapses in judgment. They don't always have enough incentive to learn what they are supposed to learn or do what they are supposed to do.

One choice is to impose more controls on people—make it harder for them to do anything with data on their own. But that can come at a cost because these control measures can be oppressive and counterproductive, changing the culture of an organization and making it too rigid, less free, and less trusting.

Good data security involves determining the appropriate level of risk. How much risk is appropriate? There is no one right answer to this question. Thoughtful data security decisions involve judgments about balancing many considerations. Data security is much more complicated, nuanced, and creative than merely checking items off a list. Although lawmakers often treat data security as a science with objective correct answers, it is much more of an art.[9]

Recall that the main goals of cybersecurity are most commonly conceptualized as protecting the "confidentiality, integrity, and availability" of data—the CIA triad.[10] While these values are useful as specific goals for policies and practices, they don't capture all of the dimensions of managing the risks involved with personal data. There is much more to data protection than maintaining confidentiality, such as addressing how personal data is shared, used, and stored.

If data security is thought of primarily in terms of risk management, it means the goals of confidentiality, integrity, and availability must be consistently balanced against the goals of information systems and the societal goals like market participation, self-expression, socialization, public health, and even democratic self-governance.

Here is where data security law can go astray. At the organizational level, over-enforcement against breached companies can skew risk management. At the systems level, notification requirements and safeguard rules don't address the need to allocate and calibrate responsibility for protection across groups of actors who contribute to insecurity. A different approach is needed.

A NEW ROLE FOR DATA SECURITY LAW

Although the current law is not adequately addressing the challenge of data security, there is an important role for the law to play. But lawmakers must take a fundamentally different approach. Currently, the law operates primarily by worsening the consequences of a breach. The hope is that intensifying the pain of breaches will deter breaches by making organizations take more steps to avoid them. But extreme deterrence is the wrong goal. As we discussed above, the goal is to encourage optimal risk management, not to avoid breaches at all costs. Because organizations that suffer breaches are not the only cause of the breaches or the only actors that can affect the risk, the law should facilitate a better management of the risk across the entire data ecosystem.

Data security law should take on the role of promoting structural change in the data ecosystem. The law should establish who is responsible for what. It should set up the right incentives; it should help shape the system in which everything operates. The key to the law's success is to look beyond the breach to the whole data ecosystem. As we will discuss later, data breaches are the product of many actors in the data ecosystem, and the law currently only focuses on a fraction of them.

An Analogy to Public Health

Data security could learn a great deal by looking through the lens of public health. The two fields actually use similar terms and concepts. Data security professionals speak to the "health" of their network.[11] They refer to mapping and monitoring their data flows as good "data hygiene."[12] "Viruses" threaten both public health and the security of networks and data.

The language of health in these settings is both appropriate and underappreciated by law and policy makers. The Oxford English Dictionary defines health as "soundness of body; that condition in which its functions are duly and efficiently discharged."[13] If we consider data networks as a body that must function efficiently, then lawmakers might benefit from an alternative approach to data security law and policy that looks beyond the health of individuals (in our case, data holders) and addresses the health of an entire populous. The field of public health looks at "the health of the population as a whole, especially as monitored, regulated, and promoted by the state (by provision of sanitation, vaccination, etc.)."[14] As Wendy Parmet notes: "[I]nfectious epidemics show that the health of an individual depends, to a great degree, on the health of others. . . . An individuals' risk of becoming ill depended in uncertain ways on the steps that the community took and the environment and conditions in which the individual lived."[15] The key lesson from public health is interdependency—we have to focus on the whole system, not play whack-a-mole with specific individuals.

Similar to combating disease epidemics, addressing the data security epidemic requires collective action. The security of our data largely depends on factors that are outside of our control and even significantly outside the control of the organizations that are responsible for storing it securely. Our approach here is inspired by Deirdre Mulligan and Fred Schneider's conceptualization of cybersecurity as a public good.[16] The scholars noted that "Public health and cybersecurity both aim to achieve a positive state (health or security) in a loosely affiliated but highly interdependent network."[17] Adam Shostack has also articulated a vision of "cyber public health" that would support public health equivalents of institutions and practices for cybersecurity.[18] "Security experts rarely give advice on the level of 'wash your hands,'" Shostack notes. "Their advice is rarely consistent with other experts, or the public. People are naturally confused and give up." He further argues that unlike in public health, where public health institutions provide useful statistics and guidance, there are "few equivalents in the world of cybersecurity."[19]

Another important feature of looking at data security from a health and wellness perspective is that, just like illnesses are inevitable, so too are security breaches. Derek Bambauer has argued that "focusing efforts principally on preventing cyberattacks is misguided: perfect security is impossible, and even attaining good security is extraordinarily difficult. Instead, cybersecurity regulation should concentrate on mitigating the damage that successful attacks cause."[20]

The Who, What, When, and How of Data Security Law

Data security law jumps in at the wrong time, is not looking to all the responsible actors, is not addressing the practices that most lead to poor security, and is not working in the right way. It is failing in four key dimensions—who, what, when, and how.

WHO

The law loves to pummel the breached organization. Of course, this is an important deterrent to keep companies from engaging in reckless security practices. But the compromised data holders are just one actor in a much larger system. Let us step back for a moment and consider the big picture. There are many actors that contribute to data breaches. They include software manufacturers that create buggy vulnerable software; makers of insecure devices that can readily be hacked; ad networks and websites that host malicious ads; platforms that don't sufficiently vet apps; consumer reporting agencies; government officials that exploit vulnerabilities; government officials that create vulnerabilities; and organizations that miseducate people, among others.

As Josephine Wolff aptly notes, the law often focuses on "the first or the most easily understood point of access—the phishing email, the dictionary attack, the unprotected wireless network."[21] What is overlooked are "all of the groups and people who play some role in enabling successful cybersecurity incidents."[22] Wolff is exactly right. The law needs to expand its scope to hold more actors accountable for data breaches.

WHAT

Almost every hack seems like the result of a technical failure or individual blunder.[23] But usually those failures or blunders were orchestrated by criminals taking advantage of a system where nobody wants to accept blame for a security lapse. The lack of accountability within these systems causes, or contributes to, a lot of breaches (or makes them more harmful).

When we step back and look at the big picture, security is about structure. It is about the structure of a data ecosystem where many actors contribute greatly to the problem and aren't held accountable. It is about the internal structure of organizations that has fragmented privacy and security. It is about the structure of products, services, and even particular security measures that are designed in ways likely to fail. Unfortunately, the law often responds with a set of reactionary jabs and band aids.

WHEN

The law most often jumps in after the breach. But this is the least effective time for the law to become involved. The multitude of actors that contribute to a breach often make their contributions long before data the breach occurs. The law's temporal focus must change. By the time a breach occurs, it's far too late. The other actors have done their damage at a very different point in the timeline. This is why focusing on the breach has severely limited the law's effectiveness.

A better strategy would be to focus on the optimal time to intervene in the life cycle of a cybersecurity incident. Sometimes that will be before the incident occurs, such as regulating design, and sometimes this will be after a breach occurs but before a risk of harm manifests itself.[24]

How

The current system is deeply flawed because it actually promotes poor security and worsens the harm caused to victims when a data breach occurs. Numerous actors play a role in data breaches beyond the organizations that suffer the breach. The market often fails to create the incentive for good security, and in many cases, the incentives encourage poor security. The reason why is because all the parties in the data ecosystem have a very strong incentive to shift the blame (and resulting liability) of a breach onto others, because they don't want to end up holding the bill.[25] Data security law right now is like a game of hot potato where no one wants to be stuck holding the potato when the timer runs out. Time and energy are wasted passing around the hot potato instead of having many hands make for a lighter load.

The law should seek to rectify this failure. The law should create rules that shape the incentives for actors and give them clear guidance on the type of activity they should be protecting against or encouraging. The law shouldn't rigidly dictate policies for all organizations, as each organization is best positioned to make decisions about establishing its own optimal security balance. The problem is that organizations often don't reach a balance that is good for society.

The law should step in to restrict organizations from establishing a balance that is bad for society. The law can also push organizations to take security measures that are more consistent with how humans behave rather than ones that are in denial of human behavior.

Additionally, the law can incentivize better design. Design is often delegated to engineers. Policymakers are sometimes wary of being too paternalistic because they think that they don't understand technology. But engineers often design technology in ways that would be secure if used by robots but are woefully insecure when used by people. Technologies are often designed in ways that exacerbate people's tendencies to be insecure rather than nudge them to be more secure.

■

Data security law must look beyond the breach. It must become more holistic about whom it holds responsible and when it becomes involved. The law can correct for the current market failure in data security; it can improve the security balance by more accurately allocating the costs of breaches to all the responsible actors; and it can be more preventative and less reactive.

Responsibility Across the Whole Data Ecosystem

They made it seem so simple. Just download the app, take a photo of yourself (the racier the better), send it to your friend or lover, and poof . . . the image or "Snap" disappears after a few seconds. But it was never that simple, and it definitely was never that safe.[1]

The popular photo sharing social media app Snapchat promised ephemeral communications but malicious actors had other plans. In the fall of 2014, hackers intercepted hundreds of thousands of pictures and videos taken by Snapchat users. After a few days of bragging and bluster, the hackers posted the photos online.

As a company already under a consent order with the FTC to protect users' privacy, Snapchat was quick to proclaim that it did nothing wrong, promptly issuing a statement that read, "We can confirm that Snapchat's servers were never breached and were not the source of these leaks." The culprit was an insecure and unauthorized third-party software program designed to let users store "disappearing" snaps. Snapchat blamed its users: "Snapchatters were allegedly victimized by their use of third-party apps to send and receive Snaps, a practice that we expressly prohibit in our Terms of Use precisely because they compromise our users' security."

Snapchat was referring to fine print buried in its terms of use that banned the use of third-party software. Snapchat didn't explain that the ban was to protect security; no reason for the ban was given. This dense, boilerplate agreement places the burden of securing against this attack on the party in the relationship least likely to have knowledge of the vulnerability—the user.

In the aftermath of a data breach, this kind of blame game is typical.[2] A legion of regulators will investigate. Insurance companies will balk. Penalties will be issued. Lawsuits will be launched. Commentators will castigate the organization for its carelessness. And, victims will often be blamed, typically for acting in predictable ways.

There are many actors lurking in the shadows. They aren't in the spotlight, but they are not bit players. These other actors are often not evil or malicious. They are doing exactly what our system allows them to do.

In this chapter, we will describe the various types of actors that contribute to data breaches and the role that each plays. The law should hold these actors more responsible for their contribution to the risk. When we speak about the law imposing more responsibility, we are not referring to a particular legal strategy for doing so. The law can impose responsibility through lawsuits, monetary penalties, prohibitions, nudges, or regulatory interventions that are more cooperative than punitive. There are plenty of tools in the law's toolbox. Our focus is on the first step, which is bringing the law to focus on risk management and to address risk throughout the entire data ecosystem.

THE ACTORS

Data breach stories often focus on the immediate events leading up to the breach. The stories typically begin with a person who makes a blunder, such as losing a device with data, failing to patch software, or falling for a phishing trick.

But there is a lot more to the story than we often hear about. In fact, what we often learn about a breach is just one chapter of a long novel. To fully understand the problem, we must read all the chapters, where we will encounter a sweeping cast of characters who each play a role in the breach.

Designers
Actors who design insecure devices and buggy software with security vulnerabilities.

Distributors
Actors who distribute security threats, such as ad networks that fail to screen out malicious ads or platforms that fail to vet insecure apps.

Amplifiers
Actors who amplify the risks by collecting and storing massive amounts of personal data, such as consumer reporting agencies and other Big Data companies.

Facilitators
Actors who facilitate bad security by creating vulnerabilities for hackers to exploit, such as government entities that demand back doors that weaken security.

Exploiters
Actors who exploit existing vulnerabilities rather than reporting them and trying to fix them.

Miseducators
Actors who train people to engage in risky behavior and that under-mine efforts to teach people safe practices.

Designers

Designers are the creators of countless devices, apps, and software programs that are riddled with security flaws. Designers usually don't intentionally make insecure products; they just don't prioritize security when designing. Instead, their energy is spent making things cheap and convenient because these are the services that the market typically rewards. Technology companies have also developed a culture of pushing a software release as soon as it works and then fixing it post-release through updates. The continual drive for updated systems and general tolerance for bugs in the software creates many issues.

DEVICE DESIGNERS

Brian Krebs, one of the leading security journalists, formerly wrote for *The Washington Post*. He later left the *Post* to write independently about security on his popular blog, KrebsOnSecurity.

One evening in 2016, a DDoS attack was launched against Krebs's website. A DDoS attack—short for a "distributed denial-of-service" attack—is one way malicious individuals use to shut down a site. They send a tsunami of traffic from other computers (usually infected with malware) to a site. The huge wave of traffic becomes too much for the computer server to handle, and the overload overwhelms the system. This floods out a website, rendering it inaccessible. DDoS attacks are automated, so millions of requests can occur in a short amount of time. On this fateful night, the DDoS attack knocked Krebs's site down.[3]

Who did this? And why? Krebs and his readers suspected that the attack was payback for Krebs' investigation into vDOS, a service that conducted DDoS attacks for hire. Krebs' investigation led to the service being shut down and to the arrest of two of its founders.[4] Unfortunately, there was no way to confirm his suspicion about the attack, as the perpetrators couldn't be found.

KrebsOnSecurity remained offline for days. Fortunately for Krebs, he had friends in high places. Ultimately, Google jumped in to rescue Krebs with Project Shield, a DDoS mitigation service for journalists and nonprofit organizations.[5]

A DDoS attack comes from multiple different computers and devices. If all the traffic were to come from one source, the attack would be easy to stop—just block the source. What makes DDoS attacks challenging is that there are swarms of sources. Hackers locate sources by briefly commandeering them and commanding them to visit a website. This is known as a "botnet"—an army of machines that are taken over briefly to preform the DDoS attack. These machines aren't a group of computers owned by hackers. Rather, they are machines owned by ordinary people, who often have no idea that their computers and devices are involved.

The attack on Krebs involved the Mirai botnet. The botnet targeted Internet-enabled security cameras, DVRs, and printers.[6] If you owned a security camera, it might have been involved in the Krebs attack, or it could be involved in another attack. You might never know. Indeed, many of your connected devices might be moonlighting as robot warriors, commanded by hackers from around the world.

The hackers arranged a two-step strategy to attack Krebs. First, they hacked into these devices so that they could take them over at will. Then, they coordinated their robot army and told all the devices to request information from the web servers at once.

Krebs dug deeper into what had happened. He discovered that one reason why the hackers could readily access the devices was because the hackers used the default factory passwords for the devices. Many devices come with a default starter password. Users are asked to change these passwords, but many devices don't force users to change them. Quite predictably, many users don't bother to do so.[7] This makes it easy for hackers to break into devices on a massive scale.

It is quite alarming how quickly KrebsOnSecurity could be shut down, and it is chilling to think this could happen to journalists or anyone voicing an idea or opinion that hackers want to silence. The attacks can disrupt businesses, take down government sites, and interrupt nearly anything. The motive might be to silence critics, punish or bully people, or wreak havoc on important services.

Krebs expressed grave concern that the Internet would be flooded with device-based DDoS attacks.[8] He was right. Just a few weeks later, a group of unknown perpetrators used the Mirai botnet to pull off a gigantic DDoS attack against Dyn.[9] Dyn is the company that controls much of the Internet's DNS infrastructure. In October 2016, it was attacked three times over the course of 12 hours.[10] The attack caused outages at dozens of popular websites, including Reddit, Spotify, CNN, Amazon, and Twitter.[11] The perpetrators of the attack remain unknown.

There are several lessons to be learned from this story. First, many devices are poorly designed for security. The term "Internet of Things" (sometimes abbreviated IoT) became popular in first decade of the 21st century to describe the growing trend of devices connected to the Internet. The trend continues to this day, where countless devices are now online, such as fire alarms, thermostats, doorbells, light switches, and appliances, among other things. All these devices pose a security risk, and they often are not designed with security in mind.[12] As Bruce Schneier notes, "Engineering teams assemble quickly to design the products, then disband and go build something else. Parts of the code might be old and out-of-date, reused again and again."[13] He concludes: "The companies involved simply don't have the budget to make their products secure, and there's no business case for them to do so."[14]

The market is failing. Consumers are not choosing devices based on security. They select them based on price, functionality, or how appealing they look. Even if consumers cared more about the security of these devices, they don't know enough to assess how secure the devices are. The manufacturer of a baby camera might declare: "Our device has reasonable security measures." But what does that mean? Manufacturers might tout their "great" or "strong" security, but these are just bald claims. How can a person assess these claims? Most consumers lack the expertise to evaluate the security of a device. Even for the experts, manufacturers often don't provide enough specific information to make a meaningful security assessment.

Moreover, the market fails to account for the fact that poor security doesn't only affect the buyers of the devices but also can cause harm to many others. The hackers attacked Krebs by using other people's insecure devices. Krebs had no say in whether a person decided to buy one device over another. Buyers often make their purchase decisions by focusing on the costs and benefits to themselves and rarely consider the costs to everyone else.

The makers of these insecure products aren't spending enough on security even though they are foreseeably jeopardizing people's data. The market isn't providing enough of an incentive to improve security. And the law, unfortunately, isn't stepping in to correct for this market failure by forcing these manufacturers to internalize their costs.

SOFTWARE DESIGNERS

Software is often designed with gaping security vulnerabilities.[15] We have almost come to expect software to be insecure. We are barraged with stories about software bugs. We are constantly being nagged to download and apply patches to our software.

When a security flaw in software results in a breach, the software manufacturer is rarely held responsible for the harm caused. There are several frameworks that collectively fail to hold software designers accountable. First and foremost, contract and tort law doctrines are intertwined in ways that routinely relieve companies from liability for insecure software.[16] Companies use exculpatory clauses to explicitly disclaim liability and argue that they are offering a service and not a good to avoid liability under express and implied warranties. Courts have generally been quite reluctant to hold developers liable for insecure software because of such deference to contractual provisions, the limited ability for plaintiffs to recover for economic loss, the unclear duties companies have under negligence law, and difficulties in causal links between conduct and harm.[17] Additionally, federal legislation does little to hold companies liable for insecure software. For example, the U.S. anti-hacking law—the Computer Fraud and Abuse Act (CFAA)—specifically provides that "No action may be brought under this subsection for the negligent design or manufacture of computer hardware, computer software, or firmware."[18]

Imagine if the software were like a regular product. Suppose your shampoo were accidentally made too acidic and could dissolve your hair and scalp. Imagine if your car could suddenly blow up. Imagine if your television was defective and could readily burst into flames. In all these situations, the makers of these products would be liable for the harms their faulty products caused.

But software usually gets a pass. Of course, judges are more likely to hold companies liable that create software that physically injures people. But the law is remarkably porous and ineffective, even under such extreme circumstances.[19] Perhaps we want some small amount of leeway for software, because it is hard to make software that isn't riddled with security bugs. But perhaps a lot of software is so poor on security because there's not enough responsibility.

Much of burden is placed on consumers, who are constantly asked to install software patches. According to Bruce Schneier, the "industry rule of thumb" is that only 25 percent install patches on the date of release and another 25 percent within the month. But 25 percent only get around to it within the year, and 25 percent don't patch at all.[20] Patching can frequently be a clunky and cumbersome process, and "many embedded devices don't have any way to be patched."[21]

To be fair, it's practically impossible to create software without any bugs and vulnerabilities. Spurring people to download and install the updates on a regular basis is like pulling teeth. It is a chore for people to keep patching, especially given how much software we are using.

Software companies also stop supporting old software, a move they refer to as "deprecating" a particular program. Unfortunately, but often for good reasons, people grow attached to old software and don't want to abandon it. People often don't have the financial resources to constantly upgrade their tools. Additionally, abandoning software might render certain data and files unusable. For example, if a person creates a video with a video editing program, the video source file could be incompatible with other programs.

If the law holds software makers more responsible for the downstream consequences of poor security choices, then software would likely become more secure. More money would be invested in security. There would be more testing before launching software. More care might be taken when determining when to stop supporting updates and how best to safely transition people to new systems.

We are not arguing that software must be perfect on security. But software should at least be up to a reasonable standard. With the proliferation of connected products and devices, so many things now have software in them and this software often has poor security. Without greater accountability, bad software can continue to flood the market and put us all at serious risk.

Distributors

Distributors are a group of actors that help distribute insecure products and services. They create places that appear safe—websites, platforms, online marketplaces—and they make it easy for individuals to find out about products and services and to purchase or use them. Unfortunately, distributors fail to adequately screen these products and services. It's akin to supermarkets stocking their shelves with tainted food.

Ad Networks

Suppose you are a cautious Internet surfer. You don't visit strange sites or anything that seems dubious or disreputable. You just go to mainstream news sites, large retailer sites, or the websites of big companies you know. You think you are safe . . . but we have bad news for you.

Imagine you are on a popular website and you see an interesting ad. You click the ad and suddenly you are thrown into a digital hell. The ad sends you to a malicious site, which infects your computer with malware.

This malady is known as "malvertising"—a mashed-up word for "malicious advertising." Malvertising involves fake ads created by hackers and fraudsters. When you click on them, the ads take you to a phishing site or a site that will infect your computer with a virus.

Many popular websites use ad networks to select and deliver ads. Ad networks are companies that serve ads on thousands of websites.[22] Instead of websites themselves selling and arranging all the ads themselves, ad networks manage the sale of advertising opportunities. Many ads are submitted to the various ad networks, and the networks often don't have time to examine each ad carefully—the system is highly automated.

The online advertising ecosystem is a remarkably complex network. It involves "publisher sites, ad exchanges, ad servers, retargeting networks and content delivery networks (CDNs). Multiple redirections between different servers occur after a user clicks on an ad. Attackers exploit this complexity to place malicious content in places that publishers and ad networks would least expect."[23]

A malicious ad might contain hidden coding that could allow a hacker to install a virus or infiltrate a computer or computer network. Once inside, the hacker can install ransomware or access data.[24]

But I only visit mainstream legitimate websites, you might think. *I can't be infected if I'm visiting only sites of large reputable companies.* If you think this, you are wrong . . . very wrong. The list of mainstream companies that have had malicious ads on their site is quite long.[25] The only way to completely protect yourself is to stay offline because there is little you can do to combat this issue. Many antivirus software programs aren't updated fast enough to catch the ads. If you visit a site with a malicious ad, your computer can be infected almost instantly. Some of the ads require you to click, but some will do damage just by being loaded up when you visit the website.

In 2017, fake Adobe Flash update ads were on Equifax's website. When people clicked the ads, their computers became infected with adware.[26] In 2019, just one malvertiser was responsible for 100 million malicious ads.[27]

Malvertisers go to elaborate lengths to make themselves look like legitimate companies. They create slick websites, LinkedIn profiles, Twitter accounts, and more. These steps make it much trickier to use automation to identify them.[28]

Ultimately, it comes down to a tradeoff that advertisers must make. Ad networks can profit more by heavily automating their operations and having weaker monitoring for security. They can increase security but at a greater expense. They could also increase security by scaling down their business. The only way they will make choices favoring more security is if they have the right incentives. Currently, the incentives created by the market and the law, however, are for them to be less secure.

PLATFORMS

In the 1980s, spending time at indoor malls was very popular. People felt safe there. The malls had security, the stores were mainstream and safe, and there were food courts.

Today, online platforms present themselves as the digital world ana-logue to malls in the 1980s. The problem is that although they appear safe, they are not. Dangerous actors lurk there, and individuals visit at their own risk.

If you go to the app store for Apple or Android, you can find a multitude of apps. Many look really neat, and it is so easy to download and use them. You might think that they are safe because they are in the store. But often they are quite risky.

Many apps have terrible security. According to one study, 43 percent of Android apps and 38 percent of Apple apps had major security flaws.[29] Another study found that 86 percent of mobile apps had a common secu-rity vulnerability that could open the door for hackers.[30]

These findings should come as no surprise because there are not many incentives for most app developers to prioritize security. They are more interested in creating what sells—exciting features and functions. Users don't know enough about security to factor it into their decisions about using apps. Thus, there isn't much market incentive to invest a lot of time or resources into security.

The app stores disclaim responsibility. Although they often claim they review apps before allowing them in the store, the app stores don't want to be held legally responsible. They simply want to review apps voluntarily and avoid being held to a particular standard.

In *Opperman v. Path*, a group of plaintiffs sued Apple for misrepre-sentation because it touted a strong commitment to privacy but didn't prevent apps from obtaining people's contacts without consent. The court threw out the case even though the court concluded that Apple misrepresented the curating of its app store and the level of security of the apps being sold there. Despite this misleading marketing, the court concluded that it wasn't extensive enough. Apple made "only a handful of statements per year, contained in 'buzz marketing' materials, press releases, statements in investor calls, and similar materials. These materials were not widely disseminated to consumers." In other words, Apple engaged in some misrepresentation, but it didn't engage in a tre-mendous amount of misrepresentation. According to the court, a little wrongdoing is okay.[31]

The court totally ignored the fact that people generally assume that they are safe in an app store. The platforms need not tout anything because they can rely on the fact that people assume the products in their stores are safe.[32]

Sometimes, the law flashes a burst of inspiration. A recent case is a cause for celebration. In *Oberdorf v. Amazon*, a court held that Amazon could be liable for a defective product sold by a third-party on Amazon's site. Oberdorf bought a collar for her dog. One day, the collar broke, and the leash snapped back and hit Oberdorf in the face, permanently blinding her in one eye. The seller of the dog collar, a third-party called "The Furry Gang," had all but vanished. The seller was unreachable, and its account on Amazon had gone inactive.

Amazon argued that it wasn't the seller of the collar because it "merely provides an online marketplace for products sold by third-party vendors." The court noted that Amazon barely vets its third-party sellers:

> Amazon's Vice President of Marketing Business admitted that Amazon generally takes no precautions to ensure that third-party vendors are in good standing under the laws of the country in which their business is registered. In addition, Amazon had no vetting process in place to ensure, for example, that third-party vendors were amenable to legal process.

The court held that Amazon should bear the responsibility for unsafe products because Amazon "exerts substantial control over third-party vendors." The court noted that "Amazon is fully capable, in its sole discretion, of removing unsafe products from its website."[33]

Much of the time, the law doesn't hold platforms accountable. Platforms like Amazon haven't yet been held responsible for selling insecure devices. Platforms often disavow responsibility for the activity that occurs on them. In the United States, Section 230 provides robust immunity for publishing content by third-parties.[34] Companies encourage activity on their platform, make money from activity on their platform, and entice people to use their platform and feel safe on it. They want all the profits and benefits without the responsibility.

A common theme in the data ecosystem is that many actors want to reap profits yet don't want to pay the costs when something goes wrong with security. The app makers don't have sufficient incentive to make secure apps. The platforms where the apps are sold don't want to be their brother's keeper, though of course many make some effort to deny access to fraudulent or insecure apps.[35] Platforms have strong incentives to point to the app makers when something goes wrong. Everyone makes money, and consumers are lulled into the false belief that they are safe when, in fact, they are not.

Amplifiers

Another group of actors amplify data security risks. *Amplifiers* sweep up people's data and store it all together, making an attractive treasure trove for fraudsters. Despite the higher risks that storing all this data creates, many amplifiers don't provide better security than anyone else.

CONSUMER REPORTING AGENCIES

Equifax is one of the big three consumer reporting agencies with personal data on hundreds of millions of people. In 2017, it had one of the largest data breaches, facilitated by a few careless errors.

In March 2017, the United States Computer Emergency Readiness Team (called US-CERT for short) sent Equifax an alert about Apache Struts, which was open-source software that Equifax used.

The Apache Software Foundation had already issued a free new version with the problem fixed. All Equifax had to do was to update to this new version. Apache Struts was used by a number of employees for a number of different applications, so multiple installations of the software had to be updated.

When the Equifax security team received the alert, they quickly sent an email around to about 400 employees informing them that if they were responsible for an Apache Struts installation, then they should update the software accordingly. But the mass email failed to include one employee who maintained a dispute portal that used the Apache Struts software. This installation wasn't updated.

A week later, Equifax scanned the network for vulnerable versions of Apache Struts, but the scan wasn't properly configured and failed to detect the Apache Struts installation on the dispute portal.

Four months later, Equifax's security team noticed some suspicious activity at the dispute portal. They later discovered that many attackers had exploited the vulnerability in the portal to break into the network. To the delight of the attackers, Equifax's network wasn't well segmented, so the attackers were able to access a lot of information. They hit the jackpot when they located administrative credentials which were stored in plain text. With these credentials, they obtained even more access to Equifax's network.

The hackers were even more gleeful when they were able to gain access to more than 145 million records, including Social Security Numbers (SSNs). Equifax's policies required that personal data be encrypted, but the SSNs were stored in plain text.[36]

This breach involves many of the themes we have discussed so far. The vulnerability was in software that required a patch. A series of careless human errors resulted in an installation of this software not being patched. There were poor practices such as failing to encrypt data—even when policies required it. The network wasn't sufficiently segmented, giving the intruders a lot more data to access. All these errors are careless human mistakes.

Of course, Equifax had made a prior statement about the quality of its data security, a statement similar to that made by many companies:

We are committed to protecting the security of your information through procedures and technologies designed for this purpose by taking these steps: We limit access to your personal information to employees having a reasonable need to access this information to provide products and services to you . . . We have reasonable physical, technical, and procedural safeguards to help protect your personal information.[37]

Statements like this are essentially meaningless to people who receive them. Everyone says they are being reasonable about security.

The FTC charged Equifax for failing to live up to its promise of reasonable security. Along with 50 states and territories, the FTC reached a settlement with Equifax, which agreed to pay $575 million (and potentially up to $700 million). This money would compensate people who suffered harm as well as pay for up to 10 years of free credit monitoring, in addition to other things. The irony is that it was users of Equifax's credit monitoring who were victimized by the breach; they would receive credit monitoring for the data compromised when they were using credit monitoring.

This particular breach involved personal data on many people who were customers of Equifax, using its credit monitoring and identity theft protection services. But most people whose data Equifax maintains are not customers. These people often have never even heard of Equifax, let alone had an account with them.

The primary business of the consumer reporting agencies is credit reporting. Their main customers aren't the people they are maintaining data about. Instead, their customers are creditors or others who want to obtain information about people. The law allows consumer reporting agencies to collect data about people and to report on their creditworthiness without people's consent. People can't even opt out.

ChoicePoint is another example of this type of actor. This was a company that had gathered extensive dossiers about individuals, mostly without their knowledge or consent. The people whose data it gathered, maintained, and analyzed weren't its customers. ChoicePoint's customers were other organizations.

The fact that people affected by breaches are often not customers presents a big problem. There isn't a sufficient market mechanism to incentivize these companies to devote extensive resources to protecting the security of personal data.

If you don't like the way that your bank treats you, you can take your money to another bank. If your doctor breaches your confidentiality, you can go to another doctor. But if a consumer reporting agency is careless with your data, you can't do anything. It can still keep and use your data.

Consumer reporting agencies began developing as early as the late 1870s.[38] With the help of computers, from the 1960s on, they grew into behemoths, processing torrents of data about hundreds of millions of people. Consumer reports contain financial information, bankruptcy filings, judgments and liens, mortgage foreclosures, checking accounts, and information from other creditors, including how well you paid back your debts in the past. Some companies also prepare investigative consumer reports, which supplement the credit report with information about an individual's character and lifestyle.

Before they were regulated by law, credit reporting agencies were notorious for their abuses. Credit reports often contained numerous errors. People had no right to check the accuracy of their credit reports or even see them. If people wanted to dispute something on their credit reports, there was often nobody they could call for help. A parade of complaints of abuse and lack of responsiveness of consumer reporting agencies sparked Congress to pass the Fair Credit Reporting Act (FCRA) in 1970.[39]

FCRA provides a set of rights to people in their credit reports. People have a right to access their credit reports, challenge inaccuracies in their credit reports, and consent for their credit reports be obtained for employment purposes.[40]

The law is good in many respects, but an incentive problem remains. Legally mandated requirements are never administered with the same zeal as profit-motivated endeavors. And, without robust enforcement of existing rules, there isn't much incentive for companies to follow the rules.

Consumer reporting agencies such as Equifax, Experian, and TransUnion process lots of data. Instead of holding these companies responsible if they make a mistake, courts often act as apologists for these companies by giving them greater leeway to make mistakes because of their vast size. The business model of these companies is to keep costs low and do things fast and at a huge volume. This isn't just the business model of consumer reporting agencies; it's increasingly the business model of many companies, especially online service platforms. Automate as much as possible, grow to an enormous size, and process a tremendous volume of data very efficiently.

Consider the case of *Sarver v. Experian*. In this case Experian reported incorrectly that Lloyd Sarver had gone bankrupt when he hadn't. The error resulted in Sarver being denied a loan from a bank. Sarver sued under the FCRA, which requires that consumer reporting agencies use "reasonable procedures to assure maximum possible accuracy."

The court tossed out the lawsuit. The court concluded that Experian gathers credit information from about 40,000 sources, and it is stored in a database "containing approximately 200 million names and addresses and some 2.6 billion trade lines. . . . The company processes over 50 million updates to trade information each day." Because Experian processes so much data, the court stated, some mistakes are bound happen, and these mistakes should be forgiven.

Sarver argued there were anomalies in his report that should have alerted Experian. The court, however, was sympathetic to Experian: "What Sarver is asking, then, is that each computer-generated report be examined for anomalous information and, if it is found, an investigation be launched." The court concluded that "given the enormous volume of information Experian processes daily," Experian shouldn't have any duty to examine each person's data for anomalies.[41]

Like many courts, the court in *Sarver* took Experian's business model as a given. With this business model, the tradeoffs make sense for a company like Experian. It must process a tremendous amount of data and doesn't want to devote too much time and too many resources to scrutinizing everyone's record. But must it have this business model? This business model works so well for Experian because it isn't paying all the costs. The business model is not so ideal for people like Lloyd Sarver, or for you or me, who can be saddled with some of the costs. Courts aren't forcing companies to internalize the costs of the harm that their errors are creating.

Simple economics will readily predict the outcome. Companies will not devote as many resources to making reports as accurate as possible and will instead continue with their high-volume business model. Because the companies don't have to pay for the harm to Sarver, they can make mistakes without internalizing the full cost.

The court is essentially telling Experian and similar companies: *Go ahead and process lots of data. The more you process, the more leeway you will have to make mistakes. We won't make you internalize the costs of the harm you cause by these mistakes.*

The same set of choices exist for data security. More time could be spent on security measures, on vetting third-party vendors, and on training employees. But companies don't want to spend too much time on these things. Business processes could be changed in ways to enhance security, but this might make them less efficient.

The other way to create an incentive is through the law. That's why FCRA was so needed. Unfortunately, it's not strong enough, especially when courts are so sympathetic to consumer reporting agencies.

Moreover, FCRA provides qualified immunity to businesses and financial institutions that furnish data to consumer reporting agencies. These organizations can't be sued for defamation, invasions of privacy, or negligence based on their reporting of information to consumer reporting agencies unless they acted with "malice or willful intent to injure."[42]

Many of the problems identity theft victims face is that there are fraudulent charges in their name. Creditors report this information to consumer reporting agencies, which is how the pollution starts to tarnish a person's records. By failing to hold furnishers of information responsible if they are negligent, FCRA isn't holding them responsible enough.

BIG DATA COMPANIES
Another problem is that many modern data-driven companies fall outside the scope of the FCRA, which hasn't kept up with information economy. The FCRA applies to any consumer reporting agency that furnishes a "consumer report." A consumer report is a communication that addresses a person's "credit worthiness, credit standing, credit capacity, character, general reputation, personal characteristics or mode of living."[43] A consumer report must be used to establish eligibility for credit, insurance, employment, or other uses defined by FCRA. This means that the FCRA

doesn't cover all Big Data enterprises, just those companies engaging in furnishing consumer reports.

Companies that analyze data can use it in different ways, many of which are not for the purposes listed under FCRA. Much of what people think of as "Big Data" activity, like predicting your shopping habits or major life decisions, doesn't involve consumer reports. The result is that the FCRA is not applicable to many businesses that maintain extensive dossiers about individuals.

A Big Data company that maintains data on millions of people doesn't have as much of a market incentive to give people rights in their data or provide robust security. The law must provide that incentive. The costs of a data breach certainly help provide some incentive, but these costs are artificially low because businesses are not internalizing all the costs borne by affected individuals or by society.

One of the data security failures of many big data companies is when they outright sell the data that hackers crave with virtually no account-ability. For example, Brian Krebs reported how a data thief "tricked an Experian subsidiary into giving him direct access to personal and finan-cial data on more than 200 million Americans."[44] All the thief had to do was pose as a private investigator and pay for access to consumer records using standard cash wire transfers. Once he got the data, the fraudster disseminated data containing SSNs, date of birth, and other records on more than 200 million Americans. This wasn't a case involving high tech circumvention of networks using exploits; it was just common fraud that companies have little legal incentive to avoid because selling data is so lucrative.[45]

Facilitators

Facilitators are actors that facilitate data breaches by providing handy tools that help hackers. Most facilitators don't intend to assist hackers, but they do so because they are so obsessed with their own goals that they don't pay attention to the secondary effects of their activities.

In the mid-1990s, national security officials under the Clinton Administration developed the Clipper Chip, a special chip to be used by telecommunications companies that would provide an encryption backdoor for the government in national security situations. The backdoor would work via "key escrow"—each chip would have an encryption key that the government would hold in escrow. National security officials wouldn't be able to use the key unless they made the appropriate showing of authority.

The Administration heavily promoted the idea of requiring the chip in devices. Companies weren't fond of the idea. Neither were consumers. Security experts raised alarm bells, pointing out some troubling vulnerabilities with the system.[46] The Clipper Chip idea soon fizzed out.

After a series of coordinated terrorist attacks in Paris in 2015, national security proponents in the United States and abroad revived the attempt to push for a backdoor to encryption. British Prime Minster David Cameron declared: "[T]he question is: Are we going to allow a means of communications which it simply isn't possible to read. My answer to that question is: 'No we must not.'"[47] President Obama echoed these statements: "If we find evidence of a terrorist plot . . . and despite having a phone number, despite having a social media address or email address, we can't penetrate that, that's a problem."[48] Then-FBI Director James Comey urged Congress for law enforcement to have special access to encrypted communications.[49]

Proponents for allowing government officials to have backdoors to encrypted communications should read Franz Kafka. Nearly a century ago, Kafka deftly captured the irony at the heart of their argument in his short story, "The Burrow." In the story, an animal builds an elaborate burrow of underground tunnels. Riddled with fear and insecurity, the creature constructs the most elaborate burrow—a maze of passages, misdirection, defenses, and so on. He becomes obsessed with building the burrow, constantly doubting its safety, constantly regretting that he didn't build it with even more defenses. He tries to make it totally secure, but one problem remains: An enemy might invade through the entrance hole.

The animal says: "At a distance of some thousand paces from this hole lies, covered by a movable layer of moss, the real entrance to the burrow; it is secured as safely as anything in this world can be secured; yet someone could step on the moss or break through it, and then my burrow would lie open, and anybody who liked . . . could make his way in and destroy everything for good."

So, the animal winds up sleeping outside the burrow to stand guard over the entrance. "My burrow takes up too much of my thoughts," the animal confesses. "I fled from the entrance fast enough, but soon I am back at it again. I seek out a good hiding place and keep watch on the entrance of my house—this time from outside—for whole days and nights. Call it foolish if you like; it gives me infinite pleasure and reassures me."

The irony (and absurdity) at the heart of the story is that the animal becomes so obsessed with his project of building the most secure burrow that he sacrifices his own security in the process.

Backdoors are a huge security risk and they undermine the effectiveness of encryption for everyone. A report by a group of leading security experts concluded that installing back doors would undermine security by creating an enormous vulnerability: "If law enforcement's keys guaranteed access to everything, an attacker who gained access to these keys would enjoy the same privilege."[50]

About 60 of the leading technology companies, including Microsoft, Alphabet, Inc. (Google's parent company), Apple, Facebook, and Twitter have vigorously critiqued backdoor proposals because of the significant security risks that backdoors present.[51]

When such a chorus of technology experts and companies point out problems, it is wise to listen. The security of all our communications is of tremendous importance—and it has national security implications. If the keys got in the hands of bad guys, our financial system could be compromised. People who have access to critical systems could be blackmailed. Key research and intellectual property could fall into the wrong clutches. Private communication is not antithetical to security—it is essential to security.

Encryption is a tool that can certainly be used by the bad guys, but it is also a tool that is primarily used to keep the bad guys out. Creating a major vulnerability will not make us more secure.

In an incident which occurred in 2016, the FBI obtained an order from a magistrate judge to force Apple to develop software to help the FBI break into an encrypted iPhone. The case arose out of the mass shooting in San Bernardino in December 2015. Two shooters killed 14 people and injured 22 people before eventually being killed in a shootout with the police. One of the shooter's phones was recovered, but the FBI couldn't unlock it.

The deceased shooter's iPhone was secured by a feature of Apple's iOS that prevented brute force attacks on the phone. Brute force attacks use software to make repeated guesses at passwords until the password is cracked. To circumvent such attacks, Apple used a feature that delayed how frequently password guessing attempts can be made. After 10 wrong guesses, the contents of the phone would be permanently inaccessible.

The FBI requested that a judge force Apple to write a new iOS to install onto the phone to get around these features. The FBI argued that a statute from 1789 gave it the authority to compel Apple to write the software.[52] The FBI convinced a magistrate judge to issue an order to compel Apple to provide "reasonable technical assistance" to the FBI. Apple vigorously opposed being forced to assist. In a letter to customers, Apple wrote: "Specifically, the FBI wants us to make a new version of the iPhone operating system, circumventing several important security features, and install it on an iPhone recovered during the investigation. In the wrong hands, this software—which does not exist today—would have the potential to unlock any iPhone in someone's physical possession." The letter further stated: "The same engineers who built strong encryption into the iPhone to protect our users would, ironically, be ordered to weaken those protections and make our users less safe."[53]

The FBI eventually hired a firm to engineer a hack to break into the iPhone, and the case was dropped. But there is nothing to stop the FBI or other law enforcement agency from trying to compel companies to break their own security features. Moreover, by hiring a firm to break the iPhone's security, the government funded the development of technology to weaken security.

Pouring money, time, and resources into weakening security might seem useful for an immediate case at hand. But in the long term, efforts like these undermine security. Government officials, if not checked, will open vulnerable backdoors to protect the front door. These moves make us less secure—often ironically in the name of security.[54]

Exploiters

Exploiters are actors who learn about vulnerabilities and use them to their advantage rather than reporting and fixing them. Exploiters are akin to those people who see something harmful but don't do anything to stop it or even warn people about it.

In 2017, a strain of ransomware known as WannaCry attacked countless computers through outdated Microsoft Windows operating systems. A look into this incident reveals that there were several actors at fault, not just the hackers and the people and organizations that failed to update their operating systems.

WannaCry was targeted at older versions of Microsoft Windows. As we discussed earlier, software companies have a common practice of "deprecating" their software—they stop supporting older versions. Many users keep using the old software because they can't afford a new version, have grown attached to their current version, have a device that can't install the necessary operating system, or have particular apps that only work on the old system. Given the severity of the attack and the number of affected computers, Microsoft rushed out a patch.

Long before the attack, the National Security Agency (NSA) had discovered the vulnerability. Unfortunately, the NSA didn't inform Microsoft because it wanted to exploit the vulnerability. Had the NSA reached out to Microsoft, the problem could have been fixed. Instead of acting to keep us safe, the NSA allowed this ticking timebomb to exist because it wanted to hack into systems itself. The NSA was believed to have created a tool to exploit the vulnerability, which was exposed in a leak online and used by hackers to carry out the WannaCry attack.[55]

Brad Smith, President of Microsoft, took the unusual step of casti-gating government officials for exploiting the vulnerability rather than re-porting it:

Finally, this attack provides yet another example of why the stockpiling of vulnerabilities by governments is such a problem. This is an emerging pattern in 2017. We have seen vulnerabilities stored by the CIA show up on WikiLeaks, and now this vulnerability stolen from the NSA has affected customers around the world. Repeatedly, exploits in the hands of governments have leaked into the public domain and caused widespread damage.[56]

Miseducators

Miseducators undermine security when their actions teach people the wrong things. Miseducators help hackers by training people to engage in the behaviors that hackers can readily exploit.

TRAINING PEOPLE TO FALL FOR HACKER TRICKS

Whenever there's a big data breach caused by a person who clicked on a suspicious link in an email, security experts roll their eyes. "People are just fools," they might mutter to themselves. It's so easy to blame people for doing foolish things, but security would be improved if we started blaming others, such as the organizations that teach people to do foolish things. In security, fools aren't born—they are *made*.

A key security tip is never to click on links in emails asking users to login. Many companies, however, send emails asking people to click on a link to log in. When companies send emails that are identical to the kind of phishing emails that hackers send, people are taught that legiti-mate companies send emails like this. In effect, people are being trained to fall for hacker tricks.

After suffering from a data breach, the firm Evernote alerted its 50 million users with an email notifying users that it had reset their passwords. The email from Evernote told users some good security wisdom: "Never click on 'reset password' requests in emails—instead go directly to the service." Ironically, in the very same email, Evernote included a password-reset link. The link didn't even go to Evernote's website. Instead, it went to "links.evernote.mkt5371.com." The sender's email address was:

v-fhbgdb_hleilamml_eahbofp_eahbofp_a@bounce.evernote.mkt5371.com

This email was indistinguishable from a phishing scam. Indeed, it practically screamed *I am a phishing email!*[57]

UNILATERAL AUTHENTICATION

It is commonplace for authentication to be unilateral. We must authenticate ourselves to organizations, but it's a one-way street. They don't authenticate themselves to us. Their failure to authenticate themselves to us contributes to so much fraud. We have been accustomed to readily trust company websites, phone calls, emails, texts, and other communications. They have trained us to trust them because it is cheaper and more convenient for them this way than if they had to authenticate themselves to us. But we really shouldn't trust them without authentication.

For example, credit card companies often call or email people to inform them about potential fraud on their cards. At first blush, this seems good—people are being informed about fraud. The problem is that a fraudster could readily be making the call or sending the email. The fraudster could ask for people's personal information, passwords, PINs, and other sensitive information by pretending to be the card company.

Organizations often expect us to just trust them whenever they call us or email us. People shouldn't be asked to give their trust so readily without a way to verify that the calls or emails are indeed coming from the companies. Companies will take steps to ensure that when consumers contact them, that consumers are who they say they are. But companies take no steps to verify that they themselves are who they say they are.

When we interact with organizations, authentication should be bilateral—companies should be developing means to authenticate themselves to us. Then, we would know to expect that a company is properly authenticated, and this would teach us how to distinguish between the imposters and actual representatives from the organizations.

Instead, organizations constantly call and email people and expect people to trust them. Fraudsters exploit this trust. This is how organizations train and prime people so that they will be easily subjected to fraudsters.

Organizations shouldn't be contacting people and asking for any personal information unless they can convincingly verify their identity so that people can distinguish them from imposters. The credit card companies that call or email should ask people to reach back out to them on the number on their cards or go directly to their websites without clicking on links in the email. So should any company that emails people—no company should be encouraging people to click on email links.

The barrage of emails and calls that people receive from organizations asking them to click this or that or to provide personal data are teaching people how to be sitting ducks for fraudsters. The cumulative effect creates a huge public harm—it weakens security for everyone, it undermines efforts to teach people good security practices, and it all but ensures that the fraudsters will find plenty of people who will fall for their schemes.

AGAINST DIGITAL TECHNOLOGY EXCEPTIONALISM

A common theme throughout our discussion of the actors who contribute to data breaches is "digital technology exceptionalism"—treating digital technology as different from other things.

The law is so enamored or flummoxed by the Internet, algorithms, and artificial intelligence that it often treats them as completely exceptional. The world has never seen anything that reduces the barrier to surveillance and communication like the Internet.[58] People are spied on, lied to, defrauded, manipulated, harassed, blackmailed, humiliated, and locked out. Yet the law is reluctant to hold organizations responsible.

Why are platforms not held more responsible for the products and services sold on them? Why is software treated so differently from other products? One reason is that digital things seem less tangible than physical ones. If a company makes a defective ladder that breaks, there's a physicality to the product, the defect, and the injury. The digital world feels intangible, less real than the world of flesh and blood and bricks and steel.

But code can kill. It can harm people in similar ways to physical items.[59] These days, more things are dependent upon software. At Black Hat and Def Con, two popular tech security events, researchers demonstrated how they could hack into pacemakers and insulin pumps. The researchers stated that they could reprogram a pacemaker to issue a shock or deny a shock.[60] Andrea Matwyshyn has written about the inherent vulnerabilities to our health and physical safety in "The Internet of Bodies."[61] Digital pills we take will communicate through sensors to our smartphones. An artificial pancreas hard-wired into the body will use software to calibrate insulin levels. The law is unprepared to deal with the individual and societal security and privacy risks of these devices. Not only have lawmakers failed to sort out the policy and legal problems of the Internet of Things generally, but they must also appropriately address what Matywyshn calls the "'legacy code' problem of software liability more generally."[62] We must stop treating digital technologies as completely distinct from other products and services.

Holding the technology industry responsible can made a big difference. Given how many devices are being hooked up to the Internet and the profound dangers that poor security can lead to, it's time we demand more from the technology industry. The software, apps, devices, and platforms they are making are no longer just the source of games and entertainment. The stakes are life and death.

When it comes to digital technologies, the law often creates a buyer-beware world. We must enter the world of digital technologies risking life and limb.

Imagine a company that opens a lion theme park where people can play with lions. Most of the lions are gentle, but occasionally there's a ferocious one that eats people alive. There's a big sign outside the place that says: "SAFETY IS OUR NUMBER ONE PRIORITY." And below that, in small print: "Enter at your own risk. We assume no liability for any injuries."

The law's response would normally be strict liability. The law would prevent the theme park from waiving liability and would not allow it to expose people to this kind of risk. But if the theme park were a technology company, the law would suddenly change its tune. The park now would be just a "meeting place" where lions "interact" with people—an exciting "social hub" for human–feline friendships. People "socialize" at their own risk. The park would just be "bringing people and lions together."

"Don't stifle innovation!" defenders will cry. "If you make the company responsible, then the lions will have to go. People love the lions. Only a few people get eaten, but most people experience great joy playing with the lions. It's their choice to accept the risk."

Outside the digital world, the law would never tolerate forcing people to take on so much risk without the theme park being held responsible. But often the law treats digital technology completely differently. It shouldn't. Incentives work the same for the physical world as they do for the digital world. This results in the law being much better at spurring the market to produce safe physical products and so poor at getting the market to produce safe digital ones. Legal regimes like negligence law are remarkably flexible and adaptable for even complex and opaque technologies like artificial intelligence.[63] But judges, lawyers, and lawmakers must continually work hard to understand the foreseeable risks of these technologies and where humans are at fault in designing and using them.

We are not arguing for a full strict liability approach or for the law to make technology companies liable for all security risks.[64] There will be always security risks with technology, and there are risks that are worth taking. The law should address *unreasonable* security risks, which are ones that are not justified by the benefits or that can readily be reduced through common industry standards and best practices.

Far too often, there are technologies on the market that have substandard security because there is hardly any incentive to invest in better security. Because of the lack of incentives, better security is often not engineered into products even when it would have been easy and inexpensive to do so. Companies that make these products should be held accountable. Products that fail to provide a reasonable amount of security should be penalized and restricted.

IT TAKES A VILLAGE

Security professionals will tell you that there is no silver bullet on computer security, short of taking every hard drive in the world and launching them into space.[65] It often takes a village to create a data breach. There are many actors in the system that lurk in the shadows, contributing to the problem yet escaping much notice and not being held responsible. These actors create risks, weaken the security of others, engage in risky activities without internalizing the harm, and create vulnerable software and devices. The law's failure to hold these actors responsible and to create the right set of incentives for them with carrots and sticks overpowers nearly all the good things that various data security laws try to do.

A lot of people are pointing fingers. For example, in her thoughtful analysis of several major breaches, Josephine Wolff contends that it is unproductive to just blame the breached organization, even when that organization is partly at fault.[66] Wolff discusses the breach of credit card data at TJX Companies, which owns the T.J. Maxx and Marshalls retail chains. Fraudsters were able to intercept and decipher wireless transmissions of data outside of store locations. She concludes: "A closer look at the full timeline of the TXJ breach reveals that the episode in fact involved several different technical vulnerabilities and companies, but by singling out one encryption protocol and one organization as fully responsible for the incident the payment card industry was able to effectively shield itself from bearing any of the blame."[67]

Finger pointing and trying to escape blame are common and predictable behaviors.[68] This is exactly where the law must become involved. A key function of the law is to determine who should be held responsible. If responsibility is properly allocated, the responsible parties start to change. They start to internalize their costs. They start to reduce the risks.

It is tempting to see bad happenings as the product of malicious rogue actors. Ascribing bad motives in this context can be counterproductive. Most actors act according to what the system incentivizes. The best way to make them act differently is to incentivize it with carrots and sticks.

Data breach risks are created by a multitude of actors throughout the entire data ecosystem. The breached organizations certainly are responsible for some of the risk, but they are one piece of the pie. To be effective, the law must aim to reduce risk throughout the whole system.

There are several ways data security law might better allocate risk to the right actors. Lawmakers can create rules holding specific and broad groups of actors accountable for data security risks. They can create and enforce data security rules for designers, distributors, amplifiers, facilitators, miseducators, and exploiters. Lawmakers can develop standards for liability. Judges can contribute by being more willing to acknowledge when these entities act unreasonably. Lawmakers can require *all* the actors to be more transparent about their operations and how they contribute to data breaches.[69] By focusing mainly on breached organizations, the law misses how many other actors are creating big security risks.

Reducing Harm
from Data Breaches

I n 2002, an identity thief began using David Lazarus's Social Security
Number to open nine different credit card accounts. The thief used the
cards to rack up debts at casinos.[1]

David reached out to the police for help, but they wouldn't help him.
Fortunately, David was a journalist and had the skills to track down the
thief and gather evidence. The thief was arrested and convicted in 2003
and was eventually deported. David thought he had won.

He was wrong. The tainted data that the thief had generated began to
take on a life of its own. David tried to buy a house, but he had trouble
obtaining a loan because of the debts that the thief had racked up. He was
told that to clear up his record, he would have to pay $4,000 of the thief's
casino debts.

After a long time fighting, many phone calls, and much stress, David
was finally able to get his loan approved. The nightmare was finally over.
In 2007, David wrote an article about how he survived this ordeal.[2]

Years passed. A decade later, David received a phone call from a debt collector for a hospital bill in Connecticut. He had never been to a hospital in Connecticut.[3] This error wasn't an innocent mistake. Nor was it a different identity thief—it was the same thief who was at it again. "And just like that, the nightmare starts again," David wrote in a follow-up article 10 years after his first article. He lamented "the near-impossibility of fully correcting erroneous online information—which I spent many hours trying to do the last time I dealt with this problem."[4]

David's case is not unusual. Identity theft is so prevalent because the law makes it so easy to perpetrate. Identity thieves can get away with fraud because companies are often not careful enough about authenticating people's identity. The thieves are hard to track down. Smart identity thieves know that identity theft is a great boondoggle, much better than bank robbery. Bank robbers get caught; identity thieves don't.

To make matters worse, identity theft is incredibly simple to do. Our data ecosystem makes it easy. To conduct an identity theft, a thief just needs a few pieces of personal data. The identity thief can then go on a massive spree of fraud. With how readily systems can be breached and with all the data already leaked from previous breaches, identity thieves live in a world abundant in riches. The Internet offers up a copious bazaar of personal data—some for sale and some for free. The thieves can readily obtain it and start using it.

The law does little to help. Laws aimed at combating identity theft are mostly ineffective. Several laws actually make the problem worse by ratcheting up the pain and suffering for identity theft victims as well as the overall harm and cost of data breaches.

THE IDENTITY THEFT EPIDEMIC

In the United States, more than 16 million people are victimized by identity theft in a single year.[5] Identity theft is a Kafkaesque nightmare, plunging victims into a bureaucratic maze that can take forever to escape from. In the early 2000s, grave concerns were raised about the burgeoning scourge of identity theft.[6] According to the FBI, in 2001 identity theft was the fastest growing form of white collar crime.[7] The problem quickly became an epidemic. Today, hardly anything has improved.

Types of Identity Theft

Identity theft is the among the most tangible and legally recognized harms resulting from a compromise in the confidentiality, integrity, or availability of personal data. To understand the full impact that data breaches have on people, it helps to have a sense of the many different kinds of identity theft.

FINANCIAL IDENTITY THEFT

Financial identity theft is the most prevalent form of identity theft. Thieves obtain credit cards or loans in the victim's name, racking up big debts. When unsuspecting victims try to obtain a loan, a job, a license, or anything requiring a credit check, the victims discover that their credit is trashed and that they owe a massive amount of debt. People can also discover that they have been victimized when they start receiving a barrage of phone calls from debt collectors.

CRIMINAL IDENTITY THEFT

In criminal identity theft, identity thieves provide the victim's information when they are arrested. Some identity thieves dupe the police with fake driver's licenses in their victim's name.[8] After their arrest, the thieves post bail and disappear. Later, victims discover that they are wanted for committing a crime. In some cases, the thief has amassed a long rap sheet of crimes in the victim's name.

One victim was repeatedly fired from jobs and had great difficulties getting hired because his criminal records were riddled with felonies, including sex crimes involving children.[9] In another case, a woman in the Air Force returned home from an overseas deployment to discover that she was wanted for injury to a child, assault, and other crimes.[10] In one instance, an identity theft victim was arrested and held in prison for more than two weeks until the police discovered that the fingerprints on the victim's records didn't match. Even then, the nightmare didn't end; it became even more horrific when the victim was arrested again based on more tainted data from the identity thief.[11]

MEDICAL IDENTITY THEFT

Another pernicious strain of identity theft is medical identity theft. According to the U.S. Department of Health and Human Services (HHS): "Medical identity theft occurs when someone steals your personal information (like your name, Social Security Number, or Medicare number) to obtain medical care, buy drugs, or submit fake billings to Medicare in your name."[12]

In one case, a person went to donate blood but was denied. A fraudster had used her Social Security Number to get treatment at an AIDS clinic.[13] In another case, a victim was billed $44,000 for surgery that he hadn't received. One incident involved a woman who was falsely listed on the birth certificate of an identity thief's baby. The baby was born addicted to meth, and the identity theft victim was wrongly pursued by child-protective services for the identity thief's baby.[14] In many cases, identity thieves use a victim's information to obtain prescriptions.[15]

The term "medical identity theft" originates from a report by Pam Dixon of the World Privacy Forum. She concluded her report by stating: "The victims who have been impacted by medical identity theft have to date been largely ignored, despite the serious consequences and harms they must face and deal with."[16] Dixon wrote this report in 2006. Since then, nothing has improved.

Most victims from medical identity theft suffer significant harm, and few are completely cured. Not only can medical ID theft create financial harm, but it can pollute medical records with false information that can jeopardize a patient's treatment. Sometimes, the errors can create life-threatening harm.[17] Imagine that you have been injured, and that you are unconscious and wheeled into the emergency room. Your medical records are riddled with errors from an identity thief—your blood type is wrong, and your allergies are incorrectly listed. There are preexisting conditions listed that you don't have. There are treatments listed that you never received. There are drugs listed that you don't take. These errors could lead to a wrong treatment that could be lethal.

Medical identity theft often takes much longer to detect than other types of fraud.[18] The longer detection period increases the value of the data to fraudsters.

CHILDREN'S IDENTITY THEFT

Identity thieves target children because they are less likely to discover the problem. In a recent example, identity thieves pretended to be teenagers in Canada to fraudulently claim thousands of dollars in government benefits.[19] There are more than one million children whose identities are stolen each year.[20] Kids are deeply wounded from identity theft because they often don't find out that it is going on until years later. When teenagers or young adults start to pay taxes, take out college loans, or get credit cards, they might discover that a thief has been conducting fraud in their name for years. Their credit will be ruined, they might owe tens of thousands of dollars, and they will have great difficulty in obtaining a loan or a credit card. If children are victims of medical identity theft, the fraud can result in astronomical health insurance premiums when they obtain their own coverage.[21]

Harms of Identity Theft

Identity theft is often brushed aside by police departments as a minor crime, but identity theft can be far more harmful than physical theft. Identity theft also has reverberations that can last for years.

COST, STRESS, ANXIETY, AND LOST TIME

Victims of identity theft suffer significant cost, stress, anxiety, and lost time to repair the damage. Some must sell possessions or borrow money to pay the expenses. Many must take time off from work or sacrifice their vacation time to clean up the mess.[22]

Victims' credit scores plummet, and they lose time trying to clean up the pollution to their credit history. Some victims have their credit cards cancelled; others see their interest rates skyrocket. Victims are often barraged with calls from collection agencies. Some victims are unable to rent an apartment or find housing, while others have trouble finding a job.[23] Medical identity theft victims can be denied health insurance coverage because thieves have used up their benefits. Some victims lose their health insurance entirely.

Cleansing one's records by clearing up the muck of bad data can be quite difficult. For example, HIPAA—the law that regulates health data— provides for a right to "amend" rather than correct one's records.[24] Patients can have notations about wrong information added to their records, but healthcare providers often don't delete incorrect data. The muck remains in the records.

Identity theft is like contracting a chronic disease that just won't go away. Victims will often have to play an endless game of "whack-a-mole" trying to shut down the fake accounts as quickly as they pop up.[25] Around 50 to 60 percent of people surveyed in recent years indicated that their identity theft issue remained unresolved. And the statistics are getting worse. In 2013, 51.1 percent reported that the identity theft remained unresolved; in 2016, the percentage had risen to 61.9 percent. In 2013, 27.5 percent resolved the issue in under six months. Only 16.8 percent resolved the issue in under six months in 2016.[26]

More than 75 percent of victims reported being "severely distressed" about the identity theft.[27] People felt angry, fearful, powerless, betrayed, embarrassed, and frustrated. Many felt anxiety. Many felt vulnerable and violated.[28]

COSTS TO ORGANIZATIONS AND TO CONSUMERS

Not only are breaches harmful to people, but they are also very costly and harmful to organizations. At first blush, some might think: *Serves these organizations right! They don't protect our data enough, and now they have to pay for it. Good! They ought to pay!*

It certainly is fair for organizations to be held accountable when they have a breach because they did something wrong or could have done something better. When organizations are at fault, they ought to feel some pain from a breach.

But the costs are often too much, don't compensate people who are harmed, don't serve to deter bad conduct, and end up hurting everyone. Organizations that suffer data breaches aren't just large, profit-hungry corporations; they are schools, colleges, hospitals, charities, and small businesses. The money schools spend on breaches is money lost from education. Money spent on hospital breaches takes away from expenditures on healthcare.

In many cases, the costs are passed along to consumers in terms of higher prices. The organizations are thus not footing much of the bill. Instead, individuals are doing so, including the very people who are identity theft victims. Moreover, these costs go primarily towards cleaning up after a breach; only a portion of the expenditure goes to improving security.

Fines by federal agencies such as the Federal Trade Commission (FTC) and state attorneys general mostly go into the coffers of the U.S. Treasury to be spent on whatever whims the government desires. Data breach victims rarely see much money or other meaningful redress from class action litigation. Instead, victims just receive endless offers of free credit monitoring that don't do much to protect them.

HOW THE LAW FAILS TO PREVENT IDENTITY THEFT

The law attempts to stop identity theft by trying to deter it with punishments after it occurs. That strategy is not working.

The law's main tool for combating identity theft has been to criminalize it. In 1998, the federal government enacted the Identity Theft and Identity Theft and Assumption Deterrence Act. The law makes it a federal crime to "knowingly transfer or use, without lawful authority, a means of identification of another person with the intent to commit, or to aid or abet, any unlawful activity that constitutes a violation of Federal law, or that constitutes a felony under any applicable State or local law."[29]

Following the federal law, most states passed their own laws criminalizing identity theft. Before 1998, only three states had such laws. By 2002, the number had grown to 44 states.[30] Today, all 50 states have criminalized identity theft.[31]

These laws are more an exercise in optics than a meaningful way to combat identity theft. Criminal law already had many tools to address identity theft prior to these laws because identity theft falls under criminal fraud laws. In other words, identity theft was a crime long before the states created special new laws to criminalize it.

The problem with using criminal law to combat identity theft is that it is too little, too late. Identity thieves are not deterred by criminal laws because they can so readily avoid detection. Identity thieves could be anywhere—in a different city, a different state, or even a different country. The thieves are very hard to track down.

Suppose you live in a city and are victimized by identity theft. You complain to the local police department. Unfortunately, the police lack the time and resources to start hunting around the world to locate the thief. They have murders, robberies, and violent crimes to solve. Identity theft isn't a priority.

Suppose you are lucky, and the police devote the time to do a thorough investigation. They track down the thief's location to a small town in another state. The police aren't going to travel to this town to find the thief. At best, they will call the police in the thief's town for help. But those police officers have their own criminal cases to investigate; their first priority is to help people in their own town, not someone who lives in a city far away.

But let us suppose that the police in the town decide to invest their time and resources to help. By the time of the investigation, which often is a long time after the fraud occurred, the thief likely is long gone. Many identity thieves are not even in a different town or state—they might be in other countries, which makes them even more difficult to track down.

The result is that hardly any identity thieves are convicted. In one estimate, only about one percent of instances of identity theft result in a conviction.[32] Identity thieves know that they will rarely ever get caught. The chorus of laws criminalizing identity theft may sound quite harmonious, but they are little more than useless background music that has barely any effect on reducing the amount of identity theft.

HOW THE LAW FACILITATES IDENTITY THEFT

The law is more than merely ineffective at preventing identity theft; the problem with the law is far worse—in fact, it's quite outrageous. The law actually facilitates identity theft.

The Worst Password Ever Created

Every year, SplashData compiles a list of the most commonly used bad passwords based on leaked passwords. Year after year, the same bad passwords dominate the list. A few shuffle up or down, but there isn't much change. Here are the most common worst 10 for 2018:

1. 123456
2. password
3. 123456789
4. 12345678
5. 12345
6. 11111
7. 1234567
8. sunshine
9. qwerty
10. iloveyou

Other popular candidates include "princess," "monkey," "password1," "welcome," and "football."[33]

These passwords are bad—really bad. But none are the worst password ever created. So, what is the worst password in all of human history?

The Social Security Number (SSN) is the worst password ever created, and it is a creation of the law. The federal government created the SSN in 1936 as part of the Social Security System. The SSN wasn't designed to be a password—it was created to be used in conjunction with a person's name to make sure that information about people with the same name wouldn't get mixed up.

Over time, unfortunately, businesses and government agencies began to use the SSN to authenticate identity. Countless companies and organizations still use people's SSNs to verify that people are really who they say they are.[34] If you know your SSN, the assumption goes, then you must be you. The irony is that the SSN was designed to be part of a username, and now it's being used as a password.[35]

Congress has sat idly by as the SSN has been misused. In 1974, when Congress passed the Privacy Act, there was a provision in the bill that would have restricted organizations from misusing SSNs. But this provision was dropped before the Privacy Act was passed.[36]

As a password, the SSN is just a nine-digit number, no better than the sixth most popular password: 123456789. Here it is as an SSN: 123-45-6789. A random string of numbers is probably not enough entropy (lack of order or predictability) to prevent the password from being guessed or otherwise cracked.[37] Professors Alessandro Acquisti and Ralph Gross found that some SSNs could be guessed through reverse engineering using public data and information from social media sites.[38]

Armed with your SSN, identity thieves can gain access to various accounts, open new accounts in your name, and engage in fraudulent transactions and attribute them to you. All this is possible because they have, in essence, obtained your password—the SSN.

But what makes an SSN a worse password than, say, the password "123"? Why is the SSN the worst password ever?

There are two reasons. First, the SSN is something that identity thieves know is used as a password, and they can readily find a person's SSN. SSNs are often in various public documents and countless record systems. Scores of data breaches have resulted in compromised SSNs, which are peddled in underground online markets on the Dark Web. SSNs are also sold legally by many companies. That's right—it's totally legal for companies to sell people's SSNs. At least with the password 123, others don't know that it is your password, and it's more difficult to find out.

Second, SSNs are quite hard to change. The beauty of passwords that you create is that if they are compromised, you can quickly change them with very little effort. Not so with SSNs, which are a tremendous hassle to change. Whenever there's a data breach involving your SSN, you now have a potentially life-long increased risk of identity theft because SSNs are so difficult to change.

Why People Can't Really Protect Themselves

Over and over again we hear the typical spiel about how people should take advantage of credit monitoring, be alert, shred their documents, guard their SSNs, and so on.[39] A list of these tips are at the end of countless news articles about data breaches. Reporters include these tips to give people hope and some sense of power that they can do something to protect themselves. Unfortunately, these tips provide false hope and an illusory sense of control.

The most important thing people can do to protect themselves is to get angry at their lawmakers for not passing the adequate laws. Without legal change, data security isn't likely to improve.

When many people hear about individuals being victimized by identity theft, they might think: *The victims must have done something wrong. I'm safe because I'm careful with my data.*

Some people take obsessive precautions to protect themselves, such as refusing to provide their SSN to organizations that request them on various forms or applications. But that is a losing battle. The law often requires organizations to collect SSNs. For example, your employer must collect your SSN. If you are hired as an independent contractor, tax law requires that you provide a W-9 form with your SSN on it. You will need to provide your SSN to open financial accounts or obtain loans or credit.

Suppose that somehow you manage to avoid giving out your SSN. You eschew employment, bank accounts, credit cards, phone service, and more. You move to a remote cabin in the woods without Internet or electricity. Are you safe? Nope. Your SSN is still out there and still widely used and available. There's often nothing you can do to remove it from public records or to stop it from being sold.

The Inadequacy of Credit Monitoring

When an organization has a data breach, it will often offer a year or two of credit monitoring to any victim who wants it. Providing free credit monitoring has become the norm. Even in breaches where credit monitoring won't be helpful or relevant, organizations offer it almost reflexively because everyone has come to expect it.

Given how often credit monitoring is offered after data breaches, one would think that it is a great cure for any harms or a vaccine against future harms. But credit monitoring isn't a cure or vaccine—it's just a limited diagnostic tool. Credit monitoring just tells you if something odd is going on in your credit reports.

Consumer reporting agencies make huge profits by selling credit monitoring. They entice people to shell out monthly subscription fees. In essence, these companies are asking you to pay money to monitor the data they have already collected about you without your consent and for their own profit—the epitome of chutzpah. Think of it this way: Imagine I decide to keep dangerous tigers in my backyard, right next to your house. I have a rather flimsy fence. I offer to install a sensor that will alert you if my tigers might enter your backyard—but only if you pay me a monthly fee. Should you really be paying money for this? Shouldn't this be my responsibility?

For example, Equifax sells a service it calls Equifax ID Patrol:

Help Better Protect Your Identity and Monitor the Credit You've
    Worked Hard to Earn
✓3-Bureau credit file monitoring
✓Lock and unlock your Equifax credit report
✓Customize alerts to stay informed about unusual activities

There's a monthly fee of $16.95.[40] But many of the offered services are free because the law requires them to be, such as the ability to lock and unlock credit reports. The law entitles people to a free copy of their credit report each year from all three consumer reporting agencies.

Jittery consumers purchase these services, thinking that they will be safe, but these services don't make people safe. They are not cures and they will not stop identity theft.

If these services really do help prevent fraud in people's records, then they should be free. The federal Fair Credit Reporting Act (FCRA) requires that consumer reporting agencies use reasonable procedures to ensure maximum possible accuracy.[41] If credit monitoring helps ensure that one's credit report is accurate and not polluted with fraudulent information, then it should be required under the law's mandate.

Credit monitoring hikes up the cost of data breaches. Organizations that have a breach must buy it for people. Credit monitoring is a great revenue source for consumer reporting agencies, but it is an added expense for organizations having a breach that is often passed to consumers in the form of higher prices. Data breaches would be cheaper if everyone already had free credit monitoring. Sadly, however, this is not how courts or regulators have interpreted the FCRA.

Irresponsible Issuers of Credit

Back in 1981, in the famous case involving an accident resulting from a defect in a Ford Pinto, it came to light that Ford knew about the design defect in the car but ignored it because it calculated that paying damages in lawsuits would cost less than fixing the design flaw.

Professor Chris Hoofnagle illustrates that the same phenomenon is happening with identity theft. Companies grant credit carelessly because it is cheap to do so. Much of the losses are sloughed off on victims because the companies aren't forced to internalize them.[42]

Identity theft often happens because companies let it happen. It is an economic decision. Companies want to make it quick and easy for people to obtain credit.

For example, you might be standing in the check-out line of a store with some expensive merchandise. The checkout clerk says: "Do you want to apply for our store credit card and receive 10 percent off?"

You are in a hurry. "How long will this take?" you ask. "I don't have a lot of time."

"It's super-fast and easy," the clerk says. "Just fill out this short application, and we can have your account created in less than a minute. And you'll get 10 percent off." Because the application process is so quick, you say "Sure."

But what if the application process took a lot longer? You might not have time to wait around. You might not want to fill out a long form and answer many questions.

This is a calculated business risk decision by companies. They know that their quick and easy process can be exploited by fraudsters. Fraud will cost them, but they will reap far more rewards by getting more people to sign up for the card.

But there's a cost that credit issuers aren't taking into account—the cost to victims of identity theft. The victims are often not their customers. These victims are the people whose identities are stolen to create fake accounts.

Hoofnagle provides data from the credit applications of six identity theft victims to show how obvious incorrect data often isn't flagged. Applications had the wrong address, wrong phone number, or wrong date of birth. Some contained multiple mistakes. One even had the victim's name misspelled. These red flags in the credit applications could readily have been identified and investigated to discover the fraud. But they were ignored.

Identity theft is a product of *deliberate* carelessness. The reason so much identity theft occurs is because it is cheaper to expose people to the risk of identity theft than to exercise more care in vetting credit applications. Courts and legislatures are also to blame because they fail to adequately recognize the harm of identity theft (or data breaches) and will not make companies internalize the full costs. The companies do their cost–benefit analysis and conclude that they can expose people to the risk of identity theft because many costs are external.

In one of the most egregious cases, *Huggins v. Citibank*, several banks negligently issued credit cards in Kenneth Huggins' name to an identity thief without investigating the accuracy of the credit card application. The thief racked up hefty charges, which were falsely attributed to Huggins. Huggins was "hounded by collection agencies" and spent much time trying to repair the damage. He was only partially able to clean up the mess.[43]

Huggins sued the banks. The banks didn't argue that they acted carefully and properly. Instead, they claimed the case should be dismissed because Huggins wasn't their customer. The court began by noting that it was "greatly concerned about the rampant growth of identity theft and financial fraud in this country." The court further noted that "we are certain that some identity theft could be prevented if credit card issuers carefully scrutinized credit card applications." However, the court then concluded that it would "decline to recognize a legal duty of care between credit card issuers and those individuals whose identities may be stolen. The relationship, if any, between credit card issuers and potential victims of identity theft is far too attenuated to rise to the level of a duty between them. Even though it is foreseeable that injury may arise by the negligent issuance of a credit card, foreseeability alone does not give rise to a duty." In sum, the court concluded that "there is no duty on the part of credit card issuers to protect potential victims of identity."

To translate the legalese, this case means that companies can make a ton of money by being very careless in issuing credit cards, and they don't have to do anything to protect people who might be harmed by their carelessness.

If courts and legislatures were to better recognize harm and force companies to internalize it, then we would see an end to the sloppy practices that allow so much identity theft to occur. Until that time, companies can be just like Ford with the Pinto.

Other courts have taken differing views.[44] But as a general matter, far too often courts aren't holding companies responsible. Because of this, identity thieves can readily open fraudulent accounts in people's names by supplying just a few pieces of information, which they can readily obtain from a data breach.

TAKING THE STING OUT OF DATA BREACHES

Data breaches cause far too much needless harm. The law can lessen or stop much of this harm. As we discussed earlier, we can't stop all data breaches. Not only is this an unrealistic goal, but it is undesirable. The obsession with stopping all breaches has worsened the problem. We can reduce the number of breaches, but we are going to have to live with some of them.

There's another way to help the problem, though. We can take much of the sting out of data breaches. They need not be so harmful to individuals or so costly to organizations. If SSNs weren't used as passwords, for example, then the SSN would just be a number and nothing more. A data breach of SSNs wouldn't cause harm.

The law should ban the use of SSNs to authenticate identity. Congress could pass such a law, but it hasn't done so, despite one of us proposing the idea at a Congressional hearing back in 2005.

However, no new law needs to be passed for change to occur. The law currently has ample tools to stop the use of SSNs as passwords. The FTC could use its enforcement power under several laws to halt the misuse of SSNs for authentication purposes. The general standard for data security for FTC enforcement is "reasonable" security. This standard is used in the

Gramm-Leach-Bliley Act (GLBA) of 1999, a law that regulates financial institutions. The FTC's broadest authority to enforce for reasonable data security is under Section 5 of the FTC Act. For the past 25 years, the FTC has enforced against unreasonable data security as a violation of the FTC Act's prohibition of "unfair or deceptive acts or practices in or affecting commerce."[45]

The misuse of SSNs as passwords is unreasonable. No security expert would argue that using SSNs to authenticate identity is a reasonable security practice, given the more effective and less dangerous alternatives for authenticating identity. The SSN should never be used as a password to authenticate identity.

Through a few enforcement actions, the FTC could fault companies that use SSNs as passwords. Other companies would then quickly take note and change their practices to avoid getting in trouble. If the FTC were to take this step, one of the best tools for identity thieves would be neutralized. Without this easy tool, many of the less sophisticated thieves would be out of luck. Of course, the more sophisticated thieves would undoubtedly try something else. But most identity thieves aren't very sophisticated; they do the crime because it is so easy.

The result, we predict, would be a significant reduction in identity theft. Countless people wouldn't be victimized and put through a harrowing, time-consuming, and costly ordeal. Data breaches would be less costly to organizations because compromised SSNs wouldn't be able to cause so much harm.

Unfortunately, we still await a federal law or FTC enforcement or rule to neutralize SSNs. The government has assigned to all of us the worst password ever created, and we can't change it. Nearly a century after the creation of the SSN, the government still won't protect us by limiting its use.

The law should also hold responsible the actors that make data breaches so harmful. Too many companies are loose about granting credit or have poor ways of authenticating identity. The law fails to force them to fully internalize the cost of their practices to individuals. As a result, fraudsters continue to take advantage of the system. The loss is borne by the individuals and the companies having the breach.

Unifying Privacy and Data Security

I n April 2015, representatives from CyTech Services, a small forensics analysis company, met with officials at the U.S. Office of Personnel Management (OPM). The CyTech employees were at OPM to demonstrate their new tool, which would perform a diagnostic scan on OPM's servers.

OPM maintains personnel records of millions of federal employees and applicants to federal jobs. Because these jobs include sensitive positions, including FBI officers and others, applicants must undergo background checks. These background checks can be very intrusive, involving questions about financial troubles, drug and alcohol use, any criminal wrongdoing, psychological information, and much more. OPM maintained records of these background checks—nearly 21.5 million records involving current federal employees and retirees. CyTech Services initiated the diagnostic scan. Everyone expected the scan to be clean.[1] Nobody was prepared for what happened next.

The scan identified odd unknown processes occurring on the server.[2] Everyone in the room was stunned. Their jaws dropped. Something was very wrong.

The House Oversight and Government Reform Committee began a massive investigation, resulting in thousands of pages of documents and transcribed interviews. After nearly a year, the Committee's investigation revealed that CyTech's demonstration wasn't the first time that OPM had learned about the intrusion.[3] In fact, OPM had discovered a breach in March 2014, more than a year earlier. Later in 2014, two breaches occurred at KeyPoint Government Solutions, a company that provided services to OPM and that had access to OPM's data. OPM failed to terminate KeyPoint's access, even though KeyPoint's credentials were used to access OPM's network.

One of the hacked OPM databases, the Central Personnel Data File, contained personnel records of current and former federal employees. The database included their Social Security Numbers, job positions, and performance evaluations.

Another hacked OPM database, the Electronic Questionnaires for Investigations Processing (e-QIP) system, contained security clearance and background check information. This data included information on 1.8 million spouses, children, and family members of security clearance applicants.[4]

OPM also maintained fingerprint data, which dated back to 2000. Initially, OPM reported that only 1.1 million fingerprint records were compromised, but it later updated the figure to 5.6 million. OPM stated that "Federal experts believe that, as of now, the ability to misuse fingerprint data is limited."[5] This statement, however, strains credulity. Many experts criticized OPM for downplaying concerns about the compromised fingerprints. One expert declared that undercover agents could be "completely compromised," noting that "a secret agent's name might be different. But they'll know who you are because your fingerprint is there. You'll be outed immediately."[6]

As far back as 2007, OPM's Inspector General Office (OIG) was delivering semi-regular audit reports to Congress criticizing OPM's security practices as a "material weakness"—the lowest possible assessment on its scale.[7] Later reports noted that "[t]he continuing weakness in OPM information security program results directly from inadequate governance. Most if not all of the [information security] exceptions we noted this year result from a lack of leadership, policy, and guidance." A 2014 information security audit also noted OPM's poor security, faulting OPM for failing to implement multi-factor authentication, which had been recommended much earlier and would have likely prevented the breach.[8] Time and again, the warnings had been made that OPM's security was poor, but nobody did anything about it.[9]

The OPM breach was not only the product of bad security practices but also of poor privacy practices. Nuala O'Connor, former head of the U.S. Department of Homeland Security's privacy office, noted that "OPM didn't have the most basic data map or a simple inventory list of its servers and databases, nor did it have an accounting of all the systems connecting to its network."[10] This is a data privacy flaw. A key dimension of protecting data is maintaining a data inventory to keep track of the data being stored and who is responsible for it.

Moreover, OPM was storing all this data in a centralized location, making it easy for the hackers to obtain a lot of data.[11] Keeping massive stores of personal information is also a privacy no-no. Even worse, OPM retained the data seemingly forever; it had data going back decades, including information about people's families. Why did it need to keep all this data and why keep it for so long?

Had OPM collected and stored less data and regularly deleted some of it, the breach wouldn't have been as damaging. Moreover, had OPM segmented the data or better restricted access to it, the hackers would have had a harder time hauling it all away. Had OPM assigned a data steward for the data, someone who would be accountable for it and who would make sure it was properly being cared for, the breach might never have occurred.

OPM maintained background check information to protect security— to prevent government personnel from being compromised and betraying the United States by giving up secrets, helping foreign governments break into computer systems, or other things. Ironically, the hacked data not only violated people's privacy but it created a grave security threat—and it continues to pose such a threat to this day. Several security experts have warned that the information in security clearance and background checks could be used to blackmail government employees in sensitive positions.[12] A former assistant director of the FBI's Criminal, Cyber, Response and Services Branch told *The Washington Post* that the OPM breach provided hackers with "very detailed information about people who hold very sensitive clearances."[13] Hackers could use this information to conduct spear phishing, targeted attempts to glean personal information to "gain access to sensitive computer accounts and even potentially conduct a physical attack or attempt extortion."[14]

The story of the OPM breach certainly reveals a stunning display of bad security practices. The story also demonstrates how poor privacy practices made the breach more possible and much worse than it should have been. In this chapter, we address the relationship between privacy and security. Good data security is almost impossible without a robust commitment to privacy values. Privacy is a key and underappreciated aspect of data security. Lawmakers and industry should break down the regulatory and organizational silos that keep them apart and strengthen our privacy rules as one way to enhance data security and mitigate breaches.

UNDERSTANDING CYBERSECURITY, DATA SECURITY, AND DATA PRIVACY

At the outset of our discussion, it is essential to understand the general scope of the domains of cybersecurity, data security, and privacy. *Cybersecurity* is generally used to broadly refer to the security of all forms of information and technical infrastructures, such as intellectual property, critical infrastructure data, trade secrets, personal data, and more.[15] *Data security* is a narrower domain that involves the security of personal data. As David Thaw observes, cybersecurity as a whole can have different goals than protecting personal data.[16] He elaborates, "The security techniques and goals for protection of strategic weapon control systems are different than the techniques and goals for an average consumer, for example, protecting their personal computer used primarily for entertainment purposes."[17]

Privacy involves, among other things, a wide array of protections of personal data. Because privacy is an important aspect of personal data, it is closer to data security, but still not entirely the same. In some formulations, privacy is a broader domain that encompasses data security, which is a subset of the protections given to personal data. It is this formulation that we prefer, as we see data privacy as a pie with many essential pieces, one of which is data security.

In many ways, the EU's terminology is better. The EU uses the term *data protection* to encompass both data privacy and data security. The EU is exactly right—data privacy and data security are both, essentially, about protecting data. The EU doesn't see privacy and security as separate domains, at least not in the same way that the United States does.

Although privacy and data security are related and intertwined, they aren't identical. As law professor Derek Bambauer observes, "Privacy establishes a normative framework for deciding who should legitimately have the capability to access and alter information. Security implements those choices."[18] Jeff Kosseff notes that security "promotes the confidentiality, integrity, and availability of public and private information, systems, and networks." Security "must address more than just the confidentiality of personal information, and also seek to protect from unauthorized alteration of data and attacks such as ransomware that cause data or systems to become unavailable."[19]

We caution against clean and rigid distinctions between privacy and data security, at least in law and policy. Much of data security involves duties and administrative policies and procedures that are similar to those for privacy. Moreover, as we argued earlier, data security is more of an art than a science, and it involves difficult policy tradeoffs just like privacy does. Although privacy and security are distinct in many ways, they have quite a lot in common. Viewing data security policy primarily as a collection of requirements for breach notifications and technical controls excludes many of the most important issues from security, and it silos privacy and security in ways that are unproductive.

THE SCHISM BETWEEN PRIVACY AND SECURITY

A major schism exists between privacy and security. This schism arose in part because data security gets lumped with cybersecurity, and much of security these days is the province of the Information Technology department.

Different Silos and Different Languages

Organizations often place privacy functions in Compliance or Legal while data security is commonly in Information Technology (IT).[20] When companies organize their departments in this way, privacy and security professionals interact less and have a lower ability to change each other's practices, habits, and fluencies. Not only do privacy and security teams infrequently speak to each other, they often speak in different languages. It's like the Tower of Babel.

Law professor Ari Waldman noticed two important issues that came up in his extensive interviews with technologists and lawyers working on privacy and security within organizations.[21] First, some corporations conflate privacy and security (and then focus only on security). Others bracket off the presumably non-security aspects of "privacy" into compliance departments with workers whose expertise is in paper trails, not privacy. Privacy is then given a meager budget, while IT departments get tasked with "security" and budgets that allow them to do their work. Then, Waldman notes, comes the magician's misdirection. Having empowered IT departments to fix security flaws, corporations then report that they are protecting their customers' privacy when, in fact, they have done quite little.[22]

Based on his interviews with technologists, Waldman observes that many technologists believe privacy merely involves providing users with notice about the company's privacy practices. Others think privacy is synonymous with encryption, which in this context is driven more by a desire to secure company data than to safeguard against consumer privacy risks. As Waldman also notes, "Few engineers remembered meeting with lawyers or privacy professionals one-on-one to discuss integrating privacy considerations into their work. Many found it difficult to design with user needs in mind; therefore, engineer-only design teams not only minimized the importance of privacy, but also missed how their designs impacted consumers."[23] This kind of organizational schism has led to a mentality around privacy and data security that ends up limiting the effectiveness of both domains.

One of the problems with separating data security and privacy is that people working in these areas cannot learn from each other. This means they often repeat the same mistakes or miss out on different ways of thinking about problems. People can get a little myopic, thinking that their little patch of responsibilities is the cosmos. This kind of narrow thinking also leads to a breakdown in cooperation where privacy interventions could help improve data security and vice versa.

Waldman's interviews with technologists reveal that the companies they work for often do very little to prioritize privacy by design. As Waldman observes, "Privacy professionals or other personnel trained in privacy rarely met with engineers and programmers, even during weeks of intense design work." Even at companies that had "privacy teams that were supposed to 'insinuate' themselves into design, high turnover, a laissez-faire attitude, and corporate silos kept privacy mostly orthogonal to design."[24]

Further, Waldman's work reveals that privacy is often deprioritized while other values take precedence. The mandate often comes from the top, where executives want engineers to prioritize "speed, agility, [and] functionality.'"[25] Waldman noted that "[i]nterviewees used words and phrases like 'hands off,' 'absent,' 'uninvolved,' and 'not really a factor,' to describe their employers' approach to privacy. Privacy is akin to security's distant cousin, whom everyone forgets to invite to the party. Even when privacy is at the party, it is relegated to the small children's table off to the side.

Beyond a lack of privacy protection, the schism between privacy and data security has resulted in organizations viewing data security mainly as an IT issue. Certainly, many components of good data security involve IT, such as encryption, firewalls, access controls, and more. But many more security issues involve a human dimension. Many security decisions involve human behavior, such as how to deal with cognitive limitations, carelessness, cheating, denial, ignorance, gullibility, and misconduct—security's seven deadly sins. Security decisions also involve policy, such as managing the tradeoff between security on the one side, and ease, convenience, and ready accessibility on the other.

We have heard people call the security side "hard" or "left-brained" and the privacy side "soft" or "right-brained." IT technologists are often not well-trained in addressing complex issues involving people and values; they are more often trained mostly in "hard" technological problems and solutions. They know how computer systems and code operate, but often they aren't sufficiently trained about how to respond to human behavior or how to think through challenging policy choices. Privacy professionals, in contrast, receive a heavier dose of training about so-called soft issues such as human behavior, values, law, and policy. We aren't fond of the terms "hard" and "soft" or "left-brained" or "right-brained," but we agree that there is certainly a distinction between the kinds of training IT and privacy professionals receive. The key difference is that privacy draws more from the humanities and data security is more steeped in engineering. For effective data security, however, both types of thinking are essential.

Privacy is (or at least should be) about much more than just effectuating peoples' personal preferences about who should have their data. Privacy is about trust, power, dignity, and the collective autonomy to set the preconditions of human flourishing.[26] In a broader sense, privacy is about all the rules that govern our personal information.[27] Data security policy similarly cannot escape a web of value-laden decisions, because it, too, requires tradeoffs guided by ethics and normative considerations.

A Schism in the Law

The schism between security and privacy also exists in the law, especially in U.S. law. Broadly speaking, the law began with a more unified view of privacy and security, but after the ChoicePoint breach, data security law spun off into a more separate domain.

In the early laws of the 1970s through 2000, data security evolved alongside and within privacy laws and frameworks. Data security is one of the original Fair Information Practice Principles (FIPPs), which were the principles proposed to address concerns with the rise of computer databases of personal information.[28] The FIPPs arose in a 1973 report by the U.S. Department of Health, Education, and Welfare (HEW) called *Records, Computers and the Rights of Citizens*.[29] The HEW report was prompted by concerns about the computerization of records, and the committee that drafted the report was charged with recommending legal and policy responses. The primary recommendation of the report was to enact a code of fair information practices to regulate all repositories of personal data. Data security was one of the main recommendations in the report: "Any organization creating, maintaining, using, or disseminating records of identifiable personal data must assure the reliability of the data for their intended use and must take reasonable precautions to prevent misuse of the data."[30]

The FIPPs have become the backbone of privacy laws around the world. In 1980, the OECD Privacy Guidelines included the "Security Safeguards Principle," which stated that "Personal data should be protected by reasonable security safeguards against such risks as loss or unauthorized access, destruction, use, modification or disclosure of data."[31] The OECD Privacy Guidelines have formed the blueprint for the EU's privacy laws, starting with various member nation's laws, then the EU Data Protection Directive, and today's General Data Protection Regulation (GDPR). Laws in the United States and around the world include many of the FIPPs. There are now more than 200 countries with data privacy laws, and most of them are built upon the FIPPs specified by the OECD.[32] Many of these privacy laws include protections for data security.

Starting in the early 2000s, a separate and more distinctive body of law around data security developed, especially in the United States. Breach notification laws and safeguards laws started popping up everywhere, and these laws focused more exclusively on data security.

Although data security is often lumped in as part of privacy and data protection regimes, it is now treated as a distinct area centered around safeguards and notification. If organizations provide notification of breaches and properly implement safeguards, in the eyes of the law, they will be seen to have fulfilled their data security obligations. The law often has stronger penalties for data security violations than for privacy violations, so when data breaches are caused by privacy problems, such as in the Cambridge Analytica case (discussed below), companies want to frame them in terms of privacy rather than security and avoid giving them the dreaded moniker of "data breach."

The classic formulation of data security is to protect the confidentiality, integrity, and availability of data—a triad often referred to with the acronym CIA. It is important to note that the first element of this triad—confidentiality—is a key dimension of privacy. Data integrity also involves privacy, as many privacy laws protect a principle called "data quality," which involves the accuracy and completeness of data.

Privacy and data security have much in common. Over time they have become estranged relatives, but they should go hand-in-hand. Recent data security breaches indicate that it is time for them to be united again.

THE FRONT DOOR AND THE BACK DOOR

Everyone is so obsessed with preventing a breach through the back door that they neglect to pay enough attention to the front door. The "back door" is a metaphor to describe the illicit break-ins by hackers or other intruders. We clearly know that they don't belong in the computer network. The "front door" describes the many people who are invited into the network or who already have access to the network.

Security focuses mostly on the back door, on keeping the bad guys from intruding. Privacy focuses mostly on the front door. The people coming into the front door often don't appear to be bad guys, but they are also a security risk. Like a nosy visitor to one's home, front-door people might start snooping into things that they are not authorized to see.

Hackers know that sometimes the easiest way to break in is through the front door, so they pose as regular customers. Recall the ChoicePoint breach that we discussed earlier. In that breach, the hackers posed as a legitimate ChoicePoint customer. They didn't need to break in—ChoicePoint opened the door and let them in. No security alarm bells went off because the hackers weren't intruding; they were customers. The problem was one that is typically in the domain of privacy—decisions about who has access to data and how it is shared. ChoicePoint was too loose about who could be its customer; it too freely shared personal data without making sure it was doing so carefully.

At the end of the day, front-door breaches and back-door breaches are both breaches, but front-door breaches are often harder to guard against. Many front-door people differ from hackers because they don't think they are doing anything wrong, or they think what they are doing is only a minor transgression.

Figure 7.1

To address back-door and front-door breaches, security and privacy must work together. Guarding the back door is all for naught if the front door is left wide open.

The Moneyball "Hack"

Jeff Luhnow, Sig Mejdal, and Chris Correa were executives with the St. Louis Cardinals major league baseball team. Luhnow and Mejdal built a database called Redbird, which contained information and statistics about players. The database adopted the Moneyball approach to baseball, which is chronicled in the bestselling book of the same name by Michael Lewis. This approach involves analyzing enormous troves of data to make baseball decisions, as opposed to the good old-fashioned technique of going with one's gut. Essentially, Moneyball is baseball's version of Big Data.

Correa and Mejdal were rivals who worked under Luhnow. Later, Luhnow left the Cardinals to become the general manager for the Houston Astros, a team that was one of the main rivals to the Cardinals in the same NL Central division.[33] Luhnow hired Mejdal to join him in Houston and named him to be head of the analytics department. There, Luhnow and Mejdal launched a similar Moneyball-style program called Ground Control.

Back in St. Louis, Correa had become head of analytics. He sought to access the scouting data Luhnow and Mejdal were gathering in Ground Control for the Astros. Correa knew Mejdal's password to Redbird because Mejdal was required to turn over his laptop and password when he left the Cardinals, and Correa figured that perhaps Mejdal, like so many other people, might reuse the same password for his other accounts, including his account for Ground Control.[34]

In March 2013, Correa tried the old password, and it worked. Over the next two-and-a-half years, Correa accessed Ground Control numerous times. He viewed scouting reports, player health information, and other data.[35]

In January 2014, Correa lost access to Ground Control when there was a system-wide password reset. But a few months later, the Astros reset all Ground Control user passwords to a default password. Correa found the default password in Mejdal's email, and he was back in.

In June 2014, the Astros were last in their division, but *Sports Illustrated* ran a feature story called "Astro-Matic Baseball" filled with praise for Mejdal and Luhnow about their Moneyball approach. The cover of the issue had an Astros player swinging his bat with the title: "Your 2017 World Series Champs." Mejdal was also featured in another article in the issue.

Perhaps sparked by the fact that his rival Mejdal was being praised even though his team was currently dead last in the division, Correa again attempted to log back into Ground Control. Correa then allegedly leaked confidential notes about Astros' trade discussions.[36] The leaks created tensions between several baseball teams and their players, and the Astros ended up apologizing individually to other teams.

It was these leaks that would be Correa's undoing. The FBI began investigating, and everything came to light.[37] The FBI discovered that Ground Control had been infiltrated from a location occupied by executives from Cardinals. The Cardinals launched an internal investigation. The hacking was traced back to Correa, who had been promoted to scouting director.

Correa was fired by the Cardinals. He was criminally charged under a federal hacking statute, and he pled guilty. He was sentenced to prison for nearly four years and ordered to pay restitution of $279,038.65. The Major League Baseball Commissioner banned Correa permanently from baseball, a sanction imposed only on a few others such as Pete Rose and players from the 1919 scandal-ridden Chicago White Sox. The Cardinals were fined $2 million, and they had to forfeit their first two picks in the draft to the Houston Astros.

"Hacking" Is Often Just Snooping

There are some who object to the word "hacking" to describe what happened here. Hacking connotes high-tech wizardry, the stuff chronicled in the movie *War Games* or regularly on TV where people can break into any network by typing for 10 seconds on a keyboard.

The methods used by Correa to access the Astros' system were not very sophisticated. Correa used some old passwords he knew from when Luhnow and others were working with the Cardinals. The passwords weren't changed when they went to the Astros. So, Correa wasn't a tech wiz, but he did know some of the ancient wisdom passed down through generations of computer fraudsters: *People often have poor password practices.* People select bad passwords, they put them on sticky notes near their computers, and they often never change them. Correa guessed correctly that Luhnow or the others didn't bother to change the password after they went from the Cardinals to the Astros.

Whether you call it "hacking" or not, the key thing for the law is that someone is accessing a computer in ways that are not authorized. This doesn't need to occur through any kind of technological acumen.

The federal Computer Fraud and Abuse Act (CFAA) imposes criminal penalties when a person "intentionally accesses a computer without authorization or exceeds authorized access, and thereby obtains . . . information from any protected computer."[38] A protected computer is defined very broadly—essentially, it includes any computer connected to the Internet.

There are a variety of different types of crimes under the CFAA depending upon the circumstances, but the foundation of all of them is unauthorized access. And based on the facts reported, there was unauthorized access. Even though the password was readily guessable—and even though it appears the Cardinals already had the list of passwords in its possession—the ease of access doesn't matter. No matter how careless Luhnow might have been with security, accessing his computer without authorization is still a crime.

Many people have the misconception that computer crime is very sophisticated, but often it isn't. Hackers often break into a system through con artistry—by tricking people into giving them their password. If you read about the exploits of reformed hacker Kevin Mitnick, the inspiration for the movie *War Games*, many of his techniques seem closer to the movie *Dirty Rotten Scoundrels*.

We don't know for sure, but we are willing to bet that Correa didn't think of himself as a hacker. Hackers are often depicted in photos as teenagers in hoodies or criminals in ninja suits. In movies and TV, hackers are sophisticated techies who can break into the most secure systems with just a few keystrokes. In heist movies, they can instantly pull up the architectural plans to the building to be robbed. A few more keystrokes gets them into the power grid.

But in real life, a large component of hacking isn't high-tech. Correa didn't use technical wizardry to break into Ground Control. He just used a password he knew. He was a snooper. But under the law, he was a hacker.

In the analog world, people do a lot of snooping. A person in the bathroom at a friend's house might peek into the medicine cabinet. A spouse might peek at their partner's diary or private papers that are sitting out on the bed. People might put their ears against the door to listen in on a conversation in the next room. These forms of non-digital snooping are not punished very severely; many instances are not even punished at all by the law.

But when it comes to digital snooping, it's a different story. Snooping into email accounts or other online accounts will violate state and federal electronic surveillance statutes which penalize many intrusions as felonies with steep prison terms.

The CFAA rightly punishes front-door snooping such as Correa's. Other forms of snooping, such as when employees of an organization look into people's records out of curiosity rather than as part of their job, are dealt with by privacy laws such as HIPAA. It is still common for most people to associate the front door with privacy and the back door with security. Understanding that the front door is also essential to security is a necessary step toward more robust security.

POOR PRIVACY LEADS TO POOR DATA SECURITY

Poor privacy will undermine even the best data security. Good privacy practices involve having more than just the bare minimum of procedural safeguards like getting consent or being transparent about data practices. To have good privacy practices an organization must severely curb its data appetite, collect only the data that is necessary and justified, delete data when it is no longer needed, and avoid data processing that threatens people's rights, exposes people to an undue risk of harm, or leads to socially detrimental effects.

Many organizations are looking for ways to try to hook everything up to the Internet, to collect more personal data, to use it in more ways, to gather it all together, and to keep it for longer, possibly forever. These are problematic privacy practices, and they are a recipe for a security Titanic. There are several ways that bad privacy can lead to bad security: (1) Weak privacy controls can lead to improper access through the front door; (2) Collecting and storing unnecessary data can make data breaches much worse; (3) Poor privacy regulation can allow for more tools and practices that compromise security; and (4) A lack of accountability over data can increase the likelihood that the data will be lost, misplaced, or misused.

Weak Privacy Leads to Front-Door Breaches

On the Sunday morning of March 18, 2018, *The Guardian* published a bombshell story: "Revealed: 50 million Facebook profiles harvested for Cambridge Analytica in major data breach."[39] The story showed how, through third-party apps on Facebook, data analytics company Cambridge Analytica extracted massive amounts of data from Facebook's users.[40] Cambridge Analytica worked for Donald Trump's election team and the Brexit campaign. Cambridge Analytica used the data that it plundered to create psychological profiles of voters, whom it then targeted and attempted to influence their voting in the 2016 Presidential election and the Brexit referendum.[41]

A big debate arose over whether Cambridge Analytica's access to the data was a data breach. People didn't even regularly use the term "data breach" until the 2000s, so it's relatively new and undefined, even though it is legally significant.[42] Nicholas Thompson, editor-in-chief of *Wired* said of the incident:

> "Breach" is a word in the tech community that means they cracked the protections, right? You got over the moat and you got in through the door. . . . Facebook, a company of engineers, [is] really proud that hasn't happened at Facebook, so if you say data is breached, to Facebook it's like, "Oh my God, that's the most offensive thing you can say." To the rest of the world, it's like, "Of course this is a breach!" Right? "They got the data!"[43]

But Facebook Vice President Andrew Bosworth declared on Twitter: "This was unequivocally not a data breach. People chose to share their data with third-party apps and if those third-party apps did not follow the data agreements with us/users it is a violation. No systems were infiltrated, no passwords or information were stolen or hacked."[44] Then in a series of later-deleted Tweets, Facebook Chief Security Officer Alex Stamos said, "The recent Cambridge Analytica stories by the *New York Times* and *The Guardian* are important and powerful, but it is incorrect to call this a 'breach' under any reasonable definition of the term. . . .We can condemn this behavior while being accurate in our description of it."[45]

Two years later, the updated top line in Facebook's first press release in response to the Cambridge Analytica scandal reads "The claim that this is a data breach is completely false. [The app developer] requested and gained access to information from users who chose to sign up to his app, and everyone involved gave their consent. People knowingly provided their information, no systems were infiltrated, and no passwords or sensitive pieces of information were stolen or hacked."[46]

Although Facebook was parsing the distinction between privacy and security, one harm was identical to the harm of a data breach—billions of pieces of personal data were compromised when they were improperly exposed to third parties.[47]

Facebook's privacy failures led to the practical equivalent of a security incident. Specifically, the failure of Facebook to meaningfully consider privacy in the design of its system and user interfaces left users vulnerable. According to scholar Ian Bogost, when a person accesses Facebook's troublesome interface that was at issue in the Cambridge Analytica scandal, "the user must accept [a third-party] app's request to share data with it as soon as they open it for the first time, even before knowing what the app does or why."[48] Facebook, not the third party, presented the request for users to consent to data practices, which made the request seem "official, safe, and even endorsed." But of course, it wasn't. Facebook simply passed data to the third party.[49] The third-party apps only once asked users (during their first use) for permission to collect and process peoples' data (including the data of their "friends"). After that, the data flowed unencrypted to the app company for years.[50] Apps were required to have privacy policies, but Facebook didn't review them. Instead, Facebook just checked to see if the link to the privacy policy went to a valid webpage.[51]

In its complaint against Facebook, the U.S. Federal Trade Commission (FTC) stated that Facebook's controls to address privacy risks created by third-party apps "did not include screening the third-party developers or their apps before granting them access to user data." Facebook inconsistently enforced its own policies.[52]

The FTC ultimately slapped Facebook with an unprecedented $5 billion fine.[53] Two Commissioners dissented, arguing that even this whopping fine wasn't enough.[54]

The Cambridge Analytica scandal demonstrates that the relationship between privacy and security is vitally important and increasingly frayed. Malicious parties compromised and exfiltrated Facebook users' data in a way that was different than your standard "hack n' breach," but to nearly the same effect. The key difference is that the third parties that filched people's data didn't bypass Facebook's technological safeguards. They used Facebook for the exact purpose for which it was designed. In other words, this was a breach that didn't occur through a break-in at the back door but through a walk-in at the front door. We can't protect data by locking it in a safe if we then give out the combination to anyone who asks for it. Although the front door is essential for security, it is often isolated in the privacy silo, where it doesn't receive the extensive resources from the security silo. For many organizations, too myopic a focus on the back door results in insufficient protection for the front door.

Unnecessary Data Makes Data Breaches Worse

Data that doesn't exist can't be compromised. The central privacy principle of *data minimization*—to collect only data necessary for the purpose at hand and to avoid retaining unnecessary data—can play a key role at minimizing the harmful effects of breaches. Many organizations collect far too much data and keep it for far too long. They should be collecting less from the outset (and designing tools incapable or discouraging of collecting more), which will soften the impact if their databases ever get breached.

For example, companies invest billions in an insatiable desire to collect as much information about you as possible so they can target you with ads (for questionable efficiency gains).[55] One such company you have probably never heard of is BlueKai, an ad tech tracking startup bought by Oracle in 2014 for over $400 million. But BlueKai has heard of you. It has amassed "one of the largest banks of web tracking data outside the federal government."[56] And, for a time "that web tracking data was spilling out onto the open Internet because a server was left unsecured and without a password, exposing billions of records for anyone to find."[57]

In another case, Ashley Madison was a popular adultery website created by Noel Biderman, a former sports agent. The website had the slogan "Life is short. Have an affair." People could create a free profile, where they would list their turn-ons, sexual preferences, and location, as well as include their photo. Male users had to pay fees to send messages to female members. Although Ashley Madison promised users that their information would be "100% discrete" if they cancelled their accounts, they had to pay an additional $19 to remove all their information from the website. By 2015, Ashley Madison claimed to have 37.6 million users in more than 46 countries.

Unfortunately for Ashley Madison and its users, a group of hackers broke into its database and posted 3.2 million records online. The aftermath of the breach was ugly. People were fired and marriages were destroyed. Some people received threats of extortion. Some people committed suicide.

Ashley Madison demonstrates in the starkest terms—through blood and death—how privacy and security are related. Protecting privacy depends upon protecting security. Moreover, good privacy rules can help keep data secure. Ashley Madison kept data it shouldn't have kept. And although Ashley Madison offered a "Full Delete" option where users could pay to remove all their information from the site, Ashley Madison actually retained the information in its database for a year. It flaunted people's trust, and everyone involved got burned.

The lesson for data security in the Ashley Madison case is that heeding the key privacy principle of data minimization can significantly lessen the harm of a data breach. As we noted earlier, data breaches can't all be stopped; they are inevitable. But their damage can be reduced by having good privacy practices.

Poor Privacy Regulation Allows for More Tools that Compromise Security

Good privacy rules will also regulate and minimize the harmful impact of manipulation and microtargeting made effective by our personal data, which can lead to massive data security vulnerabilities. Not only are surveillance ad networks vectors for the delivery of malware, but they allow criminals to use our own personal information against us to entice us to click links or share information.

Tools of surveillance, such as spyware, are regularly re-purposed by attackers to gain access to databases by stealing credentials or merely improperly accessing the same information that triggers breach notification. Privacy laws restrict spyware, but the laws thus far haven't been effective enough. As Professor Danielle Citron notes, "At least in theory . . . the providers of stalking apps could face federal and state criminal charges if it can be proved beyond a reasonable doubt that they knew or had reason to know the apps were designed to be 'primarily useful' for secret surveillance."[58] Unfortunately, Citron also observes that "[t]here have been few, if any, state prosecutions against the entities providing covert surveillance tools and a modest number at the federal level."[59]

Beyond being a grave threat to privacy, spyware also threatens data security by allowing fraudsters to obtain essential data to carry out a breach. Spyware such as keystroke loggers is often used to pilfer passwords to gain access to encrypted files.[60]

Surveillance tools like trackers and the ubiquitous devices that make up the "Internet of Things" do hackers' jobs for them. The fitness app Strava was designed to be used with fitness trackers like FitBit to record users' exercise activity and share it with others. It did that, and more. In a data visualization map released by the company that showed all the activity tracked by its users, "military analysts noticed that the map is also detailed enough that it potentially gives away extremely sensitive information about a subset of Strava users: military personnel on active service."[61] The map leaked "[s]ensitive information about the location and staffing of military bases and spy outposts around the world."[62] This is exactly the kind of information hackers break into databases to obtain.

Lawmakers and those responsible for enforcing the law should target software primarily designed to invade privacy without sufficient legitimate uses. For example, those that create and deploy spyware should be faced with civil liability and even criminal prosecution in some cases. Right now, the FTC is limited in its fight against spyware, but new privacy and security legislation could allow those harmed by spyware to pursue lawsuits against spyware makers under "means and instrumentalities" theories similar to products liability lawsuits.[63]

Lack of Accountability Leads to Compromised Data

A key component of strong privacy protection is to ensure that all repositories of personal data are mapped and have a data shepherd—a person who is responsible for looking out for that data and who is accountable for what happens to that data. Far too often, organizations don't know all the personal data that they maintain or where it is kept. Personal data can be collected in so many different ways and at many different times and places.

For example, a company can collect personal data when people submit a form to sign up for a newsletter, purchase an item, create an account, call customer service, and so on. Personal data is collected even when people visit the company's website. The company also maintains personal data about its employees. These repositories of personal data are often maintained by different departments in different places in the company. Without a shepherd, over time, the data could be forgotten, lost, or find its way outside of the security bubble and onto areas of servers that are accessible to the public.

In fact, the amount of data that is left exposed on unprotected areas of servers is shocking. The website DataBreaches.net, which has been chronicling data breaches since 2009, has covered, at the time this book was written, over 3,500 stories about the online exposure of data.[64] Just a few of the recent headlines on DataBreaches.net include "Twitter-owned SDK leaking location data of millions of users";[65] "Misconfigured cloud storage bucket exposed Pfizer drug safety-related reports";[66] "A prison video visitation service exposed private calls between inmates and their attorneys";[67] and "Dr Lal PathLabs, one of India's largest blood test labs, exposed patient data."[68] This list goes on and on.

Proper accounting for this data would have helped companies properly configure their systems to avoid exposure. Doing a data inventory and having all data assigned to data shepherds are key components of good privacy hygiene. They are also essential for strong security. If organizations don't know what data they have, where it is located, and how it should be used, then it is hard to imagine how they can keep it secure. Despite the oft-used security metaphor of locks and safes, good security isn't really about locking up data; it's more about looking after data.

THE PRIVACY COSTS OF DATA BREACHES

Poor privacy practices weaken data security, and data breaches are often data security violations as well. Likewise, poor security practices weaken privacy protections, and data breaches are often privacy violations.

The Sony Breach

Sony was planning to release a new movie, a comedy called *The Interview* that mocked North Korean leader Kim Jong-un. Apparently, in retaliation for the movie, North Korean hackers launched a major attack against Sony.

The hackers were able to break in because they were able to steal the login credentials of a Sony systems administrator through a spear phishing attack. The hacker spent several months exploring Sony's computer system trying to find ways to wreak the most havoc.[69]

On Friday, November 21, 2014, some Sony executives received an email from a group calling itself "God'sApstls" that demanded "monetary compensation" or else Sony "[would] be bombarded as a whole." The spam filters picked it up or it went otherwise unread.

The first Sony employee to log in after that weekend must have received quite the shock. A blood-red skeleton with razor fangs had conquered every single computer on the Sony lot, rendering the machines useless and sparing neither interns nor executives. Superimposed in blocky crimson letters were the words "HACKED BY THE #GOP," along with a demand to "obey" and five links that led to repositories of internal Sony records. Also included was a deadline of 11 p.m. that very night, even though GOP's demands were ambiguous.[70]

Sony hoped to keep the matter quiet, but an anonymous person posted a picture of the garish lockdown interface on Reddit, eliciting a flurry of media attention.[71] Still, at the time, Sony officials thought there wasn't much to worry about. Employees returned to their work. One Sony supervisor called it "a one-day problem."[72] No one imagined the immensity of the storm to come.

To their dismay, Sony officials learned that the hackers hadn't just vandalized them; the hackers had wreaked near total destruction. "Wiper" malware, known as "Destover" or "Wipall," erased everything stored on 3,262 of the company's 6,797 personal computers and 837 of its 1,555 servers, mixing in a "special deleting algorithm that overwrote the data seven different ways," before disabling the computers' boot software.[73]

The destruction wasn't even the worst part. The hackers had created a wound, but they wanted to maim. The hackers thus took a turn in the direction of privacy and transformed a bad breach into an utter catastrophe. On November 24, the GOP posted four unreleased Sony data files to file-sharing sites. A few days later, several journalists received an email purporting to be from "the boss of G.O.P." with links to the anonymous sharing site Pastebin, along with a password. The links led to a neatly organized set of folders containing over 26 gigabytes of unencrypted Sony personnel data, including almost 50,000 unique Social Security Numbers and detailed biographical information, compensation details, work histories, and confidential medical information.[74] They also spread the leaked details to media outlets such as Gawker, BuzzFeed, and The Verge.

The first news reports hit the Internet on December 1. Sony employees began "coming to work afraid," as multiple reports of attempted identity theft poured in.[75]

The GOP dumped more files over several days in early December 2014.[76] On December 8, the GOP finally articulated a motive, linking their actions to Sony's forthcoming The Interview, which the group called "the movie of terrorism which can break the regional peace and cause the War!" The GOP called for Sony to pull the movie or face further reprisals. In addition to the note, GOP released another round of leaked information, this time the private emails of Sony President Steve Mosko and Sony Entertainment executive Amy Pascal. In total, the group leaked over 20,000 emails addressing sensitive personal and business issues, as well as thousands of stored contact details, many of which included home addresses.[77] Pascal's emails, in particular, stirred up a media circus because many included insensitive comments about friends, associates, industry figures, and even President Obama.

Additional emails were posted on December 13 and 14, which GOP dubbed "Christmas" gifts.[78] A final leak on December 16 warned of a "bitter fate" for anyone present wherever The Interview was to be screened and invoked the September 11 attacks while warning readers to keep their distance from screenings and warning those who lived nearby to flee altogether. The actual leak consisted of over 12,000 emails and 7,000 contacts from the account of Michael Lynton, chairman and CEO of Sony.

Prior to this leak, Sony had already cancelled several media appearances involving the cast of *The Interview*, as well as most promotional events. Upon reading the December 15 warning, Sony immediately provided security for the film's actors and producers. Sony cancelled star Seth Rogen's appearances on late-night programming. Theater chains began to pull out of the film's screening. Sony later issued a press release announcing the cancellation of *The Interview*'s theatrical release—a decision that was criticized by many as cowardly. President Obama even called this decision "a mistake."[79]

December 19 brought a final communication from the GOP. In it, the group declared that Sony had suffered enough, and that they "lift[ed] the ban," allowing the *The Interview* to be released provided that Kim Jong-Un's death scene not be "too happy," and that Sony not "test [them] again." On December 24, on Google's servers, *The Interview* received an online release, earning a modest $40 million.

The Sony hack exposed a wealth of embarrassing information about both the company and its top executives. Amy Pascal apologized profusely and stepped down as co-chairwoman of Sony Pictures Entertainment and chairwoman of Sony's motion picture group.

At least two former Sony employees brought lawsuits while the leak was ongoing, though theirs and many others were later consolidated into a class action. The parties reached a settlement, approved in early 2016, which cost Sony $15 million. As part of the agreement, Sony also agreed to provide identity-theft protection through the end of 2017 and a compensation fund for class members who paid to protect themselves out of pocket.

The Sony breach was so harmful because of its privacy dimensions. This is one reason why privacy regulation is so essential to data security; not only can privacy regulation help prevent breaches, but it can also help lessen the harm that breaches cause. Typically, the privacy harm is felt by an organization's employees and customers. The Sony case is somewhat unusual in that the privacy harms were also experienced by upper management.

As we discussed in the previous chapter, the law can work to lessen privacy harm and take the sting out of many breaches. It is not clear that the law could have done much for the Sony executives, but the law could have helped the employees prevent identity theft and privacy harms.

Although it is especially difficult for the law to help prevent breaches caused by state-sponsored attacks, we highlight the Sony case because it demonstrates the enormous potential privacy implications of data breaches. Unfortunately, hackers and attackers are becoming increasingly aware of this fact, and they are finding new ways to threaten or inflict privacy harms to further their nefarious aims.

Ransomware's Grave Threat to Privacy

As we discussed earlier, ransomware is a significant data security threat. Ransomware is malicious software that encrypts the files on a computer or network. Criminal hackers then demand a ransom to decrypt the files. Otherwise, the files remain inaccessible and the data is lost.

Nearly all experts recommend that to protect against the increasingly likely threat of a ransomware attack, organizations should routinely back up their data and test the backup to make sure it works. With the data backed up, one of the main threats of the ransomware is neutralized.

A big debate with ransomware is over whether organizations should pay the ransom. Some contend that paying ransoms is the quickest way to get back up and running. Many others argue that ransoms should never be paid. They contend that the criminals will become emboldened by the payoff and might continue their extortion. Another argument against paying is that it encourages other criminals to use ransomware and sends the message that ransomware pays.[80] The main focus of the decision is on the possibility and ease of the restoration of the files. For example, in an intelligence memo, the FBI stated:

> The FBI does not advise victims on whether or not to pay the ransom. . . . Individuals or businesses that regularly backup their files on an external server or device can scrub their hard drive to remove

the ransomware and restore their files from backup. If all individuals and businesses backed up their files, ransomware would not be a profitable business for cybercriminal actors.[81]

In recent years, criminals have added a frightening new dimension to their use of ransomware. They have realized, much like the Sony hackers, that heightening the privacy harms can make the breach much worse. Hackers exfiltrate a copy of the data before they encrypt it. In typical practice, they demand a payment to provide the decryption key to the encrypted data on the victim's system. But some criminals are demanding an additional payment to destroy the copy of the data that they exfiltrated. They threaten to release the data to the public if they aren't paid.[82] Security experts refer to this practice as the "double extortion" model.

In 2016, stories began to circulate about a nasty piece of malware called "Delilah" that allowed hackers to gather personal information and webcam data from people who do sensitive things online (such as visiting pornography websites). Hackers could then use that information to blackmail those people under the threat of disclosing their secrets to the world.[83] A user on Reddit reported a similar kind of attack in 2018.[84] The criminals extorted victims into providing them with insider information at targeted companies.

In 2020, five law firms were hit with ransomware called Maze. Instead of just encrypting the data, the criminals exfiltrated it first and then posted a small amount of it online when their victims didn't pay their ransom demands. The criminals then threatened to post the remainder of the data online unless the ransom was paid. According to one article: "Recent reports have shown the hacking group behind Maze ransomware has been steadily posting the data of its victims online after the organizations fail to pay the ransom demand. A compiled list of victims shows the data of several healthcare organizations are included in those postings, despite a lack of public reporting of those incidents."[85]

Maze's double-extortion model caught on. By the end of 2020, there were approximately 20 different threat actor groups that had created leak sites where they posted victims' data to pressure them into paying ransoms.

One of the most dramatic law firm attacks involved an attack on Grubman Shire Meiselas & Sacks, an entertainment law firm with many celebrity clients. The attackers initially demanded a ransom of $21 million. When the firm refused to pay, the attackers doubled the ransom to $42 million and dumped a small sample of data. When the law firm still didn't pay, the attackers started auctioning off celebrities' files.[86]

With the introduction of the threat to publicly disclose personal data, it is much harder for victims to refuse to pay ransoms. Before the data disclosure threat, the main considerations for whether to pay the ransom had been the amount of data that would be lost and how much more quickly the victim could be back in action again. Organizations that routinely backed up their data could protect themselves. But with a copy exfiltrated and the possibility it could be dumped publicly, not paying the ransom means that people's private data will be exposed. Imagine a hospital that decided not to pay the ransom, resulting in the hackers posting all their patient records online. The hospital owes a duty to its patients to protect their data. Does this duty extend to paying the ransom to prevent the data from being exposed?

The law hasn't yet figured out an answer to this question. Much of the advice for ransomware involves urging organizations not to pay ransoms so as not to encourage future ransomware attacks. This strategy aims to further the common good by trying to dry up the criminals' revenue source, but the strategy doesn't account for the privacy harms created by leaked personal data. Ratcheting up the privacy harms has changed the ransomware playbook and has made the situation far more complicated and terrible.

IMPROVING SECURITY THROUGH STRONGER PRIVACY RULES

Lawmakers and companies should bridge data security and privacy to make them go hand-in-hand, and even be mutually reinforcing. As a first step, lawmakers should embolden privacy law to strengthen data security efforts. The rampant manipulation of people, as well as the amassing of swollen troves of personal data, not only threatens privacy but poses significant risks to security.

A holistic approach to data security law would better integrate privacy and data security. Strengthening certain controls and protections, typically found on the privacy side of the ledger, will help strengthen data security as well. Below, we provide two examples of types of privacy controls that improve security.

Maximizing Data Minimization

The idea that companies should only be able to collect and retain data that is adequate, relevant, and necessary is a bulwark against data abuse and the essence of privacy because it either prevents data from being created in the first place or compels its destruction. It also demonstrates how privacy and security must work together to achieve their separate goals.

Security can focus on how to retain data and how to protect its integrity. It can ensure that only authorized people can see data and that information doesn't get improperly accessed or leaked. Privacy focuses on difficult substantive questions such as how long the data is retained, how it can be used, and specifically who is authorized to see it and change it. Privacy focuses on determining when data should be destroyed, which is often based on regulatory requirements. Security plays a role in ensuring that the data is properly destroyed.

Lawmakers should embrace data minimization with the same zeal they embrace data security rules and for the same reasons. Although privacy and data security have slightly different functions, they work in tandem and roughly overlap to achieve the same goals.

Data Mapping

Privacy requirements such as data mapping provide awareness about potential security vulnerabilities. Data mapping shows what data is being collected and maintained, the purposes for having this data, the whereabouts of this data, and other key information. Without good data mapping, personal data is often forgotten. When this occurs, data can fall outside the security bubble or be improperly accessed, with this access not being readily detected.

Data mapping is useful for both privacy and security. Keeping track of data ensures that it remains within the security bubble and has the proper security controls. There should be data stewards with accountability for each repository of data. Security can set controls to make sure that those who should have access do and that those who shouldn't have access don't, but it is often in the realm of privacy where the determination of who should have access is made.

Recently, privacy laws have been the main driver behind organizations engaging in data mapping. Laws such as the California Consumer Privacy Act (CCPA) require that businesses provide people with the specific personal data collected about them.[87] Even more helpful than individuals knowing the specific data business have about them is the byproduct of businesses being compelled to respond to individual requests to know. To be able to respond, businesses are forced to have a better understanding and inventory of the data they possess. The CCPA doesn't directly require data mapping, but the practice becomes necessary to carry out the CPPA's obligation to respond to individual demands to know about their data.

More privacy laws should require data mapping, ideally directly rather than indirectly like the CPPA. Laws should require that organizations ensure that all personal data is accounted for and have a person assigned to be accountable for it.

∎

In addition to improving data minimization and data mapping rules, lawmakers could create improvements for data security by fortifying existing privacy preservation rules around concepts such as deidentification and rules against manipulation. Understanding the security benefits from good privacy practices could generate broader legislative support for privacy regulation. Companies would also benefit from learning not to undermine their efforts to promote security by having poor privacy practices.

Designing Security for Humans, the Weakest Link

I n the afternoon of July 15, 2020, some of the most famous and powerful people in the world appeared to suddenly become quite generous. On Twitter, Joe Biden, Barack Obama, Kanye West, Bill Gates, and Elon Musk posted messages such as the one below:

> I am giving back to the community. All Bitcoin sent to the address below will be sent back doubled! If you send $1000, I will send back $2000. Only doing this for 30 minutes.[1]

Bitcoin is a cryptocurrency that facilitates hard-to-trace transactions. This was a scam, but it worked quite well. The *New York Times* estimated that the fraudsters raked in more than $180,000.[2]

How could this have happened? How could one of the most important communication platforms in the world have been so publicly compromised?

Investigations of the incident point to a series of failures culminating in a telephone call between a hacker pretending to be from Twitter's IT department and an employee who helped the hacker by providing access to the company's customer service portal. Once the hacker tricked the employee into helping bypass Twitter's two-factor authentication protections, it was off to the races. The hackers accessed 130 accounts in a matter of hours.[3]

Humans make all kinds of terrible data security decisions. They click on dubious links. They lose their laptops or leave them unattended. They publish working login credentials to their clients' systems on public repositories like Github. They ignore warnings in browsers that important security certificates have expired. They re-use passwords. The list goes on and on.

Most data breaches are facilitated by preventable low-tech blunders. Many studies show that human error plays a role in an overwhelming number of breaches.[4] Studies and news articles often loosely say that many data breaches are "caused" by human error, but the more accurate description is many data breaches "involve" human error. Data breaches often don't occur because of just one action; they are caused by a combination of things. Human error often plays a key role.[5] Hackers may cause a breach, but they break in because humans fall for phishing schemes or fail to patch software. Even when human error isn't a major factor in a hack, humans might fail to encrypt data, thus enabling the hackers to access data they otherwise wouldn't have been able to decipher. Human error often involves the failure to prevent breaches that could readily have been stopped. For example, the previously discussed Target breach could have been prevented had humans paid attention to the blinking red lights.

Statistics on the causes of breaches are all over the place, but there is one thing that can be said with a high degree of certainty: *In most data breaches, human error has played a significant role in enabling or failing to prevent the breach.* Humans are the largest component of the data security risk equation, and they are the most challenging variable to control. It takes a lot of time and energy to even nudge human behavior, let alone change it dramatically. Security experts are not usually trained to be human behavior experts; their knowledge and experience is usually in technology, not human cognition and psychology.

Scholars have observed predictable patterns of careless human behavior in nearly every imaginable context. Yet, far too many technologies are designed in ways that not only fail to counter predictable risky human behavior but also actively encourage it. Far too many security measures are designed in ways that fail to account for human limitations. And far too many data security laws are oblivious to this problem. These laws actively encourage organizations to implement security measures that fail.

In this chapter, we focus on three broad ways that humans struggle with security. Accepting these problems and building around them will make an enormous difference for data security. The problems include:

The Bandwidth Problem
Humans lack the cognitive capabilities to perform many of the security practices they are asked to follow.

The Carelessness Problem
Humans often act carelessly. They will fail to follow security measures that are too inconvenient or difficult.

The Gullibility Problem
Humans are prone to trust, even when they ought not to.

Many security standards are checklists of various security controls, with only a few focusing on human behavior. Of those controls that involve human behavior, they often provide no guidance on how to predict, plan for, nudge, and respond to human behavior effectively. Legal rules don't do much better, often rewarding a threadbare "checklist" approach to data security, and sometimes even requiring it.

Instead, we argue that the law should encourage design that works realistically with human behavior rather than denies the realities of human nature. The law should discourage design that leads to human behaviors that create unwarranted security risks.

The law can accomplish these aims by outright restrictions or by using a mix of incentives and disincentives. The appropriate choice depends upon the context. We propose four key things that the law can require or encourage that will make a palpable difference:

Changing the Default Settings
The law can encourage or require default settings that are good for security.

Promoting Mutual Trust
The law can combat gullibility by fostering a more stable set of trust expectations; that is, when people should expect to trust an email, phone call, or website.

Encouraging Balanced Security Measures
The law can encourage a realistic balance between data security and convenience. The law should stop rewarding organizations for implementing security measures that merely look good on paper but that will fail miserably in practice.

Sending Sensible Signals
The law can encourage more secure human behavior by sending clearer signals to people about security risks.

PROBLEMS WITH PEOPLE

Organizations usually rely upon data security frameworks and standards when determining what security practices and safeguards they should be implementing. Examples include the National Institute for Standards and Technology (NIST) 800-53 and the International Standards Organization (ISO) 27001. The problem is that companies often have strong incentives to implement these standards as checklists with little regard to the human side of the equation. Consider, for example, the 20 Center for Internet Security (CIS) controls, one of the more popular sets of security controls:

Basic CIS Controls

1. Inventory and Control of Hardware Assets
2. Inventory and Control of Software Assets
3. Continuous Vulnerability Management
4. Controlled Use of Administrative Privileges
5. Secure Configuration for Hardware and Software on Mobile Devices, Laptops, Workstations and Servers
6. Maintenance, Monitoring and Analysis of Audit Logs

Foundational CIS Controls

7. Email and Web Browser Protections
8. Malware Defenses
9. Limitation and Control of Network Ports, Protocols and Services
10. Data Recovery Capabilities
11. Secure Configuration for Network Devices, such as Firewalls, Routers and Switches
12. Boundary Defense
13. Data Protection
14. Controlled Access Based on the Need to Know
15. Wireless Access Control
16. Account Monitoring and Control

Organizational CIS Controls

17. Implement a Security Awareness and Training Program
18. Application Software Security
19. Incident Response and Management
20. Penetration Tests and Red Team Exercises[6]

Although this is a great list of security controls, companies following them often do so without grappling with the complexities of human nature.

Even though security experts know well of the riskiness of human behavior, security rules and practices still aren't sensitive enough to how, and how often, people within systems make mistakes.[7] Despite the fact that security professionals know that people are imperfect, security rules and practices often fail to incorporate this knowledge. Instead, many security rules and practices are designed for perfect people. These perfect people learn and remember all of the rules. They always follow the rules, no matter how inconvenient or difficult they become. They never look at any irrelevant websites while at work. They never click on any links that are suspicious. They never cut corners. They carefully listen to their training and do everything they are told. They are always patient and careful.

But of course, people are far from perfect. Humans mess everything up. People are in a hurry, they have limited ability to remember things, they often don't pay attention and don't follow rules, and they are prone to trust when they shouldn't trust. If people were perfect, most security measures would work quite well. But it's nearly impossible to make people perfect; it is much more feasible to design security measures differently so they work with people as they are.

Figure 8.1

Policymakers are not designing data security measures with human limitations in mind. Instead of assuming the best in people, the law should prepare for the worst. Even if 99 out of 100 people are perfect, the hackers still win because they can trick one person. Data still gets lost if one person loses it. In other words, data security is a game won or lost based on the most error-prone player on your team. Sadly, on most teams, many people are competing for the title of "most likely to mess up." You can't win the game by focusing only on the good players. Hackers know this, which is why they win so often.

Data security law must confront this reality. Only by accounting for the most error-prone among us will we stand a fighting chance against the hackers.

THE BANDWIDTH PROBLEM: WHY WE ASK
THE IMPOSSIBLE WITH PASSWORDS

Imagine that you are starring in a production of Shakespeare's *King Lear*, and you are playing the king. The play starts now, the curtain is rising, but you haven't memorized your lines. You look down, and you are wearing only your underwear. . . .

You may have had nightmares similar to the one above. You are about to take a test or perform a task, but you are woefully unprepared for it. You are going to fail, and your best hope is to wake up before it happens. This type of nightmare, unfortunately, is what we are living in with many data security measures.

People are Destined to Fail with Passwords

At 33 years old, Christopher Chaney was unemployed and living in his grandmother's house. He spent his time watching movies and browsing the Internet. Having received his first computer just a few years before,

Chaney did not possess any advanced IT skills or fluency in coding. What Chaney did have, however, was an abundance of free time.[8]

In early 2008, Chaney heard that nude images of celebrity Miley Cyrus had been leaked online. Chaney was intrigued by how the images were obtained. Previously, he had learned that a hacker broke into celebrity Paris Hilton's phone by guessing her password—the name of her pet Chihuahua, Tinkerbell. On a whim, he began to compile a list of celebrities by first and last names. He then researched their personal information online, arming himself with data that would help him guess their passwords.[9]

Chaney worked his way down his list, entering names into Gmail until he found a valid celebrity email address.[10] Once he had an email address, if he couldn't guess the password, then he would turn to the "forgot my password" function. He was presented with personal security questions required to reset the account password. He then searched online across various social media platforms and other sites to find information to help him answer the questions.[11] The answers to questions, such as the name of the celebrity's pet, were fairly accessible online. When Chaney correctly answered the password recovery questions, he would reset the account password to allow him access to the account.[12]

After breaking into an account, Chaney would change the settings to automatically forward copies of all outgoing mail to his own email address.[13] When the victims regained control of their accounts, they had no idea that copies of their email were being forwarded to Chaney. Hardly anyone routinely checks their forwarding settings.[14]

Secretly receiving a copy of all emails that the celebrities sent allowed Chaney to read scores of private email messages to family, friends, physicians, attorneys, and others. He learned about people's extramarital affairs, health issues, and sex life. He could see sensitive information such as financial data and confidential movie scripts. And he could find the email addresses of other celebrities in the contact list—his next victims.

His snooping, which began in curiosity, soon turned into a compulsion. He would go on to break into at least 50 celebrity email accounts. In addition to celebrities, Chaney also started to break into other people's accounts.[15]

Among the information Chaney amassed were nude photos of several celebrities, including Scarlett Johansson, Mila Kunis, Christina Aguilera, and Renee Olstead. These images were sent in confidence by the celebrities to their significant others.[16] On several occasions, Chaney sent emails from his victims' accounts impersonating the celebrities. He leaked intimate images that Scarlet Johansson sent to her former husband, Ryan Reynolds. When their marriage began to dissolve, Chaney read their personal discussions leading up to their divorce.[17]

The leaked nude images soon made national headlines. The celebrities were shocked, devastated, and furious. According to Christina Aguilera, "[t]he feeling of security can never be given back" and "there is no compensation that can restore the feeling one has from such a large invasion of privacy."[18] Scarlet Johansson described Chaney's actions as "perverted and reprehensible."[19]

After Chaney leaked sexually provocative pictures of Renee Olstead, the former Disney actress attempted suicide on the very day the images went public.[20] Olstead was hospitalized and lost consciousness for several days. Olstead described her reaction to the violation of privacy: "[Y]ou realize that everything that you cared for—your work, your family, you know, the person that you love. . . you could lose everything because of the actions of a stranger, someone you've never met can take everything from you so fast."[21]

"I was humiliated," Olstead declared. "[T]his is the sort of thing that will haunt me for a very long time. And I realized that suddenly I wasn't the girl who works full time, is a full-time student, still manages to make the dean's list. I was the girl who was naked on the Internet."[22]

The leaked nude images sparked an FBI response. In what was referred to as "Operation Hackerazzi," the FBI investigated the source of the leaked images. The FBI closed in on Chaney, and on February 10, 2011, FBI agents searched the home Chaney was living in and seized his computers. The FBI didn't arrest him because they hoped Chaney might be able to help identify others engaging in similar conduct. The media descended upon

Chaney, who apologized and admitted that his actions caused "probably one of the worst invasions of privacy someone could experience."[23]

Nevertheless, Chaney continued to hack into celebrity accounts. Chaney was soon indicted with multiple counts of illegally gaining access and causing damage to email systems, aggravated identity theft, and illegal wiretapping. He was arrested the day after his indictment was handed down.[24]

Chaney plead guilty to unauthorized access to a protected computer to obtain information, unauthorized damage to a protected computer, and wiretapping. At his sentencing hearing, prosecutors asked for Chaney to serve six years in prison. In an unusual move, the judge increased the sentence to 10 years—beyond the prosecution's recommendation and even beyond the sentencing guidelines.[25]

This case shows how easy it is to hack into other people's accounts and snoop into their most intimate information. Chaney possessed no special knowledge of computer programming. Chaney didn't possess magical mind-reading capabilities. He was so successful because the password system is set up so that people will fail.

Time to Kill the Password?

Authentication presents one of the greatest security challenges organizations face. How do we accurately ensure that people seeking access to accounts or data are actually whom they say they are? People need to be able to access accounts and data conveniently, and access must often be provided remotely without being able to see or hear the person seeking access.

The most common approach to authentication is the use of passwords. Passwords are quite useful because they are so easy to create and replace. Passwords by themselves, however, are a very poor form of security.[26] The problem with passwords is people. People select poor passwords, reuse them on many sites, and have difficulty remembering them.[27]

As we previously mentioned, an annual list is compiled of the most widely used passwords.[28] Some perennial ones that always make the top of the list include simple words like "dragon," "monkey," "baseball," and "princess." Passwords such as "login," "password," and "letmein" are also included on the list. The password "123456" is often at the top of the list. So are "12345" and "1234."

Among experts, it is common to hear humorous stories about foolish passwords or of people writing down passwords on sticky notes and pasting them on their computer monitors. "People need to be savvier and more careful," the experts say. All this is true, but it's not people's fault. Creating and remembering so many passwords of sufficient length and complexity is beyond people's cognitive bandwidth.

Peoples' bandwidth gets depleted because authentication is needed on so many sites and systems—there are too many passwords for even those with the best memories to remember. According to one study, consumers have an average of 24 online accounts.[29] For those who use the Internet more robustly, the number of accounts is in the hundreds—accounts for health insurance sites, bank sites, investment company sites, credit card company sites, utility company sites, news sites, entertainment sites, social media sites, and merchant sites, among many others. There are also logins associated with one's place of employment and logins for devices like smart phones and laptops. The number of accounts that people have can be staggering.

To make matters worse, people are advised not to use a dictionary word or someone's name, as these can be cracked too easily.[30] Password systems often require people to use special characters, numbers, punctuation, and upper and lower case. All these add complexity to passwords, which make them harder to guess through random attempts, but they also make passwords significantly harder to remember.

These demands have resulted in users being given the Herculean task of creating a unique, complex password for every account. No one can remember all these passwords, so people ignore the advice about using unique passwords and reuse the same password or draw from a pool of a few passwords. According to a study, 73 percent of accounts use duplicate passwords, and consumers use, on average, only one unique password per every four accounts.[31]

Common approaches to authentication result in even greater unreasonable demands on human memory. Impossible isn't enough, so it must be multiplied by another impossible feat. A common (though obsolete) security practice is to change passwords frequently, and many companies force people to do so. It's hard enough to juggle dozens of balls, but now people are being asked to juggle them while riding a unicycle on a tightrope. Unsurprisingly, when people aren't forced to change their passwords, they don't. Indeed, nearly half of consumers have a password they haven't changed in more than five years.[32]

Many years ago, a company marketed a product called *Password Minder* with an infomercial that touted it as a revolutionary way to "safely store passwords." "Never lose a password," the commercial stated. "Guaranteed!"[33]

What was this miracle product? What new technology did it employ to help people remember passwords? In fact, it was just an empty notebook for people to write down their passwords.

The *Password Minder* was so mocked that eventually it was "laughed out of production."[34] But other similar products remain on the market. There's one called *I Love My Password Book!* We suggest an alternative title: *Fraudsters, Here Are All My Passwords for You in One Easy-to-Recognize Book.*

One of these types of books, *The Personal Internet Address & Password Log Book*, was at one point ranked #428 out of all books on Amazon, and was the bestselling book in Amazon's Internet and Telecommunications category.[35] To our dismay, it has done far better than any of our books. Maybe it's time to publish a password keeper book of our own.

These password notebooks are quite humorous, but critics should be laughing at themselves too. With passwords, we demand the impossible of people, and then we blame them when they fail.[36] It's quite understandable why someone would feel the need to write all their passwords down in one book. It is safer than some alternatives.

The more challenging it becomes to memorize all the passwords, the more likely people are to write the passwords down in convenient locations, thus creating additional security risks. Passwords find their way onto sticky notes near computers or in wallets or in emails or listed in text files in devices.

Impossible demands are being made on human cognition. Yet policymakers remain in denial. This isn't a problem that education can solve. People can certainly learn good password practices, but they lack the ability to implement them.

Suppose a person uses only long, complex, or unique passwords and can remember them all naturally or with the help of a password service. Is the user safe?

Nope. Fraudsters will just trick users into giving away their passwords. Even the person with the world's longest and most complex password will be defeated if they give their password to a phisher. Often, fake websites and deceptive hyperlinks look very real and easily deceive many users.

Even when users act perfectly in adopting complex, unique passwords and avoid accidental disclosure, malware can still compromise username and password credentials.[37]

Figure 8.2

The Problem with Password Recovery Questions

Password recovery questions are those questions that you set up in case you forget your password. Common questions are:

In what city were you born?
What is your mother's maiden name?
Where did you go to high school?

One problem with these questions is that the answers are sometimes leaked in security breaches. Another problem is that these answers don't change. Furthermore, these answers are easy for hackers to guess. You can create the world's best password, but a hacker can reset your password by using the recovery questions. Information such as mother's maiden name and the city of your birth are commonly available in public records. Other information, such as the name or a pet or a high school can be readily figured out by looking at social media profiles or Twitter feeds.

One company used a very clever approach to password recovery questions, asking some rather odd questions.[38] Our favorites include:

What is the favorite road on which you most like to travel?
What is your biggest pet peeve?
If you could be a character out of any novel, who would you be?
Who was your least favorite boss?
What was your childhood phone number?
What is the name of your least favorite teacher?
Where do you want to retire?
What is your dream car?
Where were you New Year's 2000?
What is the name of your most memorable stuffed animal?

Some of the questions seem like they are better suited for a psychological profile test.

Imagine what would happen if this company had a breach and leaked the answers. I'm sure hundreds of thousands of bosses will be none too pleased to learn that they are a least favorite boss.

Although we admire the effort, there's still a problem with these unconventional questions—they are difficult for people to remember. Many years later, are you going to remember where you wanted to retire when you answered your recovery questions? Or your dream car? Recovery questions must be easy to remember—easier than one's password—because the questions are designed to help people who forgot their password.

One strategy discussed is to answer the security questions with lies. But it is easy to forget the lies. So, there's a dilemma—easy-to-remember questions that might readily be guessed by hackers, or more obscure questions or wrong answers that might readily be forgotten.

It's not as though killing the password entirely would solve our problems. Password systems have proven remarkably resilient, and the alternatives have their own issues.[39] The key for policymakers is to stay constantly mindful of the costs that data security rules will impose on the people that use these systems. Advising people to be more careful is all well and good, but people are bombarded with advice about countless things throughout their day.

Security researcher Cormac Herley has argued that people rationally reject most security advice and prompts, because, in essence, the juice isn't worth the squeeze.[40] People don't see the immediate benefit of security measures but definitely feel their daily burden. If there is a harm to be suffered from poor security, the odds are that it will be borne by someone else. This makes designing beneficial security advice very hard.[41] Ultimately, for effective data security, we must avoid asking people to do things they can't do. We also shouldn't expect success if we merely ask people to do things that they are highly unmotivated to do. We must find a way to motivate people, as experience has shown that merely barking out orders isn't effective in achieving desired behavior. Effective security thus involves a realistic appreciation of human capabilities and a deep understanding of how to influence human behavior.

The Gullibility Problem: Why Phishers Catch People All the Time

In an ancient Greek myth, after fighting for years outside the walled city of Troy, Greek soldiers were still unable to infiltrate the city. So, the cunning warrior Odysseus hatched a plan.

One day, when the Trojans awakened, they saw that the Greek army outside their city walls had departed. The soldiers were all gone. Their tents and weapons were gone. Their ships were gone.

The people of Troy rejoiced. After so many years of war, the Trojans were overjoyed that the Greeks had finally given up. They noticed that on the beach was a gigantic wooden horse on wheels. They thought that the Greeks must have left this object behind, perhaps because it was too big to fit onto their ships. They wheeled the massive horse into their city as a trophy of their victory.

But it was a trick. Inside the horse were Greek soldiers, including Odysseus. Late at night, they snuck out and opened the city gate to let the other Greek soldiers in. Troy was defeated and destroyed. Today, malware that masquerades as useful software is called a "Trojan horse." The key feature of this malware is that it works through our tendency to be easily influenced, tricked, and manipulated.

Humans can be tricked more easily than they might like to believe. People are prone to trust others.[42] This is true even on the Internet.[43] When people are too trusting online, they become prime candidates for fraud and manipulation, even if they have a lot of experience on the Internet.[44] Roger Ford has argued that data analytics and modern targeting platforms make it even easier for us to be duped by data scams.[45]

Many people have proven to be too trusting and gullible when interacting online. In one example, fraudsters hacked into the email account of the CEO of Bonnier Publications, which publishes *Saveur* and *Popular Science*. From the CEO's email account, the hackers sent fake emails to employees in the accounts payable department. The emails purported to be from the CEO told the employees to wire $3 million to a bank in China.

One employee was duped by the scam. The transfer was so large that it had to be made in two payments. The employee wired $1.5 million to the bank. Then, four days later, he initiated a second transfer for the remaining $1.5 million. This time, though, the employee suddenly had some suspicions, so he called the CEO to confirm. The CEO was flabbergasted. He had never sent an email authorizing a money transfer. The second transfer was immediately stopped and recovered, but it was too late for the first transfer—$1.5 million was gone.[46]

While many scams are obvious, such as those silly "You have won the lottery" schemes, some phishers have become quite sophisticated. Under a technique called "spear phishing," savvy fraudsters use personal information about their victims to make their emails look more legitimate. And it works! A high percentage of people are fooled.

Some recent phishing scams have tricked people into losing their entire life savings. In one case, a couple was tricked into wiring their down deposit for a home into a fraudulent account. Hackers broke into the computer system of the couple's settlement company so they could learn details about the home purchase. The hackers then used this information

Figure 8.3

to impersonate emails from the settlement company to the couple. This attack is one of the fastest growing real estate cybercrimes.[47]

The average employee at a company is often not well-educated in how to spot phishing scams, especially the more sophisticated ones. Neither is the average consumer. To the hackers and phishers, the world is filled with sitting ducks. All it takes is one mistake, one lapse of judgment, and the consequences can be catastrophic for both businesses and consumers. The Twitter Bitcoin hack at the beginning of this chapter shows how dangerous our gullibility is with respect to systems that operate at scale.

In an episode of the television series *Mr. Robot*, Elliot (a hacker) is trying to break into a data storage facility called Steel Mountain, where backup tapes are located. Steel Mountain's tagline is "Impenetrable." But Elliot is undaunted. "Nothing is actually impenetrable," he says. "A place like this says it is, and it's close, but people still built this place, and if you can hack the right person, all of a sudden you have a piece of powerful malware. People always make the best exploits." Elliot goes on to say: "I've never found it hard to hack most people. If you listen to them, watch them, their vulnerabilities are like a neon sign screwed into their heads."[48]

Elliot is ultimately able to break in by targeting a low-level employee named Bill Harper. To manipulate him, Elliot needs to learn Harper's background, which he can do by searching online—an example of how privacy and security intersect. The ready availability of so much personal data makes it easy for hackers to learn about their victims so they can more effectively manipulate and trick them.

The Carelessness Problem: Why the Same Blunders Happen Again and Again

Take a moment to think about your daily routine. How many tasks do you need to undertake to meet the demands of your home, work, and social life? How long are you able to concentrate on one thing before an email comes in, a child or coworker asks for your attention, or you fall prey to mindlessly scrolling social media? People have a lot going on in their lives, which makes it difficult for them to take reasonable precautions for things that seem like a hassle, such as securing their data. This situation is true in many aspects of data security that demand peoples' time and attention.

Studies show that even when people know better, they still do careless things. They recognize a suspicious link or attachment, yet still click on it. They know they are not supposed to write down passwords on sticky notes and attach them to computers or devices, but they do so anyway. Why are people so careless? And why has the law failed to incorporate our inevitable carelessness into data security rules?

People become careless when confronted with robust security measures that are often cumbersome and inconvenient. The more inconvenient something is, the less people will do it. This means our data security frameworks and rules should be concerned with managing risk and modeling human behavior. Paradoxically, attempts to achieve perfect data security can actually weaken security because people will find end-runs around clunky security procedures. When policymakers create rules that don't factor in people's inevitable foibles and incentives to create workarounds, they get unintended consequences. We need to think of ways to better account for human behavior in designing security policy.

RETHINKING DESIGN RULES FOR TECHNOLOGIES

Although many experts realize that human fallibility is the bane of data security, information technologies are often not designed with this fact in mind. By *designing*, we mean creating something according to a plan. Design is a key aspect of good data security policy.[49] Design is everywhere, design is power, and design is political.[50] Nearly everything with technology results from a design choice, from the interface we see when we use software, to the buttons we push on devices, to the initial settings on platforms. The way humans interact with technology is at the center of so many security vulnerabilities, and design is all about structuring these interactions.

In writing about the pitiful security in most modern technological devices and systems, Bruce Schneier suggests that "Security needs to be engineered into every system, and every component of every system, from the beginning and throughout the development process."[51] We agree. The principle that Schneier is recommending is known as "security by design."

The law is several steps behind. First, only a few data security laws even try to regulate design. Most notably, Article 25 of the GDPR requires "data protection by design and by default."[52] Although the GDPR isn't very specific on what these baselines should be, at least it is a start. Beyond the GDPR, few other laws say anything about design. The law must change course and start regulating design, as doing so is crucial for strong data security.[53]

Second, the law not only must regulate design, but also must push for design that accounts for the human element. Designs that are oblivious to human behavior will fail. Security often focuses on keeping attackers *out*, rather than mitigating the errors from people who are already properly *in*. All design choices have one of two effects (and often both): They can *signal* information to people or make particular behavior *easier or harder* by imposing or reducing *transaction costs*—the expenditures of time, labor, and resources that are necessary to complete a task. Signals and transaction costs shape our mental models of how technologies work and form the constraints that guide our behavior in particular ways.[54] Design decisions make certain realities more or less likely. Companies and hackers know that the power to design is the power to exert control over people. This is because people react to signals and constraints implemented through design in predicable ways. People with the right know-how can build or leverage the design of consumer technologies to encourage desired user behavior.[55]

A concern with regulating design is that it might be too paternalistic. We don't want policymakers not versed in technology to make decisions far beyond their expertise. The regulation of design, however, need not focus on the specific details of technologies; policymakers do not need to become backseat engineers. Instead, there are some more general design requirements that the law can impose that will not be overly meddlesome but will be quite effective in designing more securely. Below, we set forth a few proposals for the types of security design requirements that follow our overarching principle, which is to design with the human element in mind.

Changing the Default Settings

Humans are prone to inertia. Most users will not take action, and design must reflect this fact. We can beg and plead with people to do things, but this nagging will fail to work consistently with many people. Bruce Schneier wisely recommends that all "devices need to be secure without much intervention by users."[56] The less work people need to do for security, the better.

One way design can have a significant effect is with default settings—the preselected options within software programs and devices. Default settings have a major impact on human behavior. Many programs, apps, and devices have initial settings that are quite insecure. For example, the default settings for many social media sites are set to maximize sharing. According to a 2015 study from Kaspersky Lab, 28 percent of social media users neglect privacy settings and leave all their posts, photos, and videos accessible to the public.[57] Not only is this setting bad for privacy, but it is also bad for security as it can lead to people exposing personal information in ways that might compromise their overall data security. Recall how Christopher Chaney was able to guess the password recovery questions of celebrities: he found their information online.

Certain apps and sites have unexpected defaults that can be very clunky to change. For example, at Venmo, a payment service, user financial transactions are public by default.[58] The process for a user to limit access to all their transactions is not very intuitive. The "Default Audience" setting only affects the visibility of the charges and payments initiated by the user. The transactions initiated by friends who have not changed the default privacy setting will still be shared publicly. To obscure all transactions, a user must hunt down and change the inconspicuous "Transactions Involving You" setting.[59]

The law could require or encourage default settings limiting the sharing of personal information online. If people want to share more, they could certainly change the settings, but many people haven't thought enough about the privacy and security consequences of the settings. As we discussed in the previous chapter, rules that strengthen privacy often also strengthen security, and a rule about the default settings is one that is often in the privacy category but can have benefits for security.

The law could also require or encourage default settings for the use of two-factor authentication for certain services or the option to automatically update software to more secure versions. If these options are not selected by default (or if the software doesn't nudge users towards using them), then users are less likely to take advantage of them.

Another way that the law can help strengthen security is to address default passwords. One of the most commonly exploited vulnerabilities in devices is the default password.[60] Many devices have a simple password by default, and it is sometimes hard-coded in. Many users never change this password, making it easy for hackers to break into devices. This is how the previously discussed DDoS attack on Krebs was perpetrated.

One solution would be to require manufacturers of devices to require that users change default passwords when they start using the device. This rule might seem like a small requirement, but it can make an enormous difference; it would remove an enormous security vulnerability in possibly hundreds of millions of devices. This requirement is based on the understanding that many people will predictably fail to change the default password on their own. But this solution carries some risks that must be addressed. Because users might choose weak passwords, device manufacturers should find ways to force users to select strong passwords. Another risk is that if the passwords are only stored locally on the device, users who forget their passwords could be completely unable to use the device. Manufacturers should address this problem by enabling a recovery system for forgotten passwords.

Our recommendation isn't an easy feat to achieve for many manufacturers, but it is something not to be ignored just because it is hard. Connected devices carry tremendous risks not just for their owners, but also for others. Manufacturers cut corners and create weak security because it is cheap, consumers don't know enough to choose secure devices, and there is no incentive for consumers to consider the security implications of the devices for other people. The market for online devices thus doesn't produce the optimal societal level of data security. The onus should be on the manufacturers to find ways to make their devices secure.

Promoting Mutual Trust

Part of the gullibility problem is that people expect to be able to trust that an organization's website, phone calls, emails, and other communications are authentic. As we discussed earlier, organizations will make people authenticate themselves so they know to trust the user. But organizations won't authenticate themselves. This leads to a perverse situation where people are constantly fooled by hackers.

Clever hackers can spoof phone numbers and email addresses. They can create fake websites that are hard to differentiate from real ones. Countless phishing attacks occur because people misplace their trust in an imposter.

Unfortunately, our system is designed to encourage people to be too trusting of the communications they receive from organizations because receiving unauthenticated communications is the norm.

Imagine if you walked into your bank and asked to withdraw money. Instead of asking for your identification or bank card, the bank teller just looked at you and said, "Yes, you sure look familiar. You are well dressed and don't look suspicious, so I'm sure you are not a fraudster. Here's your money."

Of course, no bank would do this. Organizations rightfully authenticate us when we reach out to them. But it doesn't work the other way around. Organizations don't authenticate themselves to us. When organizations initiate contact with people, they expect people to just assume that their mail, phone call, or website is legitimate. We know that people are relatively gullible and can often be easily tricked. Hackers can readily create websites and communications that look nearly identical to actual ones. Fortunately, many hackers are sloppy and make mistakes, so they leave clues. But people fall for their tricks even with these clues. Hackers who are more careful could avoid leaving many clues and fool a lot more people.

For example, suppose you bank at Big Bank. You click on a link in an email and are sent to a website. The site looks the same as what you remember when visiting Big Bank's site a few weeks ago. But you want to be careful, so you look at the site's address in the browser bar. The site's address is:

https://www.bigbank.login.com

You also receive another email that looks like it's from Big Bank. This email sends you to a site with the address:

https://www.bigbank.com/login

Which one is correct? The second one is correct. In the first, the site is actually login.com, not bigbank.com. Maybe you knew this, but many people don't. It's entirely rational for people to miss this distinction. Cormac Herley argued that "if users spent even a minute a day reading URLs to avoid phishing, the cost (in terms of user time) would be two orders of magnitude greater than all phishing losses."[61]

Countless emails from organizations have buttons that you can click to go to the site to login. But these emails can be fake ones sent by hackers, and the buttons will take you to a site that looks just like the real one. Hackers don't even need web design skills because there are numerous markets on the Dark Web where fraudsters can cheaply purchase "scampages" that mimic real websites. When you enter your login information, you will be submitting it directly to the hacker through the fake site. The hacker can then use your login credentials to go to the real site and break into your account.

Overall, it is foolish to expect busy lay people to figure out what is real and what isn't. Most people don't know enough or don't have the time to study each email or website like Sherlock Holmes. On the internet, people are sitting ducks, without adequate means to avoid being tricked.

One solution is bilateral authentication. The current authentication system is *unilateral*—it works one way, with people authenticating themselves to organizations. *Bilateral authentication* (often called "mutual" authentication) works both ways.[62] People authenticate themselves to organizations, and organizations authenticate themselves to people. With a system in which organizations authenticated themselves, people would no longer have to be Sherlock Holmes and spot some obscure detail that was off in an email or website. People would no longer assume that unauthenticated communications should be trusted. People would expect that organizations authenticated themselves.

How would this work? First, when people establish an account or relationship, they would be given a choice for certain images or passwords that an organization could provide to them to verify the organization's identity. Then, when people were contacted by the organization, or when they visited the organization's website and entered their username, they would be shown the image or password. This would verify that the organization and its website are legitimate.

Policymakers should create general rules for all organizations to follow when dealing with people. Organizations should be restricted from using certain mediums (such as email) to request particular kinds of information (such as Social Security Numbers or login information). People can remember short rules such as *No legitimate email will ever ask for your password*. It is much harder to remember the long list of things different organizations might request under certain circumstances. If legitimate organizations request Social Security Numbers or login information via email, then they confuse people. Standardizing people's expectations about what is legitimate and what is not will help close off many ways that hackers use to trick people.

Encouraging Balanced Security Measures

Counterintuitively, if security measures are *too* protective, they might lead to bad security outcomes because people create workarounds and other dangerous kludges that bypass protective systems entirely or weaken them. For example, requiring two factors for authentication is generally a good security measure. However, requiring two factors every time someone tries to login from a particular device can be counterproductive because people might grow frustrated and disable the service. Allowing people to check a box to trust certain devices after using two-factor authentication for the first time will help ease the inconvenience. In another example, which we discussed earlier, if people are forced to select passwords that are too long and complex, they will write them down on sticky notes near their computers, which opens up another major security vulnerability.[63]

Good public health frameworks are careful not to ask too much of people and instead seek to find the right balance between protection and feasibility to ensure measures can be implemented across an entire population.[64] It seems commonsensical, yet organizations regularly design their systems in ways that make us and our data less secure.

ELIMINATING IMPOSSIBLE SECURITY PRACTICES AND ADVICE
Several common security measures are not practical for people to do. The law should discourage the use of security measures that fail in this way. Instead, however, the law perversely encourages such measures. Regulators often look superficially at an organization's security, faulting organizations that don't use certain measures. Thus, security professionals might follow the same old faulty security measures because they fear that regulators will zing them for missing measures on the checklist. Regulators and the law must ensure that they stop playing a role in furthering this pathology.

If these measures were to be abandoned, what would work better? An improved strategy to help people with passwords is to use password managers to store them electronically in one account. Password manager services help people create strong, unique passwords, warn them when their passwords are bad, and save them the trouble of remembering the potentially thousands of passwords they use to access their accounts. Even these services are typically secured, at least partially, by a password themselves. Although these services are typically a better way of generating and keeping track of your passwords, like anything on the Internet, they are not without risk.

Without a password manager, we recommend different passwords at work and for personal accounts. But beyond this, we don't recommend a different password for every account. People can have hundreds of accounts, and it's not possible to remember hundreds of passwords. It is easy to find cases of password re-use and chastise people, but that's asking the impossible and scapegoating. What would be far better is to ensure that different passwords are used when it really counts—such as work accounts—and not as a matter of course.

Regarding not writing passwords down, it is impossible to remember many passwords. People must write them down. Instead of exhorting people never to write passwords down, the advice should be about *where* to write and keep them. People should not put them near the workplace computer or carry them in wallets. But suppose a person kept a list of passwords in a dresser drawer. Conceivably, a hacker could break into the person's home, rummage everywhere, and find the passwords in the dresser. But this is unlikely and is low risk. Of course, it is still a risk, and rigid approaches to security would try to stamp out this practice to eliminate the risk. The problem is that trying to reduce this low risk might ultimately induce people to engage in more risky behavior.

Good security is like good parenting. Parents soon learn to pick their battles. They can't win them all. Designing security practices to reduce all risks, even the small ones and trivial ones, can weaken human responses to risks that are more severe. The perfect becomes the enemy of the good.

Two-Factor Authentication

In security, there are other solutions to authentication problems and methods of authentication that can be used if organizations moved away from passwords alone. Many relatively cheap and easy-to-deploy methods can be used to protect against different kinds of attacks on credentials.

One means of authentication that accommodates human limitations is two-factor authentication. The essence of two-factor authentication is simple. To login, you must have something you know (usually a password), as well as one additional factor, usually something you have (e.g., your cellphone).

Two-factor authentication is promising because it has already been deployed by major companies, it protects against many different kinds of offline attacks, and it can leverage a technology that most people already constantly carry around—their cellphone. Two-factor authentication is a good way to protect against both online and offline attacks. While two-factor authentication remains vulnerable to specialized phishing and malware-based attacks, those vulnerabilities are relatively narrow and typically require the fraudster to already have a person's username and password.

Two-factor authentication is not a silver bullet that addresses all the problems with passwords. There are no useful silver bullets in data security. But there are some measures that will reduce risk.

Although many of these techniques are widely available and inexpensive, they are often not used. Change is not likely to happen fast enough without regulatory intervention. Perhaps a nudge, maybe a gentle push, or maybe a forceful shove will be needed. The law should promote security measures like two-factor authentication that are practical in light of human behavior.

ANTICIPATING HUMAN PROBLEMS

Companies often deprecate their software and Internet-connected devices and stop supporting them. They often ignore how attached people are to the tools they use. They tell people to simply stop using them. This isn't realistic. People won't just stop using old devices and programs; they often have too much invested in the software to just give it up at the command of a tech company. The difficulty in moving on is a data security problem.

Time and again, hackers have targeted deprecated software and devices, because they are no longer updated. Yet they remain connected to networks, making it easier for criminals to take advantage of unpatched vulnerabilities. These unserviced software programs and devices are like radioactive waste; they can't just be left behind or thrown away. When technology companies deprecate software, they must have a meaningful plan to transition people away from using it. Merely saying "stop" isn't good enough. Companies need to ensure that people don't lose their investments in the software, such as source files or custom software.

The law could better facilitate such reform of the deprecation process if it held technology companies more accountable.

Sending Sensible Signals

Design doesn't just facilitate or hinder tasks. It also delivers information. It communicates by sending a signal to the user of a technology.[65] Through signals, design helps define our relationships with other people and shapes our risk calculus when interacting online. These signals affect our expectations about how things work and the context within which we are acting.

Data security law focuses a lot on safeguards like encryption but hardly at all on the signals that technologies send to the people using them, like whom a communication is coming from or how a feature works or should be used. Yet, these signals are what encourage people to click certain links, share personal data, or enable certain features. Designers must engineer their systems so that the signals are understandable and that they encourage secure rather than insecure behavior.

The wrong design can send misleading signals. People will ignore signals if too many are sent or if not enough are sent. Poor signals can be a major vulnerability. Fraudsters exploit confusing, inconsistent, and ambiguous signals to trick people. In essence, poor signals make people more gullible.

MISLEADING SIGNALS

When people use devices, there is a ton of information thrown their way about the security risks of various activities. Unfortunately, this information is often vague or misleading, making it difficult for people to get a clear sense of what they should do or how vulnerable they really are.

One example is the ubiquitous padlock icon people see when they use their browser, adjust their privacy settings on social media, and enter authentication credentials.[66] The padlock is an icon of the physical manifestation of security—only those with the key get access to whatever it is protecting. But what does it mean in specific contexts online? It could mean almost anything, from the deployment of specific encryption and authentication protocols to a general warm and fuzzy sense of "security" similar to the comically vague statements in privacy policies that a "company takes your privacy and security seriously." If nothing else, padlock icons are invitations to garner consumer trust, enticing people not to worry about providing more personal information.[67] The padlock icon isn't necessarily good or bad, but it is vague and companies often use it to promise more than they deliver. Because this icon isn't regulated, the trust that it conveys is often false and prone to abuse.

Policymakers can play an important role in encouraging more useful signals and discouraging vague and misleading ones. At a minimum, regulators should provide guidance and facilitate industry coherence in security signals for users. Regulators can also do a lot more, such as applying federal and state laws against deceptive trade practices to companies that use false or misleading signals. In several cases, the FTC has alleged that technology companies using phrases like "easy to secure" and "advanced network security" were being deceptive because their products and services were insecure.[68] Icons that invoke the concept of security are conveying similar messages even though words aren't being used.

The term "security" itself also functions as a signal. Many promises made by companies about security are as vague and empty as the padlock icon. In other areas, the FTC has created rules to limit when companies can use certain terms that might mislead consumers. For example, the FTC has limited the extent to which companies can use the word "free" to describe certain products and services.[69] The use of the word "security" and icons to represent security should be similarly scrutinized.

POORLY TIMED, TOO MANY, OR NOT ENOUGH SIGNALS

Signals not only fail when they are inconsistent, vague, or misleading. Signals also fail based on the timing and frequency of their use. For example, researchers at University College London conducted a study to ascertain the effectiveness of security warnings. They found that too many warnings desensitized people to the risks. The researchers concluded that "security warnings in their current forms are largely ineffective, and will remain so, unless the number of false positives can be reduced."[70] In another study, a different group of researchers concluded that "the status quo of warning messages appearing haphazardly—while people are typing, watching a video, uploading files, etc.—results in up to 90 percent of users disregarding them."[71] Researchers at Carnegie Mellon's CyLab developed Warning Design Guidelines, which recommended that warnings be clear, concise, and accurate: "If too long, overly technical, inaccurate, or ambiguous, a warning will simply be discarded and its purpose will be lost."[72] These studies and others have repeatedly shown that security warnings are like the porridge for Goldilocks—they have to be just right. Too many warnings will work poorly, as will too few. Warnings at the wrong place and time will work poorly.

Warnings should reflect the gravity of the risk. Using similar types of warnings for low security risk and for high security risks fosters confusion; people might begin to assume that all the warnings are for low risks and can be ignored. Warnings must be implemented in ways to avoid being treated like the boy who cried wolf. Moreover, the CyLab Guidelines suggest that warnings "follow a common visual layout" because it "can be recognized faster."

Instead of better calibrating warnings to the risk, the opposite trend is occurring. Some companies are now slapping warnings on all external emails, with warnings like: EXTERNAL EMAIL—SPAM RISK. As these warnings adorn so many harmless messages, people will become desensitized to them.

Another problem is with spam filters. When going through the junk mail folder to look for any legitimate emails that have been snagged, there is often nothing to help distinguish the danger of the emails in the folder. All emails look the same even though it might be possible to identify certain ones as being far riskier to open than others.

Data security laws often fail to address signals when addressing the implementation of "reasonable safeguards." But signals play an important role in how humans think about security and in how they behave. The law should not ignore this important dimension of data security.

■

Lawmakers must do far more to encourage a more human-centric approach to designing for good data security. Good policy depends upon keeping people's foreseeable behavior front and center when creating, modifying, and enforcing data security rules. Technological systems are not self-created or self-executing. People made them, people administer them, and people use them. The more our laws and frameworks reflect this, the better off we will be.

Conclusion

The Holistic Approach

Data security is a problem that is spiraling out of control. The epidemic is growing worse each year, with no signs of abating, and the stakes couldn't be higher. More organizations are collecting more personal data. Our personal data is being used in ways that have profound effects on our lives. As more devices are being connected online, the physical world and the Internet are merging, posing risks to life and limb. Connected devices are going into our houses and even into our bodies.

As we stumble into the future, it seems as though we have fallen back to the days where pirates teemed on the seas. Criminals and fraudsters are lurking around every corner, ready to kidnap your data, post it online, break into your accounts, steal your money, pollute your credit reports, and ruin your reputation. Despite spending hundreds of millions of dollars on security each year, the most powerful companies in the world can't seem to keep the hackers out. Rome is in flames, and the barbarians have broken through the gate.

Policymakers have not stood idly by. They have rushed in to help, creating both cybersecurity frameworks and privacy rules. And in the middle lies data security—a creature born of individualistic privacy protections for personal information applied to systems of data. In a fairly short span of time, a large body of data security law has been created. Data security law currently consists of three broad types of law—breach notification laws, safeguards laws, and private litigation—all of which focus far too heavily on data breaches. This reactionary body of law rummages through the ashes of breaches, but it doesn't do enough to actually prevent breaches or reduce the harm from them. Meanwhile, the fire still rages.

In this book, we proposed a different approach to data security law. Our goal has been to rethink the foundations. Although at the surface, data breaches look like a bunch of isolated incidents, below the surface, they are symptoms of deeper interconnected problems involving the whole data ecosystem. Data security law has the potential to incorporate the best wisdom from systems-based cybersecurity frameworks and privacy rules that accommodate human behavior and aim to foster human flourishing.

Recognizing data breaches as the product of systemic problems is essential to improving the law's effectiveness. Systemic problems, if addressed structurally, can be ameliorated far more readily than countless scattered isolated problems. Instead of tackling each breach one at a time, the law can address many breaches all at once at the common source.

Looking at data security in this way—as a problem with deep roots in the structure of the data ecosystem—makes it clear that the law must take a new direction. Instead of focusing on breaches, the law must focus on the entire system of data processing and the actors within it. We call this a "holistic approach" to data security law. Lawmakers should take a page from public health law and focus on the overall "health" of the entire data ecosystem.

In many ways, the law is not only failing to improve data security but also is making the problem worse. The law is setting up bad incentives, encouraging organizations to adopt flawed security measures, providing special sanctuary to actors who are contributing factors in many breaches, facilitating practices that increase data security risks, and intensifying the harms that breaches cause. Unfortunately, the law is a big part of the problem rather than the solution.

Understood this way, it is no wonder why the problem of data security is worsening—the system's design is deeply flawed. Systemic problems will continue to relentlessly churn out the same outcomes. We could carry on with failed laws and policies, repeating the same approach after every breach in the hope that, through a miracle, something will change. Or we could take a different approach, one that focuses more on the underlying sources of the breach epidemic. Currently, the train is on the wrong track, and switching tracks will be difficult. It it is imperative we do so, however, because the train is heading toward a cliff.

We have sketched out a blueprint for a more effective role for the law to play in securing our personal data. We are not aiming to provide a fix-all solution—there are no easy answers for data security. Nor has our goal been to propose specific legislation.

Instead, we endeavor to offer a blueprint that consists of a different approach to data security law. Before lawmakers can craft specific solutions, they need broad directional guidance and a more complete way of thinking about how to protect our personal information within systems that accounts for the way people make choices and interpret signals. Below, we review some of the key parts of our blueprint.

Data security law should be more proactive and less reactive

Certain kinds of problems require proactive measures. Take food safety as an example. Lawmakers and regulators could wait until a salmonella outbreak makes people sick before holding restaurants accountable for unsanitary conditions. But that would be chasing the problem. Instead, regulators demand sanitary conditions from restaurants and require a strict set of rules regarding food preparation to ensure people will not get sick when they eat out. Everyone involved in the supply chain of food, from the farm to the restaurant table, is required to act responsibly. Inspectors from the health department don't have to wait until someone gets sick to find health code violations. Instead, they regularly inspect these businesses and hold them accountable for violations so they can make things safe before people get sick.

But data security law has largely taken the opposite approach by focusing on the breach. This reactive approach makes it very difficult for enforcement authorities to get ahead of the problem. If data security law is to succeed, it must hold actors accountable for risky behavior before breaches occur.

In a handful of cases, the U.S. Federal Trade Commission (FTC) has brought enforcement actions to companies with poor security even before they were breached.[1] These cases have woken up companies and forced them to change their approach to security before an incident occurred. Most FTC cases, however, have been brought in response to a breach, but this approach is just kicking companies when they are already down and wounded. Robust regulatory intervention before breaches would be a far more effective approach.

Data security law should craft the right incentives with a proportionate and flexible approach

Organizations and people act according to incentives. In many examples discussed throughout this book, the law fails to create incentives to engage in better data security practices, and the law even creates incentives to engage in risky practices. It is foolish to hope that somehow the incentive structure won't matter and that behavior won't follow the incentives. Lawmakers would be wise to focus on the incentives the law is creating and to expect that behavior will follow the incentives.

Because risk management is context-specific, and because technology, vulnerabilities, and threats change so rapidly, a set of rigid rules would be unworkable, burdensome, and ineffective. The law should provide sufficient flexibility so that organizations have the ability to make their own policy choices. This is why the law should focus on setting the parameters. Lawmakers should reject policy choices that fall outside the boundaries, but be careful about mandating specific measures.

Lawmakers should reserve outright restrictions and bans for the worst security practices that would not be justified under any reasonable risk management approach. In many other circumstances, lawmakers can use various hard and soft nudges to promote or discourage activities. One such way is to require certain defaults. Defaults can be overridden by user choices, but how they are set has tremendous influence. Lawmakers can hold certain organizations accountable through liability for the harms that they cause. The law can reward good data security practices by easing the penalties and costs if there is a breach. Lawmakers can also require governance measures such as data mapping to create better internal practices at organizations.

The law should recognize that data security is a systemic and societal problem, one where the effects of one's poor security can affect many others

The market is failing to deliver the optimal level of data security because the harms of poor security affect many people and organizations beyond the breached entities, and the costs of these harms are not being internalized by many of the actors that contribute to them. Not only will individuals fail to make wise informed choices about security when choosing devices or services, they also will often fail to consider the larger societal consequences of their choices. This is a situation involving market failure, and lawmakers should intervene to address it.

People's behavior regarding security is heavily shaped by how various organizations interact with them. Organizations often inadvertently teach people to engage in risky behavior. These organizations are not only weakening security for these people and for themselves, but also for many others.

In many ways, training people to engage in risky behavior is a form of pollution. Collectively, this bad training increases the most significant cause of data breaches—faulty human behavior. When individual activities create harm that extends to others, the law should intervene because the organizations causing the harm are not fully internalizing the costs.

Data security law should impose responsibility on all the actors in the data ecosystem that play a contributory role in data breaches

The most foundational step of a holistic approach to data security law is for lawmakers to broaden the accountability net to include all the actors that create data security risks. There are all kinds of actors that create risk to peoples' personal data, and even more that have the opportunity to mitigate that risk. Most of the actors that create data security risks are not forced by law to internalize it.

The law should avoid digital technology exceptionalism and start imposing the same responsibilities on digital technologies as those expected for other products and services.

Data security law should shift away from a misguided stop-all-breaches mentality and encourage more balanced and thoughtful approaches to data security

Decisions involving data security are value-laden choices about tradeoffs and should be made with an understanding of human aims and desires. Stopping all breaches is an unrealistic goal. Instead, we want good risk management. When the law obsessively pummels organizations that are breached, the law doesn't properly incentivize good risk management. The law needs a better approach to evaluate good risk management.

Data security law should work to reduce the harm of data breaches

The law should do more after a breach to lessen the pain of a breach. Breaches are inevitable and the goal of security shouldn't be to stop all breaches at any cost. This would be counterproductive. A key way the law can help is to reduce the harmfulness of breaches. Currently, however, the law fails in reducing the injuries of a breach, and often hides its head in the sand when victims seek redress. In many situations, the law makes the harm of breaches worse.

The law should avoid encouraging a mechanistic checklist approach to data security

Far too often, data security becomes a matter of ticking off items in a checklist. There are countless frameworks with numerous controls, and it is easy to fall prey to box checking rather than engaging in the more complicated and muddy balancing that good risk management requires.

The law incentivizes the pro forma checklist approach. It's far too easy for regulators to enforce by looking for missing items on a checklist than to make a more nuanced evaluation of policy choices about tradeoffs and strategies for dealing with human behavior.

Some in industry have been pushing for safe harbors, where they can avoid being faulted for breaches if they can show they have done everything on a checklist. Such safe harbors should be rejected as they can further entrench the faulty checkbox approach.

Ultimately, what matters is not just whether a particular type of security measure is implemented but *how* it is implemented. Far too often, checklists that look good on paper end up being poor in practice. For example, it's easy to check the box for security awareness training but it's far harder to implement effective training that really has an impact on behavior.

While lawmakers should seek to discourage checklist behavior, the law should still provide sufficient guidance to organizations about the basics of good data security. Lawmakers and regulators should clarify "reasonableness" standards for data security by providing more concrete guidance. To be reasonable, the policy choices must amount to sensible risk management. There can be different degrees to which organizations are willing to tolerate risk, and the law shouldn't mandate a one-size-fits-all approach. Although no one size fits all, there are organizations that engage in poor risk management, and these organizations should be penalized.

The law should encourage greater integration of privacy and security

Privacy and security go hand-in-hand. Moreover, privacy involves issues that are often quite muddy, so privacy professionals are typically more experienced in thinking about muddy issues. A major theme in our recommendations is for security thinking to become less mechanistic and to embrace the muddy balancing needed for good risk management. Privacy can contribute to data security by bringing its experience with this less formalistic way of thinking.

There are many components of privacy regulation that can strengthen security, such as data minimization, data mapping, and other requirements. Good privacy hygiene can reduce the likelihood of breaches as well as their severity.

The law should require or encourage security by design that accounts for the human element in systems

Lawmakers should take the design of information technologies more seriously because of the significant role that design plays in shaping human behavior. Some technological designs exacerbate people's carelessness or weaknesses; these designs make it easy for people to make a mistake. Some designs help nudge people to avoid mistakes.

Lawmakers are often reluctant to regulate design for fear of being too paternalistic. But there are strategies for how the law can influence design without being too rigid, such as requiring certain defaults rather than banning features or options. Lawmakers should mandate certain designs that are widely known to create unwarranted security risks, such as requiring manufacturers of devices to force users to change default passwords.

Lawmakers should promote security measures that encourage humans to behave in ways that increase security. Far too often, the law does the opposite, rewarding security measures that ignore the human element.

The law should promote a more uniform and less demanding set of security norms so that people have the right expectations and knowledge

Critics often marvel at how foolishly people behave regarding security. So many people seem to do so many unwise insecure things. In many cases, it's not people's fault. People receive inconsistent and muddled messages about security. They are taught to avoid clicking links in emails to reset their passwords, but then legitimate companies ask people to do this very thing. Lawmakers should help coordinate a more uniform approach to developing the right understanding about data security in people that doesn't place too much of a burden on them.

Lawmakers should ensure that more effective and accurate signals are sent to people about security. Bad signals can lead to insecure behavior, and good signals can greatly increase secure behavior.

■

The law should become more holistic, more strategic, and more cognizant of the role humans play in the data ecosystem. If data security law is going to stand any chance in a world of artificial intelligence, smart devices, and social media, it must move beyond the breach. Doing so will make the law much more effective and adaptive. With any luck, we will be able to stop calling every year "The Year of the Data Breach."

ACKNOWLEDGMENTS

We would like to thank the participants of the 2018 Privacy Law Scholars Conference workshop of our book proposal and chapter. We also would like to thank the following people for providing comments, reviewing drafts, and helping refine the arguments in the book: Annie Anton, Steven Bellovin, David Choffnes, Dissent Doe, Chris Hart, Chris Hoofnagle, Edward McNicholas, Paul Schwartz, Peter Swire, Charlotte Tschider, Christo Wilson, and Josephine Wolff. We are particularly grateful to Kyle Berner, Jonathan Cleary, Kayvan Farchadi, Katherine Grabar, Johanna Gunawan, Alissamariah Gutierrez, Ahmed Khalifa, Charlotte Kress, Jay Mohanka, Alexander Nally, Trevor Schmitt, Alexis Shore, and Julia Sweeney for their research assistance.

We also want to thank our agent, Susan Schulman, for her great efforts to further this project and David McBride and Holly Mitchell, our editors, for their support and flexibility throughout this project.

NOTES

CHAPTER 1

1. Michael Riley, Benjamin Elgin, Dune Lawrence & Carol Matlack, *Missed Alarms and 40 Million Stolen Credit Card Numbers: How Target Blew It*, Bloomberg, (Mar. 17, 2014), *available at* https://www.bloomberg.com/news/articles/2014-03-13/target-missed-warnings-in-epic-hack-of-credit-card-data (hereafter Riley, *Missed Alarms*).

2. Megan Clark, *Timeline of Target's Data Breach And Aftermath: How Cybertheft Snowballed For The Giant Retailer*, International Business Times, (May 5, 2014), *available at* https://www.ibtimes.com/timeline-targets-data-breach-aftermath-how-cybertheft-snowballed-giant-retailer-1580056.

3. Riley, *Missed Alarms*.

4. Riley, *Missed Alarms*.

5. Riley, *Missed Alarms*.

6. Elizabeth A. Harris, Nicole Perlroth, *For Target, the Breach Numbers Grow*, New York Times, (Jan. 10, 2014), *available at* https://www.nytimes.com/2014/01/11/business/target-breach-affected-70-million-customers.html?_r=0.

7. Riley, *Missed Alarms*.

8. Brian Krebs, *Target Hackers Broke In Via HVAC Company*, KrebsOnSecurity, (Feb. 5, 2014), *available at* https://krebsonsecurity.com/2014/02/target-hackers-broke-in-via-hvac-company/.

9. Charles Riley & Jose Pagliery, *Target will pay hack victims $10 million*, CNN Tech Blog, (Mar. 19, 2015), *available at* http://money.cnn.com/2015/03/19/technology/security/target-data-hack-settlement/.

10. Charles Riley & Jose Pagliery, *Target will pay hack victims $10 million*, CNN Tech Blog, (Mar. 19, 2015), *available at* http://money.cnn.com/2015/03/19/technology/security/target-data-hack-settlement/; Michael Riley et al., *Missed Alarms and 40 Million Stolen Credit Card Numbers: How Target Blew It*, Bloomberg News, (Mar. 17, 2014), https://www.bloomberg.com/news/articles/2014-03-13/target-missed-warnings-in-epic-hack-of-credit-card-data.

11. Brian Krebs, *Target Hackers Broke In Via HVAC Company*, KrebsOnSecurity, (Feb. 5 2014), *available at* https://krebsonsecurity.com/2014/02/target-hackers-broke-in-via-hvac-company/.

12. Chris Smith, *Expert who first revealed massive Target hack tells us how it happened*, BGR (Boy Genius Report), (Jan. 16, 2014), *available at* http://bgr.com/2014/01/16/how-was-target-hacked/.

13. Riley, *Missed Alarms*.

14. Riley, *Missed Alarms*.

15. Riley, *Missed Alarms*.

16. Riley, *Missed Alarms*.

17. Jim Daley, *Expenses From the Home Depot and Target Data Breaches Surpass $500 million*, Digital Transactions, (May 26, 2016), http://www.digitaltransactions.net/news/story/Expenses-From-the-Home-Depot-and-Target-Data-Breaches-Surpass-500-Million.

18. Chris Smith, *Expert who first revealed massive Target hack tells us how it happened*, BGR (Boy Genius Report), (Jan. 16, 2014), *available at* http://bgr.com/2014/01/16/how-was-target-hacked/.

19. *See* Brian Krebs, *Ransomware for Dummies: Anyone Can Do It*, KrebsOnSecurity (Mar. 1, 2017); Bill Brenner, *5 Ransomware as a Service (RaaS) Kits—SophosLabs Investigates*, Naked Security (Dec. 13, 2017), https://nakedsecurity.sophos.com/2017/12/13/5-ransomware-as-a-service-raas-kits-sophoslabs-investigates/.

20. Lily Hay Newman, *Atlanta Spent $2.6M to Recover From a $52,000 Ransomware Scare*, Wired, (Apr. 23, 2018), https://www.wired.com/story/atlanta-spent-26m-recover-from-ransomware-scare/.

21. Chris Bodenner, *How Easily Can Hackers Plant Evidence?*, The Atlantic, (Sept. 11, 2015), https://www.theatlantic.com/notes/2015/09/how-easy-can-hackers-plant-evidence/404863/.

22. Brian Fung, *A Snapchat Security Breach Affects 4.6 Million Users. Did Snapchat Drag Its Feet on a Fix?*, Wash. Post, (Jan. 1, 2014), https://www.washingtonpost.com/news/the-switch/wp/2014/01/01/a-snapchat-security-breach-affects-4-6-million-users-did-snapchat-drag-its-feet-on-a-fix/.

23. *See* Bruce Schneir, *Click Here to Kill Everybody: Security and Survival in a Hyper-Connected World* (2018); Andrea Matwyshyn, *The Internet of Bodies*, 61 Wm. & Mary L. Rev. 77 (2019); Scott Peppet, *Regulating the Internet of Things: First Steps Toward Managing Discrimination, Privacy, Security and Consent*, 93 Tex. L. Rev. 85 (2014); Bryant Walker Smith, *Automated Driving and Product Liability*, Michigan State Law Review, 2017 Mich. St. L. Rev. 1 (2017).

24. Elizabeth A. Harris and Nicole Perlroth, *For Target, the Breach Numbers Grow*, New York Times, (Jan. 10, 2014).

25. Kevin McCoy, *Target to Pay $18.5M for 2013 Data Breach that Affected 41 Million Consumers*, USA Today, (May 23, 2017).

26. Privacy Rights Clearinghouse, *Data Breaches*, https://www.privacyrights.org/data-breaches.

27. For a helpful guide to cybersecurity, *see* Steve Bellovin, *Thinking Security: Stopping Next Year's Hackers* (2016). Peter Swire has sought to make sense of the landscape

of cybersecurity, including the proper role of law and policy, by proposing a conceptual framework based on the multiple layers of technology and organization that make up the Internet, sometimes referred to as "the stack." *See* Peter Swire, *A Pedagogic Cybersecurity Framework*, 61 Communications of the ACM 23 (Oct. 2018), https://cacm.acm.org/magazines/2018/10/231364-a-pedagogic-cybersecurity-framework/fulltext.

28. Other important data security laws include federal statutes such as the Gramm–Leach–Bliley Act (GLBA) and the Federal Information Security Management Act (FISMA) and state laws like New York's Cybersecurity Requirements for Financial Services Companies and state breach notification and data security safeguards rules. For scholarship on data protection and cybersecurity, *see, e.g.,* Daniel J. Solove & Woodrow Hartzog, *The FTC and the New Common Law of Privacy*, 114 Columb. L. Rev. 583 (2014); Woodrow Hartzog and Daniel J. Solove, *The Scope and Potential of FTC Data Protection*, 83 Geo. Wash. L. Rev. 2230 (2015); Bill McGeveran, *The Duty of Data Security*, 103 Minn. L. Rev. 1135 (2019); Andrea M. Matwyshyn, *Privacy, the Hacker Way*, 87 S. Cal. L. Rev. 1 (2013); David Thaw, *Cybersecurity Stovepiping*, 96 Neb. L. Rev. 339 (2017); David Thaw, *Data Breach (Regulatory) Effects*, 2015 Cardozo L. Rev. De Novo 151; David Thaw, *The Efficacy of Cybersecurity Regulation*, 30 Ga. St. U. L. Rev. 287 (2014); Derek E. Bambauer, *Privacy Versus Security*, 103 J. Crim. L. & Criminology 667 (2013); Derek E. Bambauer, *Conundrum*, 96 Minn. L. Rev. 584, 585 (2011); Derek E. Bambauer, *Ghost in the Network*, 162 U. Pa. L. Rev. 1011, 1012 (2014); Derek E. Bambauer, *Schrödinger's Cybersecurity*, 48 U.C. Davis L. Rev. 791 (2015); Lauren Henry Scholz, *Information Privacy and Data Security*, 2015 Cardozo L. Rev. De Novo 107 (2015); David W. Opderbeck, *Cybersecurity, Data Breaches, and the Economic Loss Doctrine in the Payment Card Industry*, 75 Md. L. Rev. 935 (2016); Rebecca Crootof, *International Cybertorts: Expanding State Accountability in Cyberspace*, 103 Cornell L. Rev. 565 (2018).

29. Several scholars have noted the inherent complexity of the term cybersecurity itself. *See* Jeff Kosseff, *Defining Cybersecurity Law*, 103 Iowa L. Rev. 985 (2018); Andrea M. Matwyshyn, *Hacking Speech: Informational Speech and the First Amendment*, 107 Nw. U. L. Rev. 795, 845 n.99 (2013) ("Referring to all of information security, particularly in private sector contexts, as 'cybersecurity' is technically incorrect. 'Cyber' has traditionally referred to Internet-only phenomena. Information security is not solely an Internet phenomenon. Information security questions involve both computer security and physical security."); Andrea M. Matwyshyn, *CYBER!*, 2017 BYU L. Rev. 1109 (2018); David Thaw, *The Efficacy of Cybersecurity Regulation*, 30 Ga. St. U. L. Rev. 287, 291–292 (2014) ("Cybersecurity and cyber-attack are increasingly common terms in public discourse, but there is surprising disagreement as to what precisely they refer. The terms are too-often used broadly to include all of electronic crimes, military action, domestic guard/homeland security activities, corporate risk management, financial security, and a wide spectrum of other activities related to computers, the Internet, privacy, and other similar topics. I do not suggest the term is misapplied to any of these topics, but rather that more precise terms would be helpful.").

30. *See* Andrea M. Matwyshyn, *CYBER!*, 2017 BYU L. Rev. 1109, 1121 (2018) ("[E]ffective security requires vigilant coordination across institutional and legal silos wherever the particular vulnerable code has been deployed. In other words, technologically speaking, we need to fix all the vulnerable systems in both the public and the private sector because the compromise of either could potentially lead to compromise of both.").

31. For example, in this book we will explore how password complexity requirements did not serve their intended purpose and likely facilitated some breaches. For a robust exploration of how password complexity requirements went so badly, *see* David Thaw, *Cybersecurity Stovepiping*, 96 Neb. L. Rev. 339 (2017).

32. *See also* Deirdre K. Mulligan & Fred Schneider, *Doctrine for Cybersecurity*, 140 Daedalus 70 (2011) (advocating for a regulatory approach to cybersecurity modeled after public health); Elaine Sedenberg & Deirdre K. Mulligan, *Public Health as a Model for Cybersecurity Information Sharing*, 30 Berkeley Tech. L. J. 1687 (2015); Adam Shostack, *We Need a Discipline of Cyber Public Health*, Adam Shostack & Friends, (Nov. 13, 2020), https://adam.shostack.org/blog/2020/11/we-need-a-discipline-of-cyber-public-health/.

33. Wendy Parmet, Populations, *Public Health, and the Law* 192 (2009) ("effective preparedness depends on a wide array of laws that promote and protect population health not only in emergencies but also in the calm periods between the storms. In this regard, health law plays an important and often overlooked role. It helps shape the health care system, influencing whether that system has the capacity to respond to the challenges posed by a pandemic or other emergency, or whether it lacks essential attributes, such as resiliency and redundancy, leaving it overly dependent upon emergency measures. . . .").

CHAPTER 2

1. Juliana De Groot, *The History of Data Breaches*, Data Insider, (Jan. 3, 2019), https://digitalguardian.com/blog/history-data-breaches.

2. Privacy Rights Clearinghouse, *Data Breaches*, https://www.privacyrights.org/data-breaches.

3. See *infra* Chapter 3.

4. Tony Martin-Vegue, *Will the Real "Year of the Data Breach" Please Stand Up*, HackerNoon, (Jan. 4, 2018), https://hackernoon.com/will-the-real-year-of-the-data-breach-please-stand-up-744ab6f63615.

5. *Top 10 Most Visible Changes Since 2005*, SC Magazine, (Dec. 15, 2006), https://www.scmagazine.com/home/security-news/it-security-reboot-2006-the-years-top-news/.

6. Mark Jewellap, *Record Number of Data Breaches in 2007*, Assoc. Press, (Dec. 30, 2007), http://www.nbcnews.com/id/22420774/ns/technology_and_science-security/t/record-number-data-breaches/#.XVx6uOhKg60.

7. Ellen Messmer, *Details Emerging on Hannaford Data Breach*, Network World, (Mar. 28, 2008), https://www.networkworld.com/article/2284998/details-emerging-on-hannaford-data-breach.html.

8. Mark Jewell, *T.J. Maxx Theft Believed Largest Hack Ever*, NBC News, (Mar. 30, 2007), http://www.nbcnews.com/id/17871485/ns/technology_and_science-security/t/tj-maxx-theft-believed-largest-hack-ever/#.XWC8zehKg60.

9. Dawn Kawamoto, *TD Ameritrade's 6 Million Customers Hit with Security Breach*, CNET, (Nov. 26, 2007), https://www.cnet.com/news/td-ameritrades-6-million-customers-hit-with-security-breach/.

10. *Data Breaches Soar in 2008*, 2009 Computer Fraud & Security 3 (Jan. 1, 2009), https://www.sciencedirect.com/science/article/pii/S1361372309700028.

11. Linda McGlasson, *Bank of NY Mellon Breach Much Bigger than First Announced*, Bank InfoSecurity, (Aug. 29, 2008), https://www.bankinfosecurity.com/bank-ny-mellon-breach-much-bigger-than-first-announced-a-952.

12. Andy Greenberg, *The Year of the Mega Data Breach*, Forbes, (Nov. 24, 2009), https://www.forbes.com/2009/11/24/security-hackers-data-technology-cio-network-breaches.html#12bb7035d038.

13. A&L Goodbody, *European Commission Passes New E-Privacy Directive Requiring Mandatory Data Breach Notification by Public Communications Providers*, https://www.lexology.com/library/detail.aspx?g=c3d22861-a43c-4cd0-9294-b89664984101.

14. Michael Gordover, *Throwback Thursday: Lessons Learned From the 2008 Heartland Breach*, Observe IT, (Mar. 19, 2015), https://www.observeit.com/blog/throwback-thursday-lessons-learned-from-the-2008-heartland-breach/.

15. Nik Cubrilovic, *RockYou Hack: From Bad to Worse*, TechCrunch, (Dec. 15, 2009), https://techcrunch.com/2009/12/14/rockyou-hack-security-myspace-facebook-passwords/.

16. Brian Krebs, *Hackers Break Into Virginia Health Professions Database, Demand Ransom*, Wash. Post, (May 4, 2009).

17. Experian, Data Breaches in 2010: *How They Happen and What Your Organization Can do to Prepare*, (Aug. 2010), https://www.experian.com/assets/data-breach/white-papers/data-breaches-2010.pdf.

18. *See* Kim Zetter, *Countdown to Zero Day: Stuxnet and the Launch of the World's First Digital Weapon* (2014).

19. Kevin Haley, *The 2013 Internet Security Threat Report: Year of the Mega Data Breach*, Symantec Blog, (Apr. 8, 2014) https://www.symantec.com/connect/blogs/2013-internet-security-threat-report-year-mega-data-breach.

20. Diana Manos, *Health Data Breaches up 97 Percent in 2011*, Healthcare IT News, (Feb. 01, 2012), https://www.healthcareitnews.com/news/health-data-breaches-97-percent-2011.

21. Riva Richmond, *The RSA Hack: How They Did It*, New York Times, (Apr. 2, 2011).

22. Michael Gordover, *Throwback Hack: The Epsilon Email Breach of 2011*, Observe IT, (Mar. 26, 2015), https://www.observeit.com/blog/throwback-hack-the-epsilon-email-breach-of-2011/.

23. Fahmida Y. Rashid, *Epsilon Data Breach to Cost Billions in Worst-Case Scenario*, eWeek (May 3, 2011), https://www.eweek.com/security/epsilon-data-breach-to-cost-billions-in-worst-case-scenario.

24. Sydney Butler, *Dark Web History: Where Did It Come From?*, Tech Nadu, (Dec. 23, 2018), https://www.technadu.com/dark-web-history/52017/.

25. Joshuah Bearman, *The Rise and Fall of Silk Road*, Wired, (May 2015), https://www.wired.com/2015/04/silk-road-1/.

26. Tim Hume, *How FBI Caught Ross Ulbricht, Alleged Creator of Criminal Marketplace Silk Road*, CNN, (Oct. 5, 2013), https://www.cnn.com/2013/10/04/world/americas/silk-road-ross-ulbricht/index.html.

27. Joab Jackson, *Silk Road Paid Thousands in Shake-Downs from Malicious Hackers*, CIO Magazine, (Jan. 28, 2015), https://www.cio.com/article/2877013/silk-road-paid-thousands-in-shakedowns-from-malicious-hackers.html.

28. Tim Hume, *How FBI Caught Ross Ulbricht, Alleged Creator of Criminal Marketplace Silk Road*, CNN, (Oct. 5, 2013), https://www.cnn.com/2013/10/04/world/americas/silk-road-ross-ulbricht/index.html.

29. Ricardo Bilton, *2012: A Big, Bad Year for Online Security Breaches*, VultureBeat, (Sept. 17, 2012), https://venturebeat.com/2012/09/17/2012-security-breaches/.

30. Chris Velazco, *6.5 Million LinkedIn Passwords Reportedly Leaked, LinkedIn Is "Looking Into" It*, TechCrunch, (June 6, 2012), https://techcrunch.com/2012/06/06/6-5-million-linkedin-passwords-reportedly-leaked-linkedin-is-looking-into-it/?_ga=2.145624050.756657197.1566881632-1484594935.1566622469.

31. Judy Leary, *The Biggest Data Breaches in 2016*, Identity Force, (Dec. 16, 2016), https://www.identityforce.com/blog/2016-data-breaches.

32. Samuel Gibbs, *Dropbox Hack Leads to Leaking of 68M User Passwords on the Internet*, Guardian, (Aug. 31, 2016), https://www.theguardian.com/technology/2016/aug/31/dropbox-hack-passwords-68m-data-breach.

33. Danny Palmer, *What is Ransomware? Everything You Need to Know About One of the Biggest Menaces on the Web*, ZD Net (Aug. 22, 2018), https://www.zdnet.com/article/ransomware-an-executive-guide-to-one-of-the-biggest-menaces-on-the-web/.

34. Tony Bradley, *Why 2013 Was the Year of the Personal Data Breach*, PC World, (Dec. 26, 2013), https://www.pcworld.com/article/2082961/why-2013-was-the-year-of-the-personal-data-breach.html.

35. Kevin Haley, *The 2013 Internet Security Threat Report: Year of the Mega Data Breach*, Symantec Blog, (Apr. 8, 2014), https://www.symantec.com/connect/blogs/2013-internet-security-threat-report-year-mega-data-breach.

36. Haley, *Symantec Threat Report, supra* 38.

37. *Id.*

38. Brian Krebs, *Adobe Breach Impacted At Least 38 Million Users*, KrebsOnSecurity, (Oct. 29, 2013), https://krebsonsecurity.com/2013/10/adobe-breach-impacted-at-least-38-million-users/.

39. Simon Sharwood, *Adobe to Hire Security Auditor to Prevent Repeat of Password SNAFU*, Register, (Jun. 9, 2015), https://www.theregister.co.uk/2015/06/09/adobe_to_hire_security_auditor_to_prevent_repeat_of_password_snafu/.

40. HackerNoon, *Will the Real "Year of the Data Breach" Please Stand Up?* (Jan. 3, 2018), https://hackernoon.com/will-the-real-year-of-the-data-breach-please-stand-up-744ab6f63615.

41. *'Celebgate' Attack Leaks Nude Photos of Celebrities*, Verge, https://www.theverge.com/2014/9/2/6099307/celebgate-attack-leaks-nude-photos-of-more-than-100-celebrities; see generally Danielle Citron, *Hate Crimes in Cyberspace*.

42. Florida and Kentucky.

43. Tara Seals, *Home Depot to Pay $27.25m in Latest Data Breach Settlement*, InfoSecurity Magazine, (Mar. 3, 2017), https://www.infosecurity-magazine.com/news/home-depot-to-pay-2725m/.

44. Matthew Goldstein, Nicole Perlroth, and Michael Corkery, *Neglected Server Provided Entry for JPMorgan Hackers*, DealBook, (Dec. 22, 2014), https://dealbook.nytimes.com/2014/12/22/entry-point-of-jpmorgan-data-breach-is-identified/.

45. Operation Blockbuster Study, https://www.operationblockbuster.com/resources/index.html.

46. Josephine Wolff, *You'll see this message when it is too late: The Legal and Economic Aftermath of Cybersecurity Breaches* (2018).

47. Kevin Savage & Peter Coogan, et al., *The Evolution of Ransomware*, Symantec, (Aug. 6, 2015), https://www.symantec.com/content/en/us/enterprise/media/security_response/whitepapers/the-evolution-of-ransomware.pdf.

48. TrendMicro, *Year-end Review: 2014's Worst Cyber Attacks and Data Breaches*, (Nov. 24, 2014), https://blog.trendmicro.com/year-end-review-2014s-worst-cyber-attacks-data-breaches/.

49. Jon Clay, *A Year to Remember: What Can we Learn to Improve Cyber Security in 2016?* TrendMicro, (Dec. 22, 2015), https://blog.trendmicro.com/a-year-to-remember-what-can-we-learn-to-improve-cyber-security-in-2016/.

50. Susan Ladika, *Study: Data Breaches Pose a Greater Risk*, CreditCards.com, (July 23, 2014), https://www.creditcards.com/credit-card-news/data-breach-id-theft-risk-increase-study-1282.php.

51. Marianne Kolbasuk McGee, *A New In-Depth Analysis of Anthem Breach*, Bank Info Security, (Jan. 10, 2017), https://www.bankinfosecurity.com/new-in-depth-analysis-anthem-breach-a-9627.

52. InfoSec, *The Beach of Anthem Health—The Largest Healthcare Breach in History*, https://resources.infosecinstitute.com/category/healthcare-information-security/healthcare-attack-statistics-and-case-studies/case-study-health-insurer-anthem/.

53. Kate Vinton, *Premera Blue Cross Breach May Have Exposed 11 Million Customers' Medical and Financial Data*, Forbes, (Mar. 17, 2015), https://www.forbes.com/sites/katevinton/2015/03/17/11-million-customers-medical-and-financial-data-may-have-been-exposed-in-premera-blue-cross-breach/#18e0543675d9.

54. Robert Hackett, *What to Know About the Ashley Madison Hack*, Fortune, (Aug. 26, 2015), https://fortune.com/2015/08/26/ashley-madison-hack/.

55. Chris Baraniuk, *Ashley Madison: 'Suicides' Over Website Hack*, BBC News, (Aug. 24, 2015), https://www.bbc.com/news/technology-34044506.

56. Brian Krebs, *Experian Breach Affects 15 Million Consumers*, KrebsOnSecurity, (Oct. 15, 2015), https://krebsonsecurity.com/2015/10/experian-breach-affects-15-million-consumers/.

57. Olga Kharif, *2016 Was a Record Year for Data Breaches*, BLOOMBERG, (Jan. 19, 2017), https://www.bloomberg.com/news/articles/2017-01-19/data-breaches-hit-record-in-2016-as-dnc-wendy-s-co-hacked.

58. Thomas Fischer, *The Biggest and Most Impactful Data Breaches of 2016*, Data Insider, (Jan. 19, 2017), https://digitalguardian.com/blog/biggest-and-most-impactful-data-breaches-2016; Grant Gross, *The Massive Panama Papers Data Leak Explained*, Computer World, (Apr. 5, 2016), https://www.computerworld.com/article/3052218/the-massive-panama-papers-data-leak-explained.html.

59. Jacob Kastrenakes, *SEC Issues $35 Million Fine Over Yahoo Failing to Disclose Data Breach*, Verge, (Apr. 24, 2018), https://www.theverge.com/2018/4/24/17275994/yahoo-sec-fine-2014-data-breach-35-million; Olivia Beavers, *SEC Fines Yahoo $35 Million Over 2014 Email Breach*, Hill, (Apr. 24, 2018), https://thehill.com/policy/cybersecurity/384607-sec-fines-yahoo-35-million-over-2014-email-breach.

60. FBI, *Ransomware Victims Urged to Report Infections to Federal Law Enforcement*, (Sept. 15, 2016), https://www.ic3.gov/media/2016/160915.aspx.

61. Greg Otto, *Ransomware Attacks Quadrupled in Q1 2016*, FedScoop, (Apr. 29, 2016), https://www.fedscoop.com/ransomware-attacks-up-300-percent-in-first-quarter-of-2016/.

62. Richard Winton, *Hollywood Hospital Pays $17,000 in Bitcoin to Hackers; FBI Investigating*, Los Angeles Times, (Feb. 18, 2016), https://www.latimes.com/business/technology/la-me-ln-hollywood-hospital-bitcoin-20160217-story.html#.

63. Raphael Slatter, *Inside Story: How Russians Hacked the Democrats' Emails*, AP News, (Nov. 4, 2017), https://apnews.com/dea73efc01594839957c3c9a6c962b8a/Inside-story:-How-Russians-hacked-the-Democrats'-emails.

64. Online Trust Alliance, *2017 Cyber Incident & Breach Trends Report*, (Jan. 25, 2018), https://www.internetsociety.org/wp-content/uploads/2019/04/2018-cyber-incident-report.pdf.

65. *Over 5,200 Data Breaches Make 2017 an Exceptional Year for All the Wrong Reasons*, Risk-Based Security, (Feb. 6, 2018), https://www.riskbasedsecurity.com/2018/02/over-5200-data-breaches-make-2017-an-exceptional-year-for-all-the-wrong-reasons/.

66. Megan Leonhardt, *Equifax to Pay $700 Million for Massive Data Breach*, CNBC, (July 22, 2019), https://www.cnbc.com/2019/07/22/what-you-need-to-know-equifax-data-breach-700-million-settlement.html.

67. Eric Newcomer, *Uber Paid Hackers to Delete Stolen Data on 57 Million People*, Bloomberg (Nov. 21, 2017), https://www.bloomberg.com/news/articles/2017-11-21/uber-concealed-cyberattack-that-exposed-57-million-people-s-data; Josephine Wolff, *Uber's Former Security Chief Has Been Charged With Allegedly Covering Up a Data Breach. Good*, Slate, (Aug. 26, 2020), https://slate.com/technology/2020/08/uber-joseph-sullivan-charged-data-breach.html.

68. Connor Hays, *2018: The Year of the Data Breach*, Bloomberg, (Dec. 30, 2018), https://bloom.co/blog/2018--the-year-of-the-data-breach/.

69. *Alabama Becomes Final State to Enact Data Breach Notification Law*, Hunton Security Law Blog, (Apr. 3, 2018), https://www.huntonprivacyblog.com/2018/04/03/alabama-becomes-final-state-enact-data-breach-notification-law/.

70. Angelique Carson, *Dispatch from Paris: DPAs are Flooded with Complaints*, IAPP, (Feb. 13, 2019), https://www.pinsentmasons.com/out-law/news/ico-warns-over-reporting-data-breaches; https://iapp.org/news/a/dispatch-from-paris-dpas-are-inundated-flooded-with-complaints/.

71. Online Trust Alliance, *2018 Cyber Incident & Breach Trends Report*, (July 2019), https://www.internetsociety.org/resources/ota/2019/2018-cyber-incident-breach-trends-report/.

72. Vidhi Doshi, *A Security Breach in India Has Left a Billion People at Risk of Identity Theft*, Wash. Post, (Jan. 4, 2018), https://www.washingtonpost.com/news/worldviews/wp/2018/01/04/a-security-breach-in-india-has-left-a-billion-people-at-risk-of-identity-theft/.

73. Nicole Perlroth, Amie Tsang, & Adam Satariano, *Marriott Hacking Exposes Data of Up to 500 Million Guests*, New York Times, (Nov. 30, 3018), https://www.nytimes.com/2018/11/30/business/marriott-data-breach.html.

74. Gaby Del Valle, *The Marriott Hack Exposed the Passport Numbers of More Than 5 Million People*, Vox, (Jan. 4, 2019), https://www.vox.com/the-goods/2018/11/30/18119770/marriott-hotels-starwood-hack#:~:text=Marriott%20first%20disclosed%20the%20breach,hotel%20chain's%20properties%20since%202014.

75. James Sanders, *Data Breaches Increased 54% in 2019 So Far*, Tech Republic, (Aug. 15, 2019), https://www.techrepublic.com/article/data-breaches-increased-54-in-2019-so-far/.

76. David Gilbert, *Why You Should Be Worried About Getting Hacked in 2019*, Vice News, (Dec. 28, 2018), https://www.vice.com/en_us/article/8xpbyg/why-you-should-be-worried-about-getting-hacked-in-2019.

77. Risk Based Security, *From 4,000 to 40,000 Data Breaches: People are Still the Problem*, (May 3, 2019), https://www.riskbasedsecurity.com/2019/05/03/from-4000-to-40000-data-breaches-people-are-still-the-problem/.

78. Help Net Security, *In 2019, a Total of 7,098 Reported Breaches Exposed 15.1 Billion Records*, HelpNetSecurity, (Feb 11, 2020), https://www.helpnetsecurity.com/2020/02/11/2019-reported-breaches/.

79. Victoria Song, *Mother of All Breaches Exposes 773 Million Emails, 21 Million Passwords*, Gizmodo, (Jan. 17, 2019), https://gizmodo.com/mother-of-all-breaches-exposes-773-million-emails-21-m-1831833456.

80. Charlie Osborne, *Data Breach Forces Medical Debt Collector AMCA to File for Bankruptcy Protection*, ZD Net, (June 19, 2019), https://www.zdnet.com/article/medical-debt-collector-amca-files-for-bankruptcy-protection-after-data-breach/.

81. Jessica Davis, *FBI Alerts to Rise in Ransomware Attacks, Urges Victims Not to Pay*, Health IT Security, (Oct. 4, 2019), https://healthitsecurity.com/news/fbi-alerts-to-rise-in-ransomware-attacks-urges-victims-not-to-pay.

82. Jessica Davis, *Maze Ransomware Hackers Extorting Providers, Posting Stolen Health Data*, Health IT Security, (Feb. 4, 2020), https://healthitsecurity.com/news/maze-ransomware-hackers-extorting-providers-posting-stolen-health-data.

83. *Id.*

84. Privacy Rights Clearinghouse, *Data Breaches*, https://www.privacyrights.org/data-breaches.

85. Source of Data: Privacy Rights Clearinghouse, *Data Breaches*, https://www.privacyrights.org/data-breaches.

86. Online Trust Alliance, *2017 Cyber Incident & Breach Response Guide*, (Jan. 25, 2017), https://www.internetsociety.org/resources/ota/2017/2016-cyber-incident-breach-readiness-guide/.

87. Christopher Booker, *The Seven Basic Plots: Why We Tell Stories* (2006). For the curious, the plots are (1) Overcoming the monster, (2) Rags to riches, (3) The quest, (4) Voyage and return, (5) Comedy, (6) Tragedy, and (7) Rebirth.

88. Danielle Citron, *Reservoirs of Danger: The Evolution of Public and Private Law at the Dawn of the Information Age*, 80 S. Cal. L. Rev. 241 (2007).

89. Steve Ranger, *Encryption: More And More Companies Use It, Despite Nasty Tech Headaches*, ZD Net, (Apr. 20, 2015), https://www.zdnet.com/article/encryption-more-and-more-companies-use-it-despite-nasty-tech-headaches/.

90. Jessica Davis, *24% of US Health Employees Never Received Cybersecurity Training*, Health IT Security, (Aug. 21, 2019), https://healthitsecurity.com/news/24-of-us-health-employees-never-received-cybersecurity-training.

91. Online Trust Alliance, *2018 Cyber Incident & Breach Trends Report*, (July 2019), https://www.internetsociety.org/resources/ota/2019/2018-cyber-incident-breach-trends-report/.

CHAPTER 3

1. *Beck, et. al. v. McDonald, et. al.*, No. 15-1395 (4th Cir. Feb. 6, 2017).

2. Press Release, FTC, *ChoicePoint Settles* Data Security Breach Charges *to Pay $10 Million in Civil Penalties, $5 Million for Consumer Redress*, (Jan. 26, 2006), https://www.ftc.gov/news-events/press-releases/2006/01/choicepoint-settles-data-security-breach-charges-pay-10-million.

3. ACLU, *FAQ on ChoicePoint*, https://www.aclu.org/other/faq-choicepoint.

4. The Online Privacy Protection Act of 2003, Cal. Bus. & Prof. Code §§ 22575-22579 (2004).

5. California Civil Code §1798.82(g).

6. *Id.* at §1798.82(a).

7. *See* Ronald I. Raether, *There Has Been a Data Security Breach: But is Notice Required?*, American Bar Assoc.: Business Law Today, (August 2011), https://www.americanbar.org/publications/blt/2011/08/02_raether.html.

8. Sarah D. Scalet, *ChoicePoint Data Breach: The Plot Thickens*, (May 1, 2005), https://www.csoonline.com/article/2118146/choicepoint-data-breach--the-plot-thickens.html.

9. *See Data Breaches in 2005*, https://www.privacyrights.org/data-breaches?title=&taxonomy_vocabulary_11_tid%5B%5D=271.

10. In order of passage: Arkansas, North Dakota, Indiana, Montana, Georgia, Washington, Minnesota, Connecticut, Tennessee, Maine, Illinois, Nevada, Delaware, Rhode Island, Louisiana, New York, Puerto Rico, New Jersey, Ohio, North Carolina, Pennsylvania, Florida.

11. In order of passage: Wisconsin, Utah, Idaho, Nebraska, Kansas, Colorado, Arizona, Vermont, Hawaii, New Hampshire, Michigan. For more information on data breach

notification laws, *see* Charlotte A. Tschider, *Experimenting with Privacy: Driving Efficiency Through A State-Informed Federal Data Breach Notification and Data Protection Law*, 18 Tul. J. Tech. & Intell. Prop. 45 (2015).

12. Modifications to the HIPAA Privacy, Security, Enforcement, and Breach Notification Rules Under the Health Information Technology for Economic and Clinical Health Act and the Genetic Information Nondiscrimination Act, 78 Fed. Reg. 5566 (Jan. 25, 2013) (codified at 45 CFR Parts 160 and 164), https://www.gpo.gov/fdsys/pkg/FR-2013-01-25/pdf/2013-01073.pdf.

13. See, e.g, Omri Ben-Shahar & Carl E. Schneider, *The Failure of Mandated Disclosure*, 150 U. Penn. L. Rev. 647 (2011).

14. *See* Ala. Code § 8-38-1 et seq ("BREACH OF SECURITY or BREACH. The unauthorized acquisition of data in electronic form containing sensitive personally identifying information. Acquisition occurring over a period of time committed by the same entity constitutes one breach.").

15. *See* Whitman & Mattord, Principles of Information Security, (2018). (n.62) p.11; International Standardisation Organisation, ISO/IEC 27002: Code of Practice for Information Security Management (2005). International Telecommunications Union (ITU). ITU-TX.1205: Series X: Data Networks, Open System Communications and Security: Telecommunication Security: Overview of cybersecurity (2008). Available at https://www.itu.int/rec/T-REC-X.1205-200804. *See also*, Alaska Stat. § 45.48.010 et seq ("Unauthorized acquisition, or reasonable belief of unauthorized acquisition, of personal information that compromises the security, confidentiality, or integrity of the personal information maintained by the information collector.").

16. General Data Protection Regulation, Article 4(12) ("'personal data breach' means a breach of security leading to the accidental or unlawful destruction, loss, alteration, unauthorised disclosure of, or access to, personal data transmitted, stored or otherwise processed. . . .").

17. Cal. Civ. Code 17982(a).

18. California Office of Privacy Protection, Reasonable Practices on Notice of Security Breach Involving Personal Information (Jan. 2012).

19. Daniel J. Solove & Paul M. Schwartz, *Information Privacy Law* 949 (6th ed. 2018).

20. HIPAA Breach Notification Rule, 45 C.F.R. § 164.404.

21. General Data Protection Regulation, Article 33.

22. General Data Protection Regulation, Article 4.

23. General Data Protection Regulation, Article 33.

24. California, the District of Columbia, Hawaii, Illinois, Louisiana; New Hampshire, North Carolina, Oregon, South Carolina, Tennessee, and Washington currently allow for a private right of action by consumers who have been affected by a data breach. Cal. Civ. Code § 1798.84 (West 2009); D.C. Code Ann. § 28-3853(a) (LexisNexis Supp. 2009); Haw. Rev. Stat. § 487N-1 *et seq.*; 815 Ill. Comp. Stat. 530/1 *et seq.*; 2018 Louisiana S.B. 361; N.H. Rev. Stat. Ann. § 359-C:21(I) (2009); N.C. Gen. Stat. Ann. § 75-65 (2007); OR. Rev. State. Ann. § 646A.624 (West Supp. 2009); S.C. Code Ann. § 37-20-170 (Supp. 2008); Tenn. Code Ann. § 47-18-2107(h) (Supp. 2009); Wash. Rev. Code Ann. § 19.255.010(10)(9) (West 2007).

25. Bethan Moorcraft, *Are US Consumers Suffering From Data Breach Notification Fatigue?*, Insurance Business, (June 19, 2019), https://www.insurancebusinessmag.com/us/news/cyber/are-us-consumers-suffering-from-data-breach-notification-fatigue-170386.aspx; Grayson Schmidt & Ames Tribune, *Expert Warns of the Risks Posed by Data Breach Fatigue*, Government Technology, (Jan. 31, 2018), https://www.govtech.com/security/Expert-Warns-of-the-Risks-Posed-by-Data-Breach-Fatigue.html.

26. Deborah George, *Proposed New Breach Notification Rule for the Banking Industry*, JD Supra, (Jan. 8, 2021), https://www.jdsupra.com/legalnews/proposed-new-breach-notification-rule-2286096/.

27. Roger A. Grimes, *Wanted: Data Breach Risk Ratings, Because Not All Breaches are Equal*, CSO, (Sept. 13, 2018), https://www.csoonline.com/article/3304286/data-risk-ratings-because-not-all-data-breaches-are-equal.html.

28. U.S. Department of Health, Education, and Welfare, *Records, Computers, and the Rights of Citizens: Report of the Secretary's Advisory Comm. on Automated Personal Data Systems*, 41–42 (1973).

29. 44 U.S.C. § 3541 *et seq.*

30. HIPAA Privacy Rule, at 45 CFR § 164.530(c). *See generally the* HIPAA Security Rule, 45 CFR § 164.306 et seq.

31. § 164.308(a)(4).

32. *See, e.g.,* Cybersecurity Requirements for Financial Services Companies, 23 C.R.R.-N.Y. § 500.

33. Mass. Gen. Laws. Ch. 93H, Sec. 3(a) (2018), 201 Mass. Code Regs. 201 CMR 17.00 (2018).

34. Or. Rev. Stat. § 646A.600 *et seq*; Nev. Rev. Stat. § 603A.010 *et seq.*

35. *See* William McGeveran, *The Duty of Data Security*, 103 Minn. L. Rev. 1135 (2019).

36. Privacy Act, 5 U.S.C. § 552a(e)(10).

37. The FCC relied upon Sections 222(a) and 201(b) of the FCC Act. Section 222 of the Act protects the confidentiality of what is called "customer proprietary network information"—or CPNI for short. The FCC viewed inadequate data security to be a failure to protect the confidentiality of CPNI. Section 201(b) of the Act prohibits any "unjust and unreasonable" practice. The FCC viewed inadequate data security to violate this part of the Act too. These security enforcement efforts were led by Travis LeBlanc, whom *The Atlantic* called the "FCC's $365 million man" because he issued $365 million in penalties and consumer refunds in only his first year at the FCC. Brendan Sasson, *The FCC's $365 Million Man*, The Atlantic, (Apr. 26, 2015), https://www.theatlantic.com/politics/archive/2015/04/the-fccs-365-million-man/456489/.

38. *See* N.M. Stat. § 57-12C-1 et seq.; 815 Ill. Comp. Stat. 530/1 *et seq.*; Ala. Code § 8-19F-1 et seq. Other states with reasonable-security-measure requirements include Arkansas, Delaware, Florida, Nevada, Indiana, Maryland, Connecticut, New Jersey, Oregon, Rhode Island, and Utah.

39. *See, e.g.,* FTC v. Sandra L. Rennert et al., CV-S-00-0861-JBR (July 12, 2000) (settling claims against online pharmacies requiring them to "establish and maintain reasonable procedures to protect the confidentiality, security and integrity of personal information collected from consumers").

40. Letter from James C. Miller III, Chairman, FTC, to Hon. John D. Dingell, Chairman, House Comm. On Energy & Commerce (Oct. 14, 1983).

41. FTC v. Eli Lilly, No. 012-3124.

42. Decision and Order, *TJX Companies, Inc.*, 72-3055, 2008 WL 903808 (Mar. 27, 2008).

43. 15 U.S.C. § 45(n).

44. *See* Daniel J. Solove & Woodrow Hartzog, *The FTC and the New Common Law of Privacy*, 114 Colum. L. Rev. 583 (2014); Kristina Rozan, *How Do Industry Standards for Data Security Match Up with the FTC's Implied "Reasonable" Standards—And What Might This Mean for Liability Avoidance?*, IAPP (Nov. 25, 2014).

45. Most of the FTC cases have settled, but in 2015, the Wyndham Hotel chain challenged the FTC's authority to regulate data security. One of Wyndham's arguments was that the FTC's reasonableness approach was too vague to put companies on fair notice as to what they must do for adequate security. This argument was rejected by the courts, mainly because reasonableness approaches are common in the law. A few years later, however, another challenge to FTC authority resulted in some pushback against a broad reasonableness approach. In a challenge brought by LabMD, the court concluded that an FTC consent order was unenforceable because "it does not enjoin a specific act or practice. Instead, it mandates a complete overhaul of [the defendant's] data-security program and says precious little about how this is to be accomplished." Though this holding doesn't affect the FTC's power to regulate data security, it raises questions about the FTC's ability to use "reasonable" standards in its consent orders.

46. GLBA Safeguards Rule, 16 C.F.R. § 314.

47. The SEC enforced under its *Procedures to Safeguard Customer Records and Information*, 17 CFR 248.30.

48. R. T. Jones Capital Equities Management, Inc., SEC File No. 3-16827 (Sept. 22, 2015), https://www.sec.gov/litigation/admin/2015/ia-4204.pdf. In 2018, the SEC issued its first fine to a company for failing to disclose its data breach— a fine of $35 million to Yahoo for its series of breaches involving the personal data of billions of individuals. Jacob Kastrenakes, *SEC Issues $35 Million Fine Over Yahoo Failing to Disclose Data Breach*, Verge, (Apr. 24, 2018), https://www.theverge.com/2018/4/24/17275994/yahoo-sec-fine-2014-data-breach-35-million; Olivia Beavers, *SEC Fines Yahoo $35 Million Over 2014 Email Breach*, Hill, (Apr. 24, 2018), https://thehill.com/policy/cybersecurity/384607-sec-fines-yahoo-35-million-over-2014-email-breach.

49. Daniel J. Solove, *The Most Alarming Fact of the HIPAA Audits*, Privacy + Security Blog, (Nov. 3, 2014), https://teachprivacy.com/alarming-fact-hipaa-audits/. Audited companies didn't do much better of Phase 2 of HHS's study. *See* Report on 2016–2017 HIPAA Audits, https://www.hhs.gov/sites/default/files/hipaa-audits-industry-report.pdf.

50. Simon Sharwood, *Adobe to hire security auditor to prevent repeat of password SNAFU*, The Register, (June 9, 2015), https://www.theregister.com/2015/06/09/adobe_to_hire_security_auditor_to_prevent_repeat_of_password_snafu/.

51. Juha Saarien, *Adobe fined $1.3m for 2013 mega data breach*, ITNews, (Nov. 16, 2016), https://
     www.itnews.com.au/news/adobe-fined-13m-for-2013-mega-data-breach-441498.

52. Robert Schoshinski, *Equifax Data Breach: Pick Free Credit Monitoring*, FTC, (July 31,
     2019), https://www.consumer.ftc.gov/blog/2019/07/equifax-data-breach-pick-free-
     credit-monitoring.

53. Sasha Romanosky & David A. Hoffman et al., *Empirical Analysis of Data Breach
     Litigation,* 11 Journal of Empirical Legal Studies 74 (2014).

54. Daniel J. Solove & Danielle Keats Citron, *Risk and Anxiety: A Theory of Data Breach
     Harms,* 96 Tex. L. Rev. 737 (2018).

55. Lujan v. Defenders of Wildlife, 504 U.S. 555, 560 (1992).

56. Friends of the Earth Inc. v. Laidlaw Envt'l Sys., Inc., 528 U.S. 167 (2000).

57. Daniel J. Solove & Danielle Keats Citron, *Risk and Anxiety: A Theory of Data Breach
     Harms,* 96 Tex. L. Rev. 737 (2018).

58. *In re* Barnes & Noble Pin Pad Litig., No. 12–cv–8617, 2013 WL 4759588, at *5
     (N.D. Ill. Sept. 3, 2013).

59. Daniel J. Solove & Danielle Keats Citron, *Risk and Anxiety: A Theory of Data Breach
     Harms,* 96 Tex. L. Rev. 737, 767–773 (2018).

60. *Id.*

61. *Id.* at 42.

62. *Id.*

63. Reilly v. Ceridian Corp., 664 F.3d 38 (3d Cir. 2011).

64. Clapper v. Amnesty International USA, 133 S. Ct. 1138 (2013).

65. In re Sci. Applications Int'l Corp. (SAIC) Backup Tape Data Theft Litig., 45
     F.Supp.3d 14 (D.D.C. 2014).

66. *Id.*

67. *Id.*

68. Remijas v. Neiman Marcus Group, 794 F.3d 688, 695 (7th Cir. 2015).

69. *Id.*

70. *See Spokeo, Inc. v. Robins*, 136 S. Ct. 1540, 1549-50 (2016).

71. In re Ashley Madison Customer DataSec. Breach Litig., MDL No. 2669 (E.D. Mo.
     Nov. 20, 2017).

72. In re Anthem, Inc. Data Breach Litig., No. 15-02617 (N.D. Cal. prelim. approval
     June 23, 2017).

CHAPTER 4

1. For the original in-depth reporting of this story, see Lorenzo Franceschi-Bicchierai,
    The SIM Hackers, (July 17, 2018), https://motherboard.vice.com/en_us/article/
    vbqax3/hackers-sim-swapping-steal-phone-numbers-instagram-bitcoin/.

2. *Id.*

3. *Id.*

4. Bruce Schneier, *Sim Hijacking*, Schneier on Security, (Jan 21, 2020), https://
    www.schneier.com/blog/archives/2020/01/sim_hijacking.html.

5. *See* Derek E. Bambauer, *Ghost in the Network*, 162 U. Pa. L. Rev. 1011, 1012 (2014)
    (arguing that that because successful attacks are unavoidable, cybersecurity should
    focus on mitigating breaches rather than preventing them); Deirdre K. Mulligan &

Fred B. Schneider, *Doctrine for Cybersecurity*, Daedalus, Fall 2011, at 70 ("[A]bsolute cybersecurity is worthwhile but unlikely ever to be achieved. For systems that incorporate humans as users and operators, we would need some way to prevent social engineering and intentional insider-malfeasance. Prevention, here, requires overcoming the frailty of humans, which is likely to involve more than technology.").

6. Guido Calabresi, *The Gift of the Evil Deity*, in *Ideals, Beliefs, and Attitudes in the Law* (1985).

7. *See* Ido Kilovaty, *Legally Cognizable Manipulation*, 34 Berkeley Tech. L. J. (2019).

8. For more information on the misguided attempt to force a particular kind of password complexity, see Thaw, *Stovepiping, supra*.

9. *See, e.g.*, C. Herley and P. C. v. Oorschot, *SoK: Science, Security and the Elusive Goal of Security as a Scientific Pursuit*, 2017 IEEE Symposium on Security and Privacy (SP), San Jose, CA, 2017, pp. 99–120, http://ieeexplore.ieee.org/stamp/stamp.jsp?tp=&arnumber=7958573&isnumber=7958557.

10. *See, e.g.*, Cybersecurity Requirements for Financial Services Companies, 23 CRR-NY § 500.2 ("Each covered entity shall maintain a cybersecurity program designed to protect the confidentiality, integrity and availability of the covered entity's information systems."); Jeff Kosseff, *Defining Cybersecurity Law*, 103 Iowa L. Rev. 985, 988–989 (2018).

11. Take your Free Cybersecurity Self-Assessment, Microsoft, https://www.microsoft.com/cyberassessment/en ("Our Certified Microsoft Cybersecurity Experts collaborated to create a personalized Cybersecurity Healthcheck covering more than 20 security points in 4 of our key Cybersecurity categories.") (last accessed December 15, 2020).

12. *Good Cyber Hygiene Habits to Help Stay Safe Online*, Norton, https://us.norton.com/internetsecurity-how-to-good-cyber-hygiene.html (last updated Jan 23,2021); *Cyber Hygiene: 10 Basic Tips For Risk Mitigation*, Sentinel One (Dec. 4, 2018), https://www.sentinelone.com/blog/practice-these-10-basic-cyber-hygiene-tips-for-risk-mitigation/.

13. "health, n.1." OED Online. Oxford University Press, December 15, 2020.

14. Public Health, Oxford English Dictionary (last accessed December 15, 2020).

15. Wendy E. Parmet, *Populations, Public Health, and the Law* 11 (2009).

16. Deirdre K. Mulligan & Fred B. Schneider, *Doctrine for Cybersecurity*, Daedalus, Fall 2011, at 70, 75–78; *see also* Elaine Sedenberg & Deirdre K. Mulligan, *Public Health as a Model for Cybersecurity Information Sharing*, 30 Berkeley Tech. L. J. 1687 (2015).

17. *Id.*

18. Adam Shostack, *We Need a Discipline of Cyber Public Health*, Adam Shostack & Friends, (Nov. 13, 2020), https://adam.shostack.org/blog/2020/11/we-need-a-discipline-of-cyber-public-health/ ("We have public health institutions at many scales: local, national and international. They are defining, gathering and distributing statistical measures. Those measures include most prominently deaths, but also hospital admissions, and for some diseases doctor diagnoses. We have guidance for the public. We have few equivalents in the world of cybersecurity. We do not know how many computers have malware on them. We do not know what the

equivalent of deaths are: is it systems lost to ransomware? What if they were backed up? We do not study means of infection or transmission rates.").

19. *Id.* ("Because we cannot quantify how computers are compromised, or the causes, it is hard to justify answers to the question of "what should developers know about security?" We know there are aspects of security developers must consider, but the time and attention of developers is a scarce resource. Educating and training them effectively is dependent on prioritization, and for that we need cyber public health and its measurement capabilities.").

20. Derek E. Bambauer, *Ghost in the Network*, 162 U. Pa. L. Rev. 1011, 1019 (2014).

21. Wolff, *supra* at 12.

22. Wolff, *supra* at 13.

23. Wolff, *supra* note at 15. According to Wolff, the finger almost always initially gets pointed at problems like "poor encryption, improperly configured firewalls, . . . out-of-date software . . . [or] careless users who made the mistake of clicking on a phishing email, or opening an attachment, or failing to change default passwords." *Id.*

24. Wolff argues that "the elements of these security incidents that are most susceptible to the kinds of intervention that cut off an entire stage of the attack and thereby halt the 'kill chain' are often related to public policy and legal intervention." Importantly, these interventions often, if not usually, are not proximate to the "breach" itself, legally defined. Wolff, *supra*, 208.

25. *See* Wolff, *supra* at 208.

CHAPTER 5

1. Ingrid Lunden, *Snapchat: Our Servers Were Not Breached In The 'Snappening'*, *Blame 3rd Party Apps*, TechCrunch, (Oct. 10, 2014), https://techcrunch.com/2014/10/10/snapchat-our-servers-were-not-breached-in-the-snappening-blame-3rd-party-apps/?guccounter=1.

2. Wolff, *supra* at 13 ("Much of what becomes clear in the aftermath of breaches is how complicated and ill-defined the liability regimes for these incidents are—and how that translates into everyone trying to shift blame onto each other and no one being willing to take on even some small piece of the overall defensive posture lest they should end up shouldering the entire responsibility alone.").

3. Gareth Colefield, *Security Man Krebs' Website DDoS Was Powered by Hacked Internet of Things Botnet*, Register, (Sept. 26, 2016), https://www.theregister.co.uk/2016/09/26/brian_krebs_site_ddos_was_powered_by_hacked_internet_of_things_botnet/.

4. Brian Krebs, *KrebsOnSecurity Hit with Records DDoS*, KrebsOnSecurity Blog, (Sept. 21, 2016, *available at* https://krebsonsecurity.com/2016/09/krebsonsecurity-hit-with-record-ddos/).

5. Darren Pauli, *Google Rushes in Where Akamai Fears to Tread, Shields Krebs After World's-worst DDoS*, Register, (Sept. 26, 2016), http://www.theregister.co.uk/2016/09/26/google_shields_krebs/.

6. Daniel Shugrue, *620 + Gbps Attack—Post Mortem*, Akamai Blog, (Oct. 5, 2016), *available at* https://blogs.akamai.com/2016/10/620-gbps-attack-post-mortem.html.

7. Brian Krebs, *Who Makes the IoT Things Under Attack?*, KrebsOnSecurity Blog, (Oct. 3, 2016), *available at* https://krebsonsecurity.com/2016/10/who-makes-the-iot-things-under-attack/.

8. *See* Krebs *supra*.

9. Nicky Woolf, *DDoS Attack that Disrupted Internet Was Largest of Its Kind In History*, Experts Say, *The Guardian*, (Oct. 26, 2016), https://www.theguardian.com/technology/2016/oct/26/ddos-attack-dyn-mirai-botnet.

10. Scott Hilton, *Dyn Analysis Summary Of Friday October 21 Attack*, Dyn Blog, (Oct. 26, 2016), *available at* http://dyn.com/blog/dyn-analysis-summary-of-friday-october-21-attack/.

11. Berkeley Lovelace Jr., *Friday's Third Cyberattack on Dyn 'Has Been Resolved,' Company Says*, CNBC, (Oct. 21, 2016), *available at* http://www.cnbc.com/2016/10/21/major-websites-across-east-coast-knocked-out-in-apparent-ddos-attack.html.

12. Woodrow Hartzog, *Privacy's Blueprint: The Battle to Control the Design of New Technologies* (2018); Woodrow Hartzog & Evan Selinger, *The Internet of Heirlooms and Disposable Things*, 17 N.C. J. of Law & Tech. 581 (2016).

13. Bruce Schneier, *Click Here to Kill Everybody: Security and Survival in a Hyper-Connected World* 39 (2018).

14. Schneier, *Click Here, supra* at 39.

15. *The Software Industry Delivers Appliances With Known Vulnerabilities*, Cyber Security Intelligence, (Oct. 13, 2020), https://www.cybersecurityintelligence.com/blog/the-software-industry-delivers-appliances-with-known-vulnerabilities-5252.html

16. *See, e.g.*, Rebecca Crootof, *The Internet of Torts: Expanding Civil Liability Standards to Address Corporate Remote Interference*, 69 Duke L.J. 583 (2019); Stacy-Ann Elvy, *Hybrid Transactions and the Internet of Things: Goods, Services, or Software?*, 74 Wash. & Lee L. RevV. 77, 82–86 (2017) (discussing the difficulty of applying the Uniform Commercial Code to Internet of Things because the hardware and software service are interdependent); Michael D. Scott, *Tort Liability for Vendors of Insecure Software: Has the Time Finally Come?*, 67 Md. L. Rev. 425 (2008); *see also* Derek Bambauer & Oliver Day, *The Hacker's Aegis*, 60 Emory L. J. 1051 (2011).

17. *Id.*

18. 18 U.S.C. § 1030(g). Michael D. Scott, *Tort Liability for Vendors of Insecure Software: Has the Time Finally Come?*, 67 Md. L. Rev. 425 (2008); *see also* Derek Bambauer & Oliver Day, *The Hacker's Aegis*, 60 Emory L. J. 1051 (2011).

19. *See, e.g.*, Rebecca Crootof, *The Internet of Torts: Expanding Civil Liability Standards to Address Corporate Remote Interference*, 69 Duke L.J. 583 (2019).

20. Bruce Schneier, *Click Here to Kill Everybody: Security and Survival in a Hyper-connected World* 36 (2018); *see also* Woodrow Hartzog, *Privacy's Blueprint: The Battle to Control the Design of New Technologies* (2018).

21. Schneier, *Click Here, supra*, at 37.

22. Sophie C. Boerman, Sanne Kruikemeier & Frederik J. Zuiderveen Borgesius, *Online Behavioral Advertising: A Literature Review and Research Agenda*, 46 J. of Advertising 363, 363 (2017).

23. *What is Malvertising*, Imperva, https://www.imperva.com/learn/application-security/malvertising/ (last accessed May 6, 2021).

24. Dilan Samarasinghe, *Malvertising*, Center for Internet Security, https:// www.cisecurity.org/blog/malvertising/.

25. Steven Melendez, *A New Wave Of Bad Ads Is Hijacking Even Top-Tier Websites*, *Fast Company*, (Jan. 18, 2018), https://www.fastcompany.com/40516897/ a-new-wave-of-bad-ads-is-hijacking-even-top-tier-websites.

26. Jonathan Crowl, *The Rise of Malicious Ads: How They Hurt Brands and What Marketers Can Do*, Content Standard, (Feb. 21, 2018), https://www.skyword.com/ contentstandard/marketing/the-rise-of-malicious-ads-how-they-hurt-brands- and-what-marketers-can-do/.

27. Catalin Cimpanu, *Hong Kong Malvertiser Blamed for Malicious Ads that Invaded Microsoft Apps*, ZD Net, (July 17, 2019), https://www.zdnet.com/article/hong- kong-malvertiser-blamed-for-malicious-ads-that-invaded-microsoft-apps/.

28. Dan Goodin, *Here's Why the Epidemic of Malicious Ads Grew So Much Worse Last Year*, Ars Technica, (Jan. 23, 2018), https://arstechnica.com/information- technology/2018/01/malvertising-factory-with-28-fake-agencies-delivered-1- billion-ads-in-2017/.

29. Taylor Armerding, *Mobile Apps: Still Insecure By Default*, Forbes, (June 27, 2019), https://www.forbes.com/sites/taylorarmerding/2019/06/27/mobile-apps-still- insecure-by-default/#72379b6a3b24.

30. Alison DeNisco Rayome, *How 85% of Mobile Apps Violate Security Standards*, Tech Republic, (Oct. 4, 2018), https://www.techrepublic.com/article/how-85-of-mobile- apps-violate-security-standards/.

31. *Opperman v. Path*, 87 F.Supp.3d 1018 (N.D. Cal. May 14, 2014); *Opperman v. Path*, Order Denying Motion for Class Certification (N.D. Cal, July 25, 2017), https:// www.courthousenews.com/wp-content/uploads/2017/07/AppleNoCert.pdf.

32. App stores represent a significant bottleneck to disrupt the breach kill chain. Jonathan Zittrain identified one of the virtues of the "walled garden" or "non- generative" approach represented by these app stores to be security (even though he identified a significant number of drawbacks from such a constrained envi- ronment). Jonathan Zittrain, *The Future of the Internet and How to Stop It* (2008) ("[W]e have grown weary not with the unexpected cool stuff that the generative PC had produced, but instead with the unexpected very uncool stuff that came along with it. Viruses, spam, identity theft, crashes: all of these were the consequences of a certain freedom built into the generative PC. As these problems grow worse, for many the promise of security is enough reason to give up that freedom.").

33. *Oberdorf v. Amazon*, 930 F.3d 136 (3rd. Cir. 2019).

34. 47 U.S.C. § 230. Although Section 230 has some relevance when platforms are sought to be treated as publishers of third party content, the conduct we specifi- cally target has roots in products liability as well as distributor liability. See *Lemon v. Snap*, D.C. No. 2:19-cv-04504-MWF-KS, Opinion, http://cdn.ca9.uscourts.gov/ datastore/opinions/2021/05/04/20-55295.pdf; *MacPherson v. Buick Motor Co*. 217 N.Y. 382, 111 N.E. 1050 (1916).

35. *See, e.g.,* Apple Platform Security, App Security Overview, https://support.apple.com/ guide/security/app-security-overview-sec35dd877d0/web.

36. The facts are from the allegations in the FTC's complaint in *FTC v. Equifax*, https://www.ftc.gov/system/files/documents/cases/172_3203_equifax_complaint_ 7-22-19.pdf.

37. Quoted in *id.*

38. Josh Lauer, *Creditworthy: A History of Consumer Surveillance and Financial Identity in America* (2017).

39. Daniel J. Solove, *The Digital Person: Technology and Privacy in the Information Age* 67 (2004).

40. The Fair Credit Reporting Act, Pub. L. No. 90-32, 15 U.S.C. §§ 1681 *et seq.*

41. Sarver v. Experian Information Solutions, 390 F.3d 969 (7th Cir. 2004). Fair Credit Reporting Act § 1681e(b).

42. FCRA, § 1681h(e).

43. FCRA, §1681(a).

44. Brian Krebs, *Experian Lapse Allowed ID Theft Service Access to 200 Million Consumer Records*, KrebsOnSecurity, (March 10, 2014), https://krebsonsecurity.com/2014/ 03/experian-lapse-allowed-id-theft-service-to-access-200-million-consumer-records/.

45. Dorthy Atkins, *Experian Hid Major Data Breach*, Blood, Hurst, & O'Reardon, (Dec. 10, 2019), https://bholaw.com/experian-hid-major-data-breach/.

46. Hal Abelson, Ross Anderson, Steven Michael Bellovin, Josh Benaloh, Matt Blaze, Whitfield Diffie, John Gilmore, Peter G. Neumann, Ronald L. Rivest, Jeffrey L. Schiller & Bruce Schneier, *The Risks of Key Recovery, Key Escrow, and Trusted Third-Party Encryption* (1997), https://academiccommons.columbia.edu/doi/ 10.7916/D8GM8F2W.

47. Rowena Mason, *UK Spy Agencies Need More Powers, Says Cameron, Guardian*, (Jan. 12, 2015), http://www.theguardian.com/uk-news/2015/jan/12/ uk-spy-agencies-need-more-powers-says-cameron-paris-attacks.

48. Will Oremus, *Obama Wants Tech Companies to Install Backdoors for Government Spying*, Slate, (Jan. 19, 2015), https://slate.com/technology/2015/01/obama-wants-backdoors-in-encrypted-messaging-to-allow-government-spying.html.

49. Spencer Ackerman, *FBI Chief Wants 'Backdoor Access' to Encrypted Communications to Fight Isis*, Guardian, (July 8, 2015), http://www.theguardian.com/technology/ 2015/jul/08/fbi-chief-backdoor-access-encryption-isis.

50. Daniel J. Solove, *Security Experts Critique Government Access to Encrypted Data*, TeachPrivacy, (July 14, 2015), https://teachprivacy.com/security-experts-critique-government-access-encrypted-data/.

51. Samuel Gibbs, *Apple, Google and Microsoft: Weakening Encryption Lets the Bad Guys In*, Guardian, (Nov. 23, 2015), http://www.theguardian.com/technology/ 2015/nov/23/apple-google-microsoft-weakening-encryption-back-doors.

52. The All Writs Act, 28 U.S.C. § 1651, provides: "(a) The Supreme Court and all courts established by Act of Congress may issue all writs necessary or appropriate in aid of their respective jurisdictions and agreeable to the usages and principles of law. (b) An alternative writ or rule nisi may be issued by a justice or judge of a court which has jurisdiction."

53. Apple, *A Message to Our Consumers* (Feb. 16, 2016), https://www.apple.com/customer-letter/.

54. *See* Hal Abelson, Ross Anderson, Steve Bellovin, Josh Benaloh, Matt Blaze, Whitfield Diffie, John Gilmore, Matthew Green, Susan Landau, Peter Neumann, Ron Rivest, Jeff Schiller, Bruce Schneier, Michael Specter, and Danny Weitzner, *Keys Under Doormats: Mandating insecurity by requiring government access to all data and communications*, CSAIL Technical Reports, (July 6, 2015), http://dspace.mit.edu/handle/1721.1/97690.

55. *Ransomware Attack 'Like Having a Tomahawk Missile Stolen', Says Microsoft Boss*, Guardian, (May 14, 2017), https://www.theguardian.com/technology/2017/may/15/ransomware-attack-like-having-a-tomahawk-missile-stolen-says-microsoft-boss.

56. Brad Smith, *The Need For Urgent Collective Action to Keep People Safe Online: Lessons From Last Week's Cyberattack*, (May 14, 2017), https://blogs.microsoft.com/on-the-issues/2017/05/14/need-urgent-collective-action-keep-people-safe-online-lessons-last-weeks-cyberattack/.

57. Paul Wagenseil, Evernote Breaks Own Security Rule in Data-Breach Email, TechNewsDaily, (Mar. 4, 2013), http://www.mnn.com/green-tech/computers/stories/evernote-breaks-own-security-rule-in-data-breach-email.

58. *See* Ryan Calo, *Robotics and the Lessons of Cyberlaw*, 103 Calif. L. Rev. 513 (2015); Woodrow Hartzog & Fred Stutzman, *The Case for Online Obscurity*, 101 Calif. L. Rev. 1 (2013); Jessica Silbey & Woodrow Hartzog, *The Upside of Deep Fakes*, 78 Md. L. Rev. 960 (2019) (arguing that deep fakes are symptoms of much deeper and long-existing problems).

59. *See* Rebecca Crootof, *The Internet of Torts: Expanding Civil Liability Standards to Address Corporate Remote Interference*, 69 Duke L.J. 583 (2019).

60. Ms. Smith, *Hacking Pacemakers, Insulin Pumps and Patients' Vital Signs in Real Time*, CSO, (Aug. 12, 2018), https://www.csoonline.com/article/3296633/hacking-pacemakers-insulin-pumps-and-patients-vital-signs-in-real-time.html.

61. *See* Andrea Matwyshyn, *The Internet of Bodies*, 61 William & Mary L. Rev. (2019).

62. *Id.* at 88.

63. *See* Andrew Selbst, *Negligence and AI's Human Users*, 100 B.U. L. Rev. 1315 (2020).

64. Given the difficulties of proving causation and harm thresholds, strict liability in combination with a functional insurance scheme could approximate a risk-based approach by forcing a redistribution of the costs of a breach as a way for organizations to minimize and calibrate risk. *See, e.g.,* Danielle Keats Citron, *Reservoirs of Danger: The Evolution of Public and Private Law at the Dawn of the Information Age*, 80 S. Cal. L. Rev. 241, 242 (2007); Mark A. Geistfeld, *Protecting Confidential Information Entrusted to Others in Business Transactions: Data Breaches, Identity Theft, and Tort Liability*, 66 DePaul L. Rev. 385, 387–88 (2017)("[t]he rule *388 of strict liability supplies the necessary means for customers to adequately enforce the tort duty obligating businesses to adopt reasonable precautions for protecting entrusted confidential information."); Justin (Gus) Hurwitz, *Cyberensuring Security*, 49 Conn. L. Rev. 1495, 1500 (2017) ("[I]mposing strict liability on firms hosting consumer data would achieve the key purposes of cyber insurance that have so far remained elusive, and it would do so in a way that addresses some of the

key challenges generally facing the use of strict liability to address cybersecurity is-sues.") Bryan Choi has suggested and professionalizing software development and developing a concept of "crashworthy code" to help courts ascertain when tech-nology design decisions and practices are unreasonable or uncustomary. Bryan H. Choi, *Crashworthy Code*, 94 Wash. L. Rev. 39 (2019); Bryan H. Choi, *Software as a Profession*, 33 Harv. J. L. & Tech. 557 (2020).

65. Wolff, *supra*, at 208. Wolff argues that a corollary to this wisdom is that "there is no single bulletproof defender who can, unilaterally, prevent all compromises and detect every breach." Id.

66. Josephine Wolff, *You'll see this message when it is too late: The Legal and Economic Aftermath of Cybersecurity Breaches* (2018).

67. *Id.*

68. Justin (Gus) Hurwitz, *Cyberensuring Security*, 49 Conn. L. Rev. 1495, 1508 (2017). ("This multiplicity of actors makes establishing cybersecurity responsibility dif-ficult. Each of the actors has some legitimate argument that at least some of the others bear responsibility for almost any cyber-incident. . . . The response to any security incident will invariably be to assign blame to any number of other parties.")

69. *Id.* at 1174. ("[W]e can expect insurers will do even more to drive adherence to a predefined duty of data security. Many experts agree that making these insurance policies more affordable—and therefore more widespread—will require better in-formation for insurers to use in making more efficient risk assessments, and more uniform recommendations for what minimum security measures insurers should require of policyholders.")

CHAPTER 6

1. David Lazarus, *An Advocate for Readers, A Name You Can Trust*, L.A. Times, (Aug. 12, 2007), https://www.latimes.com/archives/la-xpm-2007-aug-12-fi-lazarus12-story.html.

2. *Id.*

3. David Lazarus, *The Guy Who Stole My Identity 15 Years Ago Just Resurfaced in My Life*, L.A. Times, (Aug. 8, 2017), https://www.latimes.com/business/lazarus/la-fi-lazarus-identity-theft-20170808-story.html.

4. *Id.*

5. Sandra Parsons, An Identity Theft Victim Speaks, *MoneyTips*, https://www.moneytips.com/an-identity-theft-victim-speaks.

6. Bob Sullivan, *Your Evil Twin: Behind the Identity Theft Epidemic* (2003); Daniel J. Solove, *Identity Theft, Privacy, and the Architecture of Vulnerability*, 54 Hastings L.J. 1227 (2003).

7. Jennifer Lee, *Fighting Back When Someone Steals Your Name*, New York Times, (Apr. 8, 2001), at C8.

8. Steve Weisman, *When Identity Thieves Commit Crimes in Your Name*, USA Today, (May 21, 2016), https://www.usatoday.com/story/money/columnist/2016/05/21/when-identity-thieves-commit-crimes-your-name/84383670/.

9. *Id.*

10. Wayne Carter, *Identity Theft Victims May Have a Criminal Record and Not Know It*, NBC-Dallas Fort Worth Channel 5, (Oct. 16, 2017), https://www.nbcdfw.com/news/local/identity-theft-victims-may-have-a-criminal-record-and-not-know-it/42957/.

11. Identity Theft Resource Center, *ID Theft Leads to Multiple Arrests of an Innocent Man*, (July 16, 2014), https://www.idtheftcenter.org/id-theft-leads-to-multiple-arrests-of-an-innocent-man/.

12. U.S. Department of Health and Human Services, *Medical Identity Theft*, https://oig.hhs.gov/fraud/medical-id-theft/.

13. Laura Shin, *Medical Identity Theft: How The Health Care Industry Is Failing Us*, (Aug. 31, 2014), http://fortune.com/2014/08/31/medical-identity-theft-how-the-health-care-industry-is-failing-us/.

14. Lisa Fletcher & Betsy Kulman, *How a Stolen ID Made One Woman the Mother of a Meth-Addicted Baby*, Al Jazeera, (Jan. 6, 2016), http://america.aljazeera.com/watch/shows/america-tonight/articles/2016/1/6/how-a-stolen-id-made-one-woman-the-mother-of-a-meth-addicted-baby.html.

15. Michael Ollove, *The Rise Of Medical Identity Theft In Healthcare*, Stateline, (Feb. 7, 2014), http://kaiserhealthnews.org/news/rise-of-indentity-theft/.

16. Pam Dixon, *Medical Identity Theft: The Information Crime that Can Kill You*, World Privacy Forum, (May 3, 2006). http://www.worldprivacyforum.org/2006/05/report-medical-identity-theft-the-information-crime-that-can-kill-you/.

17. HHS further states: "Medical identity theft can disrupt your life, damage your credit rating, and waste taxpayer dollars. The damage can be life-threatening to you if wrong information ends up in your personal medical records." HHS, *Medical Identity Theft*, supra.

18. Shawn Radcliffe, *Patients Beware: Hackers Are Targeting Your Medical Information*, Healthline, (Aug. 1, 2019), http://www.healthline.com/health-news/hackers-are-targeting-your-medical-information-010715#4.

19. Natasha Kumar, *Teens Victims of ECP Fraud*, The Times Hub (Jan. 21, 2020), https://thetimeshub.in/teens-victims-of-ecp-fraud/3703/.

20. Kelli B. Grant, *Identity Theft Isn't Just an Adult Problem. Kids are Victims, Too*, CNBC, (Apr. 24, 2018), https://www.cnbc.com/2018/04/24/child-identity-theft-is-a-growing-and-expensive-problem.html.

21. Dan Munro, *New Study Says Over 2 Million Americans Are Victims Of Medical Identity Theft*, Forbes, (Feb. 23, 2015), http://www.forbes.com/sites/danmunro/2015/02/23/new-study-says-over-2-million-americans-are-victims-of-medical-identity-theft/.

22. Identity Theft Resource Center, *Identity Theft: The Aftermath 2017*, https://www.idtheftcenter.org/images/page-docs/Aftermath_2017.pdf.

23. *Id.*

24. HIPAA Privacy Rule, 45 CFR §164.526 (a)(1).

25. Anna Bahney, *Identity Theft Nightmares: 'I've Spent My Lifetime Building Up My Credit'*, CNN Money, (Sept. 29, 2017), https://money.cnn.com/2017/09/29/pf/identity-theft/index.html.

26. Identity Theft Resource Center, *Identity Theft: The Aftermath 2017*, https://www.idtheftcenter.org/images/page-docs/Aftermath_2017.pdf.

27. *Id.*

28. *Id.*

29. Identity Theft and Identity Theft and Assumption Deterrence Act, 18 U.S.C. § 1028.

30. U.S. General Accounting Office, Identity Theft: Greater Awareness and Use of Existing Data Are Needed, H.R. Rep. No. GAO-02-766, at 6 (2002).

31. National Conference of State Legislatures, *Identity Theft*, https://www.ncsl.org/research/financial-services-and-commerce/identity-theft-state-statutes.aspx.

32. David Lazarus, *An Advocate for Readers, A Name You Can Trust*, L.A. Times, (Aug. 12, 2007), https://www.latimes.com/archives/la-xpm-2007-aug-12-fi-lazarus12-story.html.

33. John Hall, *SplashData's Top 100 Worst Passwords of 2018*, SplashData, (Dec. 13, 2018), https://www.teamsid.com/splashdatas-top-100-worst-passwords-of-2018/. Two years later, the most popular passwords didn't change much. *See Top 200 most common passwords of the year 2020*, NordPass, https://nordpass.com/most-common-passwords-list/ (last accessed Mar. 17, 2021).

34. Farai Chideya, *The Way We Use Social Security Numbers Is Absurd*, FiveThirtyEight, (Oct. 15, 2015), https://fivethirtyeight.com/features/the-way-we-use-social-security-numbers-is-absurd/.

35. Haje Jan Kamps, *Fingerprints and SSN Numbers are Usernames, Not Passwords*, https://medium.com/@Haje/ssn-is-a-username-not-a-password-aa9b9d9f48ad.

36. Daniel J. Solove, *The Digital Person: Technology and Privacy for the Digital Age* (2004).

37. See, e.g., M. Yıldırım & I Mackie, *Encouraging users to improve password security and memorability*. Int. J. Inf. Secur. 18, 741–759 (2019). https://doi.org/10.1007/s10207-019-00429-y; David Thaw, *Cybersecurity Stovepiping*, 96 Neb. L. Rev. 339 (2017).

38. Alessandro Acquisti & Ralph Gross, *Predicating Social Security Numbers From Public Data*, (July 7, 2009), https://www.pnas.org/content/106/27/10975.full.

39. Tony Bradley, *5 Things All Anthem Customers Should do After the Massive Data Breach*, PCWorld, http://www.pcworld.com/article/2880611/5-things-all-anthem-customers-should-do-after-the-massive-data-breach.html.

40. Equifax ID Patrol, https://www.equifax.com/personal/products/identity-theft-protection/.

41. Fair Credit Reporting Act, 15 U.S. Code § 1681e(b).

42. Christopher Hoofnagle, *Internalizing Identity Theft*, 13 UCLA J. of L. & Tech. 1 (2009).

43. *Huggins v. Citibank*, 585 S.E.2d 275 (S.C. 2003).

44. *Wolfe v. MBNA America Bank*, 485 F. Supp. 2d 874 (W.D. Tenn. 2007).

45. Daniel J. Solove & Woodrow Hartzog, *The FTC and the New Common Law of Privacy*, 114 Colum. L. Rev. 583 (2014).

CHAPTER 7

1. Sean Gallagher, *Report: Hack of Government Employee Records Discovered by Product Demo*, Ars Technica, (June 11 2015), https://arstechnica.com/security/2015/06/report-hack-of-government-employee-records-discovered-by-product-demo/.

2. United States. Cong. House. Committee on Oversight and Gov. Reform. Letter to the Hon. Devin Nunes, Chairman, and the Hon. Adam Schiff, Ranking Member, Permanent Select Committee on Intelligence—Evidence Obtained By Committee Debunks Claim That CyTech Was First to Discover OPM Data Breach, (May 26 2016). 114th Cong. (letter from Elijah E. Cummings, Ranking Member, U.S. Congress), https://democrats-oversight.house.gov/sites/democrats.oversight.house.gov/files/documents/2016-05-26.EEC%20to%20HPSCI%20Re.CyTech.pdf.

3. *Id.*

4. *Id.*

5. *Id.*

6. Jose Pagliery, *OPM Hack's Unprecedented Haul: 1.1 Million Fingerprints*, CNN Tech Blog, (July 10, 2015), http://money.cnn.com/2015/07/10/technology/opm-hack-fingerprints/.

7. *Id.*

8. U.S. Office of Personnel Management, Office of the Inspector General, Office of Audits, *Final Audit Report: Federal Information Security Management Act Audit FY 2014*, U.S. Office of Personnel Management, (Nov. 12, 2014), https://www.opm.gov/our-inspector-general/reports/2014/federal-information-security-management-act-audit-fy-2014-4a-ci-00-14-016.pdf.

9. David Auerbach, *The OPM Breach Is a Catastrophe*, Slate, (June 16, 2015), http://www.slate.com/articles/technology/future_tense/2015/06/opm_hack_it_s_a_catastrophe_here_s_how_the_government_can_stop_the_next.html.

10. Nuala O'Connor, *Why the OPM Breach Is Unlike Any Other*, CDT, (June 22, 2015), https://cdt.org/insights/why-the-opm-data-breach-is-unlike-any-other/.

11. For example, Derek Bambauer argues that "disaggregation" should be a key design principle for data security. Disaggregation "splits information into multiple, separated data stores. The loss of any single store, or perhaps several of them, does not confer all of an organization's information upon an attacker." Derek E. Bambauer, *Ghost in the Network*, 162 U. Pa. L. Rev. 1011, 1052 (2014).

12. Kim Zetter & Andy Greenberg, *Why the OPM Breach is Such a Security and Privacy Debacle*, Wired, (June 11, 2015), *available at* https://www.wired.com/2015/06/opm-breach-security-privacy-debacle/.

13. Ellen Nakashima & Lisa Rein, *Chinese Hackers Go After U.S. Workers' Personal Data*, Wash. Post, (July 10, 2014), http://wapo.st/1kJBCuc?tid=ss_tw.

14. *Id.*

15. *See generally* Jeff Kosseff, *Defining Cybersecurity Law*, 103 Iowa L. Rev. 985 (2018); Andrea M. Matwyshyn, *CYBER!*, 2017 BYU L. Rev. 1109 (2018); Andrea M. Matwyshyn, *Hacking Speech: Informational Speech and the First Amendment*, 107 Nw. U. L. Rev. 795, 845 n.99 (2013); David Thaw, *The Efficacy of Cybersecurity Regulation*, 30 Ga. St. U. L. Rev. 287, 291–92 (2014).

16. David Thaw, *Data Breach (Regulatory) Effects*, 2015 Cardozo L. Rev. De Novo 151, 154–55 (2015).

17. Thaw also noted that there are different cybersecurity risk profiles for at least for different kinds of entities ranging from military and critical infrastructure to non-sensitive private entities, not all of which implicate privacy concerns. *Id.* ("Defining

the unit of analysis that a cybersecurity law or regulation seeks to address is critical. Approaches necessary for military environments may be ill-suited—or possibly even damaging—to ordinary consumer-based commercial environments. This Essay proposes a four-part classification for entities: (1) Military, intelligence, and other high-reliability or sensitive government operations; (2) Privately operated "critical infrastructure," utilities, communications networks, and other infrastructure operated by private entities but requiring high-reliability operations or utilizing meaningful sensitive information; (3) Public and other government operations, which are not otherwise sensitive or high-reliability; (4) Non-critical/non-sensitive private entities, private entities that neither require high-reliability operations nor utilize meaningful amounts of sensitive information.").

18. Derek E. Bambauer, *Privacy Versus Security*, 103 J. Crim. L. & Criminology 667, 668–69 (2013). For additional thoughts on the difference between privacy and cybersecurity, see Justin (Gus) Hurwitz, *Cyberensuring Security*, 49 Conn. L. Rev. 1495, 1547 (2017) ("Critically, the task of 'security' is fundamentally different from that of 'privacy.' Security is about prohibiting unauthorized parties from accessing or using data or systems; privacy is about prohibiting authorized parties from exceeding the use of data to which they have been given access."); Jeff Kosseff, *Hacking Cybersecurity Law*, 2020 U. Ill. L. Rev. 811, 814 (2020) ("Cybersecurity laws often are conflated with privacy laws, as there is significant overlap. Cybersecurity laws, however, must address more than just the confidentiality of personal information, and also seek to protect from unauthorized alteration of data and attacks such as ransomware that cause data or systems to become unavailable. Cybersecurity laws also must focus not just on financial harms, but any threats to national security or individual privacy or safety."); Lauren Henry Scholz, *Information Privacy and Data Security*, 2015 Cardozo L. Rev. De Novo 107, 109 (2015) ("an institution's interest in its own data security is not necessarily consonant with the information privacy interests of the individuals whose personal information is housed."); Andrea M. Matwyshyn, *Cyber!*, 2017 B.Y.U. L. Rev. 1109, 1141 (2017) ("Unlike security, which focuses on properties of systems, privacy analysis uses a particular person—not a technical system—as the focal point of analysis. Privacy relates to the negotiated rights and privileges of a (usually) human person in her own information and her choice to engage in its selective transmission under certain terms.").

19. Jeff Kosseff, *Defining Cybersecurity Law*, 103 Iowa L. Rev. 985, 988–89 (2018).

20. *See* Lauren Henry Scholz, *Information Privacy and Data Security*, 2015 Cardozo L. Rev. De Novo 107, 115 (2015) ("[I]nformation privacy and data security can be siloed into very different parts of professional practice.").

21. Ari Waldman, *Industry Unbound* (2021); Ari Ezra Waldman, *Designing Without Privacy*, 55 Hous. L. Rev. 659, 664 (2018); *see also* Kenneth A. Bamberger & Deirdre K. Mulligan, *Privacy on the Ground* (2015).

22. *Id.*

23. Ari Ezra Waldman, *Designing Without Privacy*, 55 Hous. L. Rev. 659, 664 (2018).

24. *Id.*

25. *Id.*

26. *See* Daniel J. Solove, *Understanding Privacy* (2008); Neil Richards, Why Privacy Matters (2021); Lisa Austin, *Enough About Me: Why Privacy is About Power, not Consent (or Harm)*, in *A World Without Privacy?*, (Cambridge Press, Austin Sarat, ed. 2015); Julie E. Cohen, *What Privacy is For*, 126 Harv. L. Rev. 1904 (2013); Woodrow Hartzog & Neil Richards, *Privacy's Constitutional Moment and the Limits of Data Privacy*, 61 B.C. L. Rev. 1687 (2020).

27. *See* Neil Richards, *Four Privacy Myths, A World Without Privacy?*, (Cambridge Press, Austin Sarat, ed. 2015); Woodrow Hartzog, *The Inadequate, Invaluable Fair Information Practices*, 76 Md. L. Rev. 952, 961 (2017).

28. Robert Gellman, *Fair Information Practices: A Basic History*, https://bobgellman.com/rg-docs/rg-FIPshistory.pdf.

29. U.S. Department of Health, Education, and Welfare, *Records, Computers and the Rights of Citizens* (1973).

30. U.S. Department of Health, Education, and Welfare, *Records, Computers and the Rights of Citizens* (1973).

31. *Id.* (citing http://www.oecd.org/internet/ieconomy/oecdguidelinesontheprotection ofprivacy andtransborderflowsofpersonaldata.htm).

32. *See* Woodrow Hartzog, *The Inadequate, Invaluable Fair Information Practices*, 76 Md. L. Rev. 952, 958 (2017); Graham Greenleaf, *Asian Data Privacy Laws* (2014).

33. Michael S. Schmidt, *Cardinals Investigated for Hacking Into Astros' Database*, New York Times, (June 16, 2015), https://www.nytimes.com/2015/06/17/sports/baseball/st-louis-cardinals-hack-astros-fbi.html?smid=pl-share&_r=0.

34. Lindsey Adler, *Feds: Cardinals Hacker Probably Leaked To Deadspin As Revenge For Astros' Sports Illustrated Cover*, Deadspin, (Jan. 30, 2017), http://deadspin.com/feds-cardinals-hacker-probably-leaked-to-deadspin-as-r-1791778599.

35. Derrick Goold, *Cardinals' Pain is Astros' Gain as MLB Levels Penalties for Hacking*, St. Louis Post-Dispatch, (Jan 31, 2017), http://www.stltoday.com/sports/baseball/professional/mlb-hammers-cardinals-first-two-draft-picks-million-go-to/article_bfe37c71-a48c-57be-98ed-1c5dec2eee93.html.

36. *United States v. Christopher Correa*, Sentencing Memo of the United States, https://www.scribd.com/document/337801597/45-2#.

37. Chris Cwik, *Former Cards Employee Pleads Guilty in Hacking Scandal*, Yahoo News, (Jan. 8, 2016), http://sports.yahoo.com/blogs/mlb-big-league-stew/report--former-cardinals-employee-to-plead-guilty-in-hacking-scandal-171723289.html.

38. Computer Fraud and Abuse Act, 18 U.S.C. § 1030. For more background about the Act, see Orin S. Kerr, *Cybercrime's Scope: Interpreting "Access" and "Authorization" in Computer Misuse Statutes*, 78 N.Y.U. L. Rev. 1596 (2003).

39. Carole Cadwalladr & Emma Graham-Harrison, *Revealed: 50 million Facebook Profiles Harvested for Cambridge Analytica in Major Data Breach*, Guardian, (Mar. 17, 2018), https://www.theguardian.com/news/2018/mar/17/cambridge-analytica-facebook-influence-us-election.

40. Ian Bogost, *My Cow Game Extracted Your Facebook Data*, Atlantic, (Mar. 22, 2018), https://www.theatlantic.com/technology/archive/2018/03/my-cow-game-extracted-your-facebook-data/556214/ ("It's not just that abusing the Facebook platform for deliberately nefarious ends was easy to do (it was). But worse, in those

days, it was hard to avoid extracting private data, for years even, without even trying.").

41. Carole Cadwalladr & Emma Graham-Harrison, *Revealed: 50 Million Facebook Profiles Harvested for Cambridge Analytica in Major Data Breach*, Guardian, (Mar. 17, 2018), https://www.theguardian.com/news/2018/mar/17/cambridge-analytica-facebook-influence-us-election.

42. Google Books Ngram viewer shows almost no regular use of the term data breach until the early 2000s. *See* https://books.google.com/ngrams/graph?content=data+breach&year_start=1800&year_end=2008&corpus=15&smoothing=3&share=&direct_url=t1%3B%2Cdata%20breach%3B%2Cc0; 44 U.S.C. § 3542; US Dept of Commerce, *Standards for Security Categorization of Federal Information and Information Systems*, http://csrc.nist.gov/publications/fips/fips199/FIPS-PUB-199-final.pdf.

43. *Id.*

44. Alex Sundby, *Facebook's Fight Against the Phrase "Data Breach"*, CBS News, (Mar. 19, 2018), https://www.cbsnews.com/news/facebook-cambridge-analytica-was-it-a-data-breach/.

45. *Id.*

46. Paul Grewal, *Suspending Cambridge Analytica and SCL Group From Facebook*, Facebook Newsroom, (Mar. 16, 2018), https://about.fb.com/news/2018/03/suspending-cambridge-analytica/.

47. Ian Bogost, *My Cow Game Extracted Your Facebook Data, Atlantic,* (March 22, 2018), https://www.theatlantic.com/technology/archive/2018/03/my-cow-game-extracted-your-facebook-data/556214/.

48. *Id.* ("The part of the Facebook website where apps appear, under the blue top navigation (as seen above), introduces further confusion. To the average web user, especially a decade ago, it looked like the game or app was just a part of Facebook itself. The page is seamless, with no boundary between the site's navigational chrome and the third-party app. If you look at the browser address bar while using a Facebook app on the website, the URL begins with "apps.facebook.com," further cementing the impression that the user was safely ensconced in the comforting, blue cradle of Facebook's care.").

49. *Id.*

50. *Id.* ("For years, these transmissions were even conducted unencrypted, until Facebook required apps to communicate with its service over a secure connection.").

51. Ian Bogost, *supra.*

52. In the Matter of Facebook, Inc., No. C-4365 (July 24, 2019).

53. *See* In the Matter of Facebook, Inc., No. C-4365 (July 24, 2019); *see also* FTC Press Release, "FTC Imposes $5 Billion Penalty and Sweeping New Privacy Restrictions on Facebook," (July 24, 2019), https://www.ftc.gov/news-events/press-releases/2019/07/ftc-imposes-5-billion-penalty-sweeping-new-privacy-restrictions.

54. *Id.*

55. *See* Tim Wu, *The Attention Merchants* (2016).

56. Zack Whittaker, *Oracle's BlueKai Tracks You Across the Web. That Data Spilled Online*, TechCrunch, (June 19, 2020), https://techcrunch.com/2020/06/19/oracle-bluekai-web-tracking/.

57. *Id.*

58. Danielle Keats Citron, *Spying Inc.*, 72 Wash. & Lee L. Rev. 1243, 1249–50 (2015) ("Under federal law, it is a crime to manufacture, sell, or advertise a device knowing or having reason to know that the design of the device renders it "primarily useful" for the covert interception of electronic, wire, or oral communications. Twenty-five states and the District of Columbia have similar criminal statutes.").

59. *Id.*

60. See Kim Zetter, *Everything We Know About How the FBI Hacks People*, Wired, (May 15, 2016), https://www.wired.com/2016/05/history-fbis-hacking/ (detailing how the FBI deployed a keystroke logger called "Magic Lantern" to access encrypted data by capturing encryption keys).

61. Alex Hern, *Fitness Tracking App Strava Gives Away Location of Secret US Army Bases*, Guardian, (Jan. 28, 2018), https://www.theguardian.com/world/2018/jan/28/fitness-tracking-app-gives-away-location-of-secret-us-army-bases.

62. *Id.*

63. *See* Woodrow Hartzog, *Privacy's Blueprint: The Battle to Control the Design of New Technologies* (2018); James Grimmelmann, *Privacy as Product Safety*, 19 Widener L. J. 793 (2010); Danielle Keats Citron, *Spying Inc.*, 72 Wash. & Lee L. Rev. 1243 (2015).

64. *See Data Protection Commission Fine on Tulsa Child and Family Agency Confirmed in Court*, (Nov. 6, 2020), https://www.databreaches.net/category/breach-types/exposure/.

65. Joseph Cox, *Twitter-Owned SDK Leaking Location Data of Millions of Users*, DataBreaches.net, (Oct. 21, 2020), https://www.databreaches.net/twitter-owned-sdk-leaking-location-data-of-millions-of-users/.

66. *Misconfigured Cloud Storage Bucket Exposed Pfizer Drug Safety-Related Reports-Researchers*, DataBreaches.net, (Oct. 20, 2020), https://www.databreaches.net/misconfigured-cloud-storage-bucket-exposed-pfizer-drug-safety-related-reports-researchers/.

67. Zack Whittaker, *A Prison Video Visitation Service Exposed Private Calls Between Inmates and Their Attorneys*, DataBreaches.net, (Oct. 11, 2020), https://www.databreaches.net/a-prison-video-visitation-service-exposed-private-calls-between-inmates-and-their-attorneys/.

68. Zack Whittaker & Manish Singh, *Dr Lal PathLabs, One of India's Largest Blood Test Labs, Exposed Patient Data*, DataBreaches.net, (Oct. 8, 2020), https://www.databreaches.net/dr-lal-pathlabs-one-of-indias-largest-blood-test-labs-exposed-patient-data/.

69. Operation Blockbuster Study, https://www.operationblockbuster.com/resources/index.html.

70. Mark Seal, *An Exclusive Look at Sony's Hacking Saga*, Vanity Fair, (Mar. 2015), http://www.vanityfair.com/hollywood/2015/02/sony-hacking-seth-rogen-evan-goldberg (hereafter Vanity Fair).

71. "I used to work for Sony Pictures. My friend still works there and sent me this. It's on every computer all over Sony Pictures nationwide", Reddit.com, (Nov. 24, 2016), https://www.reddit.com/r/hacking/comments/2n9zhv/i_used_to_work_for_sony_ pictures_my_friend_still/ (author deleted, even in earliest archived snapshots).

72. *See* Vanity Fair *supra*.

73. Peter Elkind, *Inside the Hack of the Century, Part 1*, Fortune, (June 25, 2015), http:// fortune.com/sony-hack-part-1/.

74. A Breakdown and Analysis of the December 2014 Sony Hack, Risk-Based Security, (Dec. 5 2014), https://www.riskbasedsecurity.com/2014/12/a-breakdown-and-analysis-of-the-december-2014-sony-hack/.

75. *See* Vanity Fair *supra*.

76. Kim Zetter, *Sony Got Hacked Hard: What We Know and Don't Know So Far*, Wired, (Dec. 3 2014), https://www.wired.com/2014/12/sony-hack-what-we-know/.

77. *See* Risk-Based Security *supra*.

78. Nolan Feeney, *Sony Asks Media to Stop Covering Hacked Emails*, Time Tech, (Dec. 15 2014), http://time.com/3633385/sony-hack-emails-media/.

79. *See* Vanity Fair *supra*.

80. Mathew J. Schwartz, *Ransomware: Is It Ever OK to Pay?*, BankInfo Security, (Apr. 13, 2016), https://www.bankinfosecurity.com/ransomware-ever-okay-to-pay-a-9036.

81. *FBI Cyber Division Responses to Senator Wyden's Questions on Ransomware*, (Feb. 8, 2016), https://www.wyden.senate.gov/imo/media/doc/FBI%20Response%20on%20 Ransomware.pdf.

82. Cyber Extortion: Ransomware vs Extortionware, Alpine Security, https:// alpinesecurity.com/blog/cyber-extortion-ransomware-vs-extortionware/.

83. Darlene Storm, *Delilah Malware Secretly Taps Webcam, Blackmails and Recruits Insider Threat Victims*, ComputerWorld, (July 18, 2016), https:// www.computerworld.com/article/3096250/delilah-malware-secretly-taps-webcam-blackmails-and-recruits-insider-threat-victims.html; Delilah Ransomware is a 'Blackmailware' That Blackmails You for Information, The Windows Club, (July 22, 2016), https://news.thewindowsclub.com/delilah-ransomware-blackmailware-blackmails-information-85034/; https://www.hotspotshield.com/blog/hackers-use-delilah-malware-blackmail/.

84. Lawrence Abrams, *BlackMailware Found on Porn Site Threatens to Report Users are Spreading Child Porn*, BleepingComputer.com, (Jan. 25, 2018), https:// www.bleepingcomputer.com/news/security/blackmailware-found-on-porn-site-threatens-to-report-users-are-spreading-child-porn/.

85. Jessica Davis, *Maze Ransomware Hackers Extorting Providers, Posting Stolen Health Data*, HealthITSecurity, (Feb. 4, 2020), https://healthitsecurity.com/ news/maze-ransomware-hackers-extorting-providers-posting-stolen-health-data.

86. Dissent Doe, *Law firm discloses ransomware attack*, DataBreaches.net, (Oct. 12, 2020), https://www.databreaches.net/law-firm-discloses-ransomware-attack/.

87. California Consumer Privacy Act, Cal. Civ. Code §§ 1798.100-1798.199 (2018).

CHAPTER 8

1. Sheera Frenkel, *A Brazen Online Attack Targets V.I.P. Twitter Uses in a Bitcoin Scan*, New York Times, (*last updated* July 17, 2020), https://www.nytimes.com/2020/07/15/technology/twitter-hack-bill-gates-elon-musk.html.

2. Kate Conger & Nathaniel Popper, *Florida Teenager is Charged as 'Mastermind' of Twitter Attack*, New York Times, (*last updated* Sept. 1, 2020), https://www.nytimes.com/2020/07/31/technology/twitter-hack-arrest.html.

3. Catalin Cimpanu & Zero Day, *How the FBI Tracked Down the Hackers*, ZDNet, (Aug. 1, 2020), https://www.zdnet.com/article/how-the-fbi-tracked-down-the-twitter-hackers/.

4. *See* Jeff Hancock and Tessian, *The Psychology of Human Error* (2020), https://www.tessian.com/research/the-psychology-of-human-error/ (88 percent of breaches involved human error); Tony Pepper, *Alarming Statistics Show Human Error Remains Primary Cause of Personal Data Breaches*, Realwire, (Aug. 20, 2019) (60 percent of breaches involved human error), https://www.realwire.com/releases/alarming-statistics-show-human-error-remains-primary-cause-of-data-breaches.

5. Aimee O'Driscoll, *The Role of Human Error in Cybersecurity: What the Stats Tell Us*, Comparitech, (Oct. 8, 2020). https://www.comparitech.com/blog/information-security/human-error-cybersecurity-stats/.

6. Center for Internet Security (CIS), *The 20 CIS Controls & Resources*, https://www.cisecurity.org/controls/cis-controls-list/.

7. Paul Ohm referred to this dynamic in the context of potential adversarial actors as the "myth of the superuser." Paul Ohm, *The Myth of the Superuser: Fear, Risk, and Harm Online*, 41 U.C. Davis L. Rev. 1327 (2008).

8. Tim Walker, *You've Been Swatted: How Hackers are Infiltrating the Homes of A-List Celebrities*, Independent, (Mar. 2, 2013), http://www.independent.co.uk/life-style/gadgets-and-tech/features/youve-been-swatted-how-hackers-are-infiltrating-the-homes-of-a-list-celebrities-8513561.html; David Kushner, *The Hacking of Hollywood*, Backchannel, (Nov. 23, 2015), https://backchannel.com/the-hacking-of-hollywood-51c25895512f.

9. *Id.*

10. *Id.*

11. Brief for Respondent at 7, United States v. Chaney, 628 Fed. Appx. 492 (9th Cir. 2015); David Kravets, Scarlett Johansson Hacker Gets 10 Years, Wired, (Dec. 17, 2012), https://www.wired.com/2012/12/scarlett-johansson-hacker/; Alex Myers, *Celeb Hacker Christopher Chaney Says Getting into Emails was Easy*, Daily Caller, (Apr. 26, 2012), http://dailycaller.com/2012/04/26/celeb-hacker-christopher-chaney-says-getting-into-emails-was-easy/.

12. Walker, *supra.*

13. Alan Duke, *Nude Scarlett Johansson Pic, Hacking Celebs' E-Mail Gets Man 10 Years in Prison*, CNN, (Dec. 18, 2012), http://www.cnn.com/2012/12/17/showbiz/hackerazzi-sentenced.

14. *Accused Celebrity Hacker: 'I deeply Apologize. . . It Eats at Me'*, CNN, (Oct. 13, 2011), http://www.cnn.com/2011/10/13/showbiz/hacking-arrest/index.html.

15. Kushner, *supra*; *Accused Celebrity Hacker: 'I deeply Apologize. . . It Eats at Me'*, CNN, (Oct. 13, 2011), http://www.cnn.com/2011/10/13/showbiz/hacking-arrest/index.html; David Kravets, *Scarlett Johansson Hacker Gets 10 Years*, Wired, (Dec. 17, 2012), https://www.wired.com/2012/12/scarlett-johansson-hacker/; Kim Zetter, *Alleged Celeb Hacker Glad He Got Caught; Was Addicted to Hacking*, Wired, (Oct. 31, 2011), https://www.wired.com/2011/10/hacker-glad-he-got-caught/.

16. David Kravets, *Scarlett Johansson Hacker Gets 10 Years*, Wired, (Dec. 17, 2012), https://www.wired.com/2012/12/scarlett-johansson-hacker/; Kim Zetter, *Alleged Celeb Hacker Glad He Got Caught; Was Addicted to Hacking*, Wired, (Oct. 31, 2011), https://www.wired.com/2011/10/hacker-glad-he-got-caught/; Kusher, *supra*.

17. Kushner, *supra*. *'Hollywood Hacker' Who Targeted Scarlett Johansson Given 10 Years in Jail*, Guardian, (Dec. 17, 2012), https://www.theguardian.com/technology/2012/dec/17/hollywood-hacker-christopher-chaney-10-years-jail.

18. *Christopher Chaney, So-Called Hollywood Hacker, Gets 10 Years for Posting Celebrities' Personal Photos Online*, CBS, (Dec. 18, 2012), http://www.cbsnews.com/news/christopher-chaney-so-called-hollywood-hacker-gets-10-years-for-posting-celebrities-personal-photos-online/.

19. Walker, *supra*.

20. CBS, *supra*.

21. Brief for Respondent, *supra* at 7.

22. Brief for Respondent, *supra* at 23.

23. Zetter, *supra*.

24. CNN *supra*; Brief for Respondent, *supra*.

25. OTRC: Christopher Chaney, *Celebrity Hacker, Sentenced to 10 Years in Prison*, ABC7 Eyewitness News, (2017), http://abc7.com/archive/8923789/.

26. J. Bonneau, C. Herley, P. C. van Oorschot, & F. Stajano, *The Quest to Replace Passwords: A Framework for Comparative Evaluation of Web Authentication Schemes*, IEEE Symposium on Security and Privacy (SP) 553, 567, 20–23 May 2012.

27. R. Morris & K. Thompson, *Password Security: A Case History*, Comm. ACM 22, 11, 594–97 (1979); A. Adams & M. Sasse, *Users are Not the Enemy*, Comm. ACM 42, 12, p. 41–46, (1999); C. Herley & P. C. van Oorschot, *A Research Agenda Acknowledging the Persistence of Passwords*, IEEE Security & Privacy, 10, 1, pp. 28–36, 2012; Blase Ur, et al., *Helping Users Create Better Passwords*, USENIX, 37(6): 51–57 (2012).

28. *Announcing Our Worst Passwords of 2015*, TeamPassword, (Jan. 19, 2016) https://www.teamsid.com/worst-passwords-2015/.

29. *TeleSign Consumer Account Security Report*, Telesign, (June 3, 2015), https://www.telesign.com/resources/whitepapers/telesign-consumer-account-security-report/.

30. Bruce Schneier, *Choosing Secure Passwords*, Schneier on Security, (Mar. 3, 2014), https://www.schneier.com/blog/archives/2014/03/choosing_secure_1.html.

31. *TeleSign Consumer Account Security Report*, Telesign, (June 3, 2015), https://www.telesign.com/resources/whitepapers/telesign-consumer-account-security-report/.

32. *Id.*

33. *Password Minder Infomercial* (more information about the infomercial is here): http://www.infomercial-hell.com/blog/2013/03/11/password-minder/.

34. Casey Johnston, *Password Minder: The Blank Notebook that Got Laughed Out of Production*, ARS Technica, (May 16, 2013), http://arstechnica.com/gadgets/2013/05/password-minder-the-blank-notebook-that-got-laughed-out-of-production/.

35. *Internet, Groupware, & Telecommunications*, Amazon, http://www.amazon.com/gp/bestsellers/books/3705/ref=pd_zg_hrsr_b_1_4_last%20%28last%20visited%20July%2023,%202015%29.

36. Cormac Herley, *So Long, and No Thanks For the Externalities: The Rational Rejection of Security Advice by Users*, NSPW '09: Proceedings of the 2009 Workshop on New Security Paradigms Workshop, September 2009, pages 133–144, https://doi.org/10.1145/1719030.1719050.

37. *See* Brian Krebs, *Anthem Breach May Have Started in April 2014*, KrebsOnSecurity, (Feb. 15, 2015), http://krebsonsecurity.com/2015/02/anthem-breach-may-have-started-in-april-2014/.

38. Daniel J. Solove, *The Funniest Password Recovery Questions Ever and Why Even These Don't Work*, Privacy + Security Blog (Oct. 2, 2016), https://teachprivacy.com/the-funniest-password-recovery-questions-and-why-even-these-dont-work.

39. See Cormac Herley & Paul van Oorschot, *A Research Agenda Acknowledging the Persistence of Passwords*, IEEE Security & Privacy, (January/February 2011).

40. Herley, *So long, supra.*

41. *Id.* ("most security advice simply offers a poor cost-benefit tradeoff to users and is rejected. Security advice is a daily burden, applied to the whole population, while an upper bound on the benefit is the harm suffered by the fraction that become victims annually. When that fraction is small, designing security advice that is beneficial is very hard.")

42. *See, e.g.,* Stephen Greenspan, *Annals of Gullibility: Why We Get Duped and How to Avoid It* (2008); Joseph Paul Forgas, *Why are Some People More Gullible Than Others?*, Phys.org, (Mar. 31, 2017), https://phys.org/news/2017-03-people-gullible.html ("In most face-to-face situations, the threshold of acceptance is fairly low, as humans operate with a "positivity bias" and assume most people act in an honest and genuine way.").

43. *See, e.g.,* David Gefen Izak Benbasat et al., *A Research Agenda for Trust in Online Environments*, J. of Mgmt. Info. Sys., 24:4, 275–286, (2008) DOI: 10.2753/MIS0742-1222240411.

44. *See, e.g.,* Stefano Grazioli & Sirkka L. Jarvenpaa, *Perils of Internet Fraud: An Empirical Investigation of Deception and Trust with Experienced Internet Consumers*, IEEE Transactions On Systems, Man, and Cybernetics—Part A: Systems and Humans, Vol. 30, No. 4, July 2000; Emma J. Williams & Amy Beardmore et al., *Individual Differences in Susceptibility to Online Influence: A Theoretical Review*, 72 Comp. in Human Behavior 412 (2017).

45. Roger Ford, *Data Scams*, 57 Hou. L. Rev. 111 (2019).

46. Keith J. Kelly, *Magazine Publisher Loses $1.5M in Cyberfraud*, New York Post, (June 16, 2015), https://nypost.com/2015/06/16/magazine-publisher-swindled-out-of-1-5-million-in-cyber-fraud/.

47. Kenneth R. Harney, *Hackers Prey on Home Buyers, with Hundreds of Millions of Dollars at Stake*, Washington Post (Nov. 1, 2017), https://www.washingtonpost.com/realestate/hackers-prey-on-home-buyers-with-hundreds-of-millions-of-dollars-at-stake/2017/10/30/0379dcb4-bd87-11e7-97d9-bdab5a0ab381_story.html.

48. *Mr. Robot*, Season 1, Episode 5, "3xpl0its.wmv."

49. "Design," *Merriam-Webster Online Dictionary* (2016), http://www.merriam-webster.com/dictionary/design.

50. Woodrow Hartzog, *Privacy's Blueprint* (2018).

51. Schneier, *Click Here, supra.*

52. General Data Protection Regulation Article 25.

53. Under a proposal in the American Law Institute's *Principles of the Law, Data Privacy*, also requires organizations to articulate a framework for privacy and security by design, whereby "A personal data user shall analyze the privacy and security implications early on in the development of any new products, services, or processes that have a reasonable likelihood of involving privacy or security issues." The Principles also recommend a commitment to default settings with a rigorous impact assessment regarding how the default settings of any new product or service implicate and appropriately address privacy and security and that the outcome of that assessment reasonably "be reflected in the final default setting choices that are made." American Law Institute, *Principles of the Law, Data Privacy* §18, at 101–02 (2019). The reporters on the project were Paul M. Schwartz and Daniel J. Solove.

54. Signals can also modulate transaction costs themselves. Weak signals burden users with the cost of finding more information. Strong signals reduce the burden of retrieving information. For example, buttons with labels send signals to users that make the decision as to when to press the button easier.

55. *Id.*

56. Schneier, *Click Here, supra*, at 107.

57. Kate Kochetkova, *Users Are Still Too Careless in Social Networks*, Kaspersky Lab Daily, (Feb. 3, 2016), https://blog.kaspersky.com/social-networks-behaviour/11203/; Evan Selinger & Woodrow Hartzog, *Why Is Facebook Putting Teens at Risk?*, Bloomberg, (Oct. 24, 2013), http://www.bloomberg.com/view/articles/2013-10-24/why-is-facebook-putting-teens-at-risk-.

58. Aran Khanna, *Your Venmo Transactions Leave a Publicly Accessible Money Trail*, Huff Post, (Oct, 30, 2015), http://www.huffingtonpost.com/aran-khanna/venmo-money_b_8418130.html; http://internet.gawker.com/heres-the-number-one-reason-to-set-your-venmo-account-t-1687461730.

59. Khanna, *supra*, Huff Post, (Oct. 30, 2015), http://www.huffingtonpost.com/aran-khanna/venmo-money_b_8418130.html.

60. *See, e.g.*, Steve Ranger, *IoT Security Crackdown: Stop Using Default Passwords and Guarantee Updates, Tech Companies Told*, ZD Net, (May 1, 2019), https://www.zdnet.com/article/iot-security-crackdown-stop-using-default-passwords-and-guarantee-updates-tech-companies-told/; Sue Poremba, *Will Weak Passwords Doom the Internet of Things (IoT)?*, Security Intelligence, (Feb. 13, 2020), https://securityintelligence.com/articles/will-weak-passwords-doom-the-internet-of-things-iot/; *Careful Connections: Keeping the Internet of Things Secure*, FTC, https://

www.ftc.gov/tips-advice/business-center/guidance/careful-connections-keeping-internet-things-secure; Thomas Pahl, *Stick with Security: Require Secure Passwords and Authentication*, FTC, (Aug. 11, 2017), https://www.ftc.gov/news-events/blogs/business-blog/2017/08/stick-security-require-secure-passwords-authentication.

61. Herley, *So long, supra*.

62. *See, e.g.*, John Spacey, *3 Examples of Mutual Authentication*, Simplicable, (Nov. 4, 2016) https://simplicable.com/new/mutual-authentication.

63. For an in-depth analysis of the problems with a certain approach to password complexity, *see* David Thaw, *Cybersecurity Stovepiping*, 96 Neb. L. Rev. 339, 349 (2017).

64. *See* Parmet, *supra*.

65. Hartzog, *supra*.

66. *Introduction to HTTPS*, The HTTPS-Only Standard, https://https.cio.gov/faq/ (*last visited* June 8, 2016); *HTTPS Everywhere*, Electronic Frontier Found. (*last visited* June 8, 2016) https://www.eff.org/https-everywhere.

67. Hartzog, *supra*.

68. *See* FTC v. D-Link Corp., Complaint for Permanent Injunction and Other Equitable Relief, Claim FTC File No. 132 3157, https://www.ftc.gov/system/files/documents/cases/d-link_complaint_for_permanent_injunction_and_other_equitable_relief_unredacted_version_seal_lifted_-_3-20-17.pdf.

69. *See* Guide Concerning Use of the Word "Free" and Similar Representations, 16 CFR Part 251; *Gut Check: A Reference Guide for Media on Spotting False Weight Loss Claims*, FTC, https://www.ftc.gov/tips-advice/business-center/guidance/gut-check-reference-guide-media-spotting-false-weight-loss.

70. Kat Krol & Matthew Moroz et al., *Don't Work. Can't Work? Why it's Time to Rethink Security Warnings*, IEEE, (2012), https://ieeexplore.ieee.org/stamp/stamp.jsp?tp=&arnumber=6378951.

71. *People Disregard Security Warnings on Computers Because They Come at Bad Times, Study Finds*, ScienceDaily, (Aug. 17, 2016), https://www.sciencedaily.com/releases/2016/08/160817142911.htm.

72. Lujo Bauer & Christian Bravo-Lillo et al., *Warning Design Guidelines*, CyLab, (Feb. 5, 2013), https://www.cylab.cmu.edu/_files/pdfs/tech_reports/CMUCyLab13002.pdf.

CHAPTER 9

1. In the Matter of Microsoft Corp., No. 012-3240 (FTC 2002); In re Guess.com, Inc., No. 022-3260 (FTC 2003).

For the benefit of digital users, indexed terms that span two pages (e.g., 52–53) may, on occasion, appear on only one of those pages.

Figures and tables are indicated by *f* and *t* following the page number.